MOVIE LOCATIONS

A Guide to Britain & Ireland

MARK ADAMS

BOXTREE

First published in 2000 by Boxtree, an imprint of Macmillan Publishers Ltd, 25 Eccleston Place, London, SW1W 9NF and Basingstoke

www.macmillan.co.uk

Associated companies throughout the world

ISBN 0 7522 7169 5

A CIP catalogue record for this book is available from the British Library

Designed and typeset by Dan Newman/Perfect Bound Ltd

Printed by Bath Press

Picture acknowledgements:
© Angelus Films, photograph by David Appleby: p9. BBC/BFI: pp98–9. BFI: pp50, 171, 200–1. BFI Stills, Posters and Designs: p61. Carlton/Canal+: p228. © 1999 Danjaq, LLC and United Artists Corporation, all rights reserved: pp219, 220–1, 224–5. Enigma Films/BFI: p100. Fugitive Features/Rank Film Distributors/BFI: pp26–7. HandMade Films/BFI: p142. Heritage Hotels: p43. Huntley Film Archives/Dalton Nicholson Collection: p96, 148–9, 210–1. Jaap Buiterdijk/FilmFour: p129. Moviestore Collection: pp11, 12, 22, 24, 30–1, 32, 52–3, 54, 55, 56–7, 72–3, 74–5, 76, 80–1, 90–1, 92–3, 101, 103, 104, 114–5, 126–7, 128, 130–1, 132–3, 134–5, 138–9, 150–1, 152–3, 154–5, 157, 158, 168–9, 173, 176–7, 180–1, 182–3, 190–1, 193, 194–5, 205, 206–7, 208–9, 215, 232, 234–5, 238–9. The National Trust Photographic Library/Rupert Truman: p241. Palace Pictures/BFI: p213. Palace Pictures/HandMade Films/BFI: pp58–9. Pathé/BFI: p106–7. Rank Film Distributors/BFI: pp62–3. The Samuel Goldwyn Company/BBC/BFI: p83. Tomboy-Gruber Brothers/Kobal Collection: pp110–1. Universal Pictures International/BFI: pp34–5. Wilton House Trust: p70.

biography

MARK ADAMS HAS WRITTEN FOR A NUMBER OF FILM TRADE magazines including *Variety*, *Moving Pictures International* and *The Hollywood Reporter*. He was Head of Programming at the National Film Theatre in London for six years until 1998, Deputy Director of the London Film Festival for two years, helped launch the Noosa Film Festival in Australia in 1999, and currently helps programme the Flanders International Film Festival in Ghent, Belgium. His favourite movie is *The Thin Man*, and he firmly believes that William Powell and Myrna Loy (and Asta the dog) had the greatest of all film relationships. He supports Leicester City Football Club and lives in Stoke Newington in North London (uncomfortably close to Arsenal). His favourite British movie location is the beach featured at the start of *A Matter of Life and Death*, which can be found at... well, read on for further details.

bibliography

I HAVE READ, ENJOYED AND OCCASIONALLY DRAWN ON THE following: *Variety, The Hollywood Reporter, Screen International, Moving Pictures International, Premiere, Movieline, Empire, Neon* and *Sight & Sound*, as well as the following books.

An Autobiography of British Cinema by Brian McFarlane (Methuen, 1996).
The Carry On Companion by Robert Ross (Batsford, 1996).
Check Book 4 (British Film Commission, 1998).
Filmed in Cornwall by Sue Craig & David Fitzgerald (Bossiney Books, 1999).
From Limelight to Satellite edited by Eddie Dick (BFI Publishing, 1990).
Halliwell's Film and Video Guide (HarperCollins, 1999).
The Hammer Story by Marcus Hearn & Alan Barnes (Titan Books, 1998).
If They Move, Kill 'Em! The Life and Times of Sam Peckinpah by David Weddle (Faber and Faber, 1996).
London on Film: 100 Years of Filmmaking in London by Colin Sorenson (Museum of London, 1996).
Magic Hour by Jack Cardiff (Faber and Faber, 1997).
Notting Hill: The Script by Richard Curtis (Hodder and Stoughton, 1999).
On Location: The Film Fan's Guide to Britain and Ireland by Brian Pendreigh (Mainstream, 1995).
Saving Private Ryan by Steven Spielberg & David James (Boxtree, 1998).
Sense and Sensibility: The Diaries by Emma Thompson (Bloomsbury, 1996).

Thanks also due to the ever-excellent Internet Movie Database website: www.imdb.com

acknowledgements

PROFOUND AND PROFUSE THANKS ARE DUE TO THE FOLLOWING: my wife Bridget for putting up with me; my children Jake (10) and Charlie (8) for watching films with me and for being cool little dudes; Emma Marriott at Boxtree for shaping and watching over everything; Tina McFarling at The Film Council for being wonderful all of the time; Dick Fiddy, Clare Norton-Smith and Julie Pearce at the NFT for being so helpful and so remarkable; Sophie Edwards and Jenny Nathan at the British Tourist Authority for planting the seeds; Sara Squire (FilmFour) and Cathy Dunkley (*The Hollywood Reporter*) for being good friends and constant sources of support; Chris Pickard (The Brazilian Embassy) for being there that night in Cannes; Jonathan Rutter (McDonald and Rutter) for loads of help; Marion Pilowsky (UIP) for being the one and only; Hayley Castle at FilmFour Intl., for playing with the kids and always smiling; Richard Wallace (The *Mirror*) for history going back way too far; Arun Singh (OBE) for loving movies and for being an OBE; my parents Pat and Tony for letting me watch too many old movies on television; the Pedgrift family (and assorted partners, husbands and children) for being great supporters; Gordon and Gail, and Al and Jenny for being the best of friends, and Fiona Hill and Jane Turney because they are great. Thanks also to: The London Film Commission, BFI, Buena Vista, The British Council, National Film Theatre, Eon Productions, UIP, Warner Bros., Columbia TriStar, 20th Century Fox, Pathé Distribution, Icon Film Distribution, Entertainment Film Distributors, FilmFour, Alliance Releasing, the British Film Commission, and the whole UK and Ireland Film Commission network (good luck to you all). Plus all of those I have inadvertently forgotten.

NOTE FOR THE READER

The years given after film titles are dates of production,
not cinema release dates.

contents

foreword
by alan parker

THE FIRST TIME I VISITED LIMERICK IN APRIL 1998, I WAS ARMED WITH a bunch of maps that we had downloaded from one of the *Angela's Ashes* fan websites. I thought this particular website was all the more remarkable because it was Japanese. Why a culture so different from the Irish one should have been so taken by Frank McCourt's story intrigued me no end. I walked the streets that had been so carefully mapped out and lovingly flagged by the Japanese fans who were obviously obsessed with every detail of Frank's book.

I write now having finished the film, with the 'In Search of the McCourts' obsession gaining even more momentum. 'Walking Tours' are regularly advertised: 'Daily at 2.30 pm,' the flyers pronounce, 'Individual Walks, Four punts per person!' Bands of 'McCourties', clutching their much-thumbed copies of Frank's memoir, regularly walk up Barrack Hill in search of Roden Lane, baffled that it's no longer there. (I couldn't find it either, and so we built it as a set in Dublin, which, as with most film sets, lasted as long as it took to get the all-clear from Technicolor.)

In the main, however, my generation of film-makers prefer (if somewhat perversely) to shoot in real streets, in cold castles and up to our knees in muddy bogs. I'm sure that films such as *Notting Hill, Braveheart, Shakespeare in Love* and *Elizabeth* draw attention to the UK and Ireland, and show off the history, architecture and countryside of the regions to spectacular effect.

If you're a film fan you'll be fascinated by this book, which looks behind the scenes of filming on location, and reveals exactly where some of the wonderful films shot in the UK and Ireland have been filmed. From the

stunning coastline of Ireland and the lush valleys of Wales to the glorious Highlands of Scotland and the stately homes of England, when it comes to finding the perfect backdrop for a film Britain and Ireland are a film-maker's dream.

△ Alan Parker, film director and chairman of the UK's Film Council.

Alan Parker

introduction

IT IS EASY TO UNDERSTAND WHY THE SIGHT OF A BEAUTIFUL SUNSET over a picturesque castle or a vision of the sun irradiating a golden beach makes you yearn for a holiday (or at least a visit) to that spot. But combine that image with a glamorous movie star (or at the very least an English actor or actress) and magnify it on the big screen and it is clear that you have a recipe for success.

Nothing is more fun than watching a movie and spotting the locations that act as the backdrop to the storyline. We've all done it. Watched a London-set movie and worked out that a character couldn't (and shouldn't have) have made their way from Leicester Square to Piccadilly Circus via Buckingham Palace. Or wondered why a character has wandered down an Edinburgh Street and miraculously found themselves standing on the edge of Loch Ness. Okay, so you finally have to admit that movie storylines aren't usually there to make a lot of sense, but they can help to remind us (or, more often than not, reveal) just how wonderful the landscape of the UK and Ireland truly is.

Initially it may be a vicarious experience, as you sit in the cinema with a box of popcorn or at home armed with a remote control – but how often do you find yourself watching the credits right to the end just to find out exactly where that stunning stately home, magnificent castle, beautiful beach or beautiful town really is?

According to official figures, many people do just that – and later visit the spot. It is estimated that the three Scottish-set hit movies *Braveheart*, *Rob Roy* and *Loch Ness* accounted for between £7 and £15 million in extra tourist revenue, and a paper in the 'Annals of Tourism Research' noted that

a location featured in a successful film can expect visitors to increase by 54% over the next four years.

A quick break for a few facts:

△ Hugh Grant and the film crew take a quiet walk along Portobello Road, in *Notting Hill*.

- Saltram House in Devon saw visitor numbers rise by 39% in 1996, over 1995. This was entirely due to the film *Sense and Sensibility*, as the house had not been marketed in any other way.

- Dyrham Park, Chippenham, Wiltshire, the location of *The Remains of the Day*, had a 9% boost in tourism following the release of the film.

- The Crown Hotel in Amersham repeatedly has calls to book the room that was the setting for the first romantic love scene with Hugh Grant and

△ Billy Connolly and Judi Dench in a scene from *Mrs Brown*.

Andie MacDowell in *Four Weddings and a Funeral*, and is booked up months in advance.

- Grimethorpe, the colliery town that was used in the 1996 film *Brassed Off*, saw a 50% increase in visitors following the release of the film.

- Following the international success of the Sheffield-set comedy *The Full Monty*, there is now an official tour around sites featured in the film.

- The disused power station at Trawsfynydd in Wales, the setting for *First Knight*, saw visitors increase from 37,015 in 1993 to 42,452 a year later when the film had been released.

- Osborne House on the Isle of Wight, the setting for the final scenes of *Mrs Brown*, has seen a 25% increase in tourism since the film was released.

Certainly there is something quite inspiring about being in a spot where you know a film has been shot. Whether it is standing outside that blue door where Hugh Grant and Julia Roberts started their love affair in *Notting Hill*; walking on Holkham Beach in Norfolk and imagining the beautiful closing scene in *Shakespeare in Love*; standing in awe in stunning York Minster and recalling the coronation scene in *Elizabeth*; looking up at the clock at Carnforth Station and tearfully recalling the unrequited love in *Brief Encounter*; or even sitting in the restaurant in Wellington Street, central London, where Andie MacDowell counted her previous lovers while Hugh Grant looked on in befuddled embarrassment.

As a rule a film will leave little behind to remind you that any given spot was actually the location for a movie. Granted, David Lean and his crew left remnants of the village set for *Ryan's Daughter* behind them, but generally you have to use your imagination to recreate what was staged up there on the silver screen. In truth, that is actually the fun of it. Movies are all about using your imagination, and at the same time as you are standing on the edge of Loch Ness and recalling the wonderful scenes from *The Private Life of Sherlock Holmes*, that self-same imagination might help Nessie rise from the waves.

The locations can also have an impact on the cast and crew who film there: Julie Christie was so taken with Dorset during filming of *Far From the Madding Crowd* that she vowed to live in the country; Ken Loach was so shaken by the hardships of Glasgow while shooting *Carla's Song* that he decided to return later to make a film about the city's problems, and eventually made *My Name is Joe*.

There are, of course, difficulties when it comes to shooting on location. While there may be a shared language with American production companies, when it comes to filming in the UK a few problems may be encountered along the way. First and foremost is the weather! What a director wants when he or she is filming outdoors at a specific location is guaranteed consistency of weather. This is the obvious reason why California, and the Los Angeles region in particular, became the home of the American film industry: practically guaranteed sunshine. Quite unlike the UK and Ireland... to the extent that some film-makers come here specifically for fog, clouds and rain.

In the past other problems were voiced by companies filming here on location; complaints about food, petty officialdom, poor communications and intransigent unions were commonplace. Things have changed. The food is better (well, in some restaurants); the film commission network has eased the pain of red tape; telecommunications and transportation are world-class; and the craftsmen, technicians and performers are among the best in the world. Even government has gradually been doing its bit by easing tax burdens with a commitment to help major productions film in the UK and Ireland.

Film-makers from overseas have repeatedly proven keen to make use of English locations, crews and talent when it comes to making their films. George Lucas, who directed *Star Wars* in the UK, produced the *Indiana Jones* films here, and returned a couple of years ago to make *Star Wars: The Phantom Menace*, said: 'I came back to do *The Phantom Menace* because I have done all of my big-budget movies here – you have great acting talent, great crews, and a lot of ability to do large-scale productions like the ones I have been doing over the years. I don't think there was any question we would come back here on *The Phantom Menace*.'

Producer Frank Marshall, who has worked on the *Indiana Jones* films as well as *Who Framed Roger Rabbit?* adds: 'I've produced several movies in the UK. It has always been a wonderful experience. What I like about it is it is sort of one-stop shopping – you have everything available that you would need. From terrifically talented actors and craftsmen to wonderful locations, and good stages and post-production facilities.'

And while California may offer sunshine and easy access to the Hollywood studios, it can't come up with the grand country houses, ancient castles, enchanting sleepy villages, lush rolling countryside and distinctively elegant beaches (okay, granted, there are a few nice beaches in California). Producers may be tempted by the thought of their dollar going much further in countries like Russia, The Czech Republic, Bulgaria and other European countries, but things like food, communications, security and keeping their stars happy are also paramount concerns. It is easy to see why the UK and Ireland are popular choices.

Writer-director Anthony Minghella, who made *The English Patient*, *Truly Madly Deeply* and most recently *The Talented Mr Ripley*, is from the Isle of Wight. He has commented: 'Oddly, the geography of Britain has been under-exploited in films. I think we are only just beginning to realise we have wonderful islands. The landscapes of this place are under-exploited in films. The Isle of Man, Ireland, Scotland – there are so many fantastic landscapes available."

And he is, of course absolutely right. The UK and Ireland do offer wonderful options for film-makers. Over the years hundreds of films have been shot throughout these islands, making glorious use of valleys in Wales, peaks in Scotland, beaches in Cornwall, castles in Ireland and even the Thames in London. Only recently we had the sight of Pierce Brosnan as James Bond battling his way along the River Thames in the nineteenth Bond film *The World Is Not Enough*. From the historic Houses of Parliament and Tower Bridge to the new designs of Docklands and the

Millennium Dome – Bond came blasting by them all, showing off a flash of London to brilliant effect.

However, anyone who has come across a film or television crew filming on location will realise what a massive undertaking it involves. Trucks and vans containing lighting, cameras, electrical generators, make-up, props, costumes, catering (the most important vehicle on any location shoot) and dressing rooms can often take up streets. When a movie crew comes to town you certainly know about it. It should therefore come as no surprise to appreciate the lasting effect a location shoot can have on any locality. Sometimes people object to the noise, clutter and sheer scale of the movie-invasion, but it is certainly a talking point and can equally lead to a great deal of pride about the way a locality may be reflected on the big screen. Certainly it can mean a good deal of additional revenue into a town or village particularly if a film is based there for some weeks. Shops, bars, restaurants and hotels all benefit enormously from a crew's arrival, and if the film proves to be a hit there can be a lasting impact, with tourists returning year after year to visit the spot where their favourite film was shot.

To ease the location-shooting process, most films (especially those coming in from overseas) will have a location manager to oversee finding and securing that perfect castle, house, hill or village. These managers often come armed with extensive knowledge of the best places to shoot and a contacts book full of the names and numbers of all of the key people involved. They will work closely with the appropriate film commission, local authority, police force or private individual to make sure that when the crew arrives all will run smoothly.

This book will take you on a tour of the UK and Ireland, and in many cases take you behind the scenes of a movie and its locations. It is, of course, virtually impossible to mention every film ever shot in the UK and Ireland, or to list every location utilized – but there should be more than enough here to enthrall you, and possibly even encourage you to make a trip and relive that movie moment for real.

Mark Adams

london

ITS HISTORY, THE AVAILABILITY OF EXPERIENCED AND PROFESSIONAL talent, or even the notion of 'Cool Britannia': whatever the reason, London is one of the hottest spots in the world for filming. Big-budget American producers have a natural leaning towards a city with which they feel a close link and, more important, where a common language is spoken. London's position, too, means that the city is the perfect stopping-off point for further trips into mainland Europe as well as Eastern Europe.

London is also packed with some of the best shops in the world, has a reputation for culinary skills, and offers a wealth of actors and craftsmen. And not only are there wonderful and distinctive locations, but the vital support structure of editors, effects, costumes, musicians and designers are all easily available.

An estimated 200 stages (a stage is the studio space on which film sets are built) are available via 60 studios of varying sizes across London, in all amounting to some 1.5 million square feet of shooting space. The impressive London Film Commission, at its offices in Tottenham Court Road, offers a library detailing thousands of locations, has the ability to negotiate appropriate discounts and can generally try to cut through that often-present red tape.

London itself is, of course, packed with distinctive historical landmarks, such as Tower Bridge, the Houses of Parliament, Trafalgar Square, the Tower of London and many more. Yet it also has the ability to morph into other locations, and has often been used by film-makers searching for lookalike venues. The city has been Vietnam in *Full Metal Jacket*, Moscow in *GoldenEye* and Argentina in *Evita*, to name just a few of many.

The River Thames, which occasionally features in films, had a massive boost when the thrilling opening-action sequence of the nineteenth James Bond film, *The World Is Not Enough*, was shot along the river. Meanwhile London's elegant parks often turn up in both period and contemporary films, and the city's architecture can spring surprises, offering a wide range of styles and some buildings with modest and inconsequential exteriors blessed with fascinating and provocative interiors.

In the 1950s and 1960s you couldn't move for films being shot in London. In the 1950s the Ealing comedies and *Carry On...* films were more often than not shot in the suburbs rather than the centre of the city. But things started changing in the 1960s when London was swinging, and film-makers wanted to show the rocking city streets and funky clubs as well as the more well-known London tourist spots.

The coming of the 1970s and 1980s led to councils being much more careful of the more obvious sights being used by film-makers, and the police were wary of directors taking a few too many liberties when it came to demands for streets to be closed and venues made available to them. It wasn't unknown – and still isn't – for film crews to use guerrilla-style tactics to close down a street quickly, get an important shot and head off before the police caught on. And in these days of lightweight cameras, it has become easier to position a camera in a car and drive around the centre of London to get those typical shots of Piccadilly Circus, Leicester Square, Trafalgar Square and the rest.

The gradual redevelopment of London has also caused problems for film-makers. No longer can a film-maker like Stanley Kubrick find a spot in Docklands to re-create his own vision of Vietnam (for his film *Full Metal Jacket*) and places like Bankside, County Hall and Shad Thames near Tower Bridge have all been developed, with trendy apartments and cool restaurants taking the place of nice empty spots much loved by film-makers.

The arrival of the London Film Commission has certainly changed things; a single body that can offer advice, information and contacts is vital for the professional use of London by film-makers. But London is also becoming

The City Barge, Chiswick

In *Help!*, the second Beatles film, the group were filmed at Strand on the Green in Chiswick and are seen coming along Post Office Alley and on to the Thames footpath. To escape the villains (led by Leo McKern) pursuing them, they head into The City Barge. When they go through the doors, though, they are on a set built at nearby Twickenham Studios. For tax reasons, *Help!* was shot mainly overseas, and this sequence is one of the few scenes filmed in the UK. In the previous Beatles film, *A Hard Day's Night*, Ringo has a pub experience when he pops into the Turk's Head pub (in Winchester Road, close to Twickenham Studios) when he should be readying himself for a televised concert.
Film: *Help!*

daily more crowded, more developed and more complicated. It is estimated that it can cost between £3,000 and £4,000 a day to shoot in London, when the costs of the location and parking and the price of having a policeman on duty are added up.

Yet despite these provisos, London is still one of the coolest places in which to film, and the major productions shot in the city over the past few years are proof that overseas interest is far from waning. London as a film-making centre has a long history, stretching back to the late nineteenth century, when the Victorians were able to see the first 'animated photographs' of their great city. Ever since then London – by the mere fact that the majority of the UK's film studios and production centres were based there – has been a popular spot for film-makers.

The wonderfully titled *The Arsenal Stadium Mystery* (1939) was filmed – no surprise here – at Arsenal Stadium in Highbury. Directed by Thorald Dickinson, the film features Arsenal playing a charity match against a team named the Trojans. One of the players collapses and is found to be dead. Cue the arrival of Inspector Slade (Leslie Banks) of Scotland Yard to investigate the case. The other big Arsenal film was to come many years later, in 1997, when Nick Hornby's book *Fever Pitch* was made into a movie. Directed by David Evans, it starred Colin Firth as the Arsenal fan whose love for the team gets in the way of his love for Ruth Gemmell, and was filmed at Fortismere Secondary School (both characters are teachers), in Maidenhead and at Arsenal Stadium.

London Apprentice, Old Street

In this well-made drama with a twist in the tail, the Metro Bar where Dil (played by Jaye Davidson) worked as a singer was in fact the East London bar, the London Apprentice. The exterior scenes were in reality just a vacant lot. Elsewhere in the film, the pub where Miranda Richardson plans an IRA hit was actually the Lowndes Arms in Belgravia.

Film: *The Crying Game*

In the classic Ealing comedy *Hue and Cry* (1946), the climax where gangs of children join to foil a gang of thieves at supposedly Ballard's Wharf, Wapping, was actually shot near Southwark Bridge. *The Blue Lamp* (1949) was shot around Paddington Green, and the film included the now-closed Paddington Green Police Station. Filming also took place at Kilburn.

Michael Powell's controversial *Peeping Tom* (1960), starring Carl Buhm, Moira Shearer and Anna Massey, shot scenes just north of Oxford Street in Newman Passage and at Rathbone Place. The opening memorial-service scene of *Lawrence of Arabia* (1962) was filmed at St Paul's Cathedral, while Lawrence's fatal motorcycle accident was shot at Cobham, Surrey. *The Knack* (1965), a Swinging Sixties film directed by Richard Lester and starring Rita Tushingham, Ray Brooks and Michael Crawford, was shot in Kensington,

Shepherd's Bush, Holland Park School, Lancaster Gate, Victoria Coach Station and Ruislip Lido.

Even John Wayne made it to the UK to make the cop movie *Brannigan* (1975), directed by Douglas Hickox and co-starring Lesley-Anne Down and Mel Ferrer. It is very much a tour-guide-to-London crime-movie, with even the poster images featuring Tower Bridge looming behind Wayne.

Shad Thames near Tower Bridge was dressed to look like the nineteenth-century East End for *The Elephant Man* (1980). The much-admired British crime-film *The Long Good Friday* (1980), directed by John MacKenzie and starring Bob Hoskins, Helen Mirren and Eddie Constantine, was shot at Paddington Station, Heathrow Airport, and most memorably on the Thames and at St Katharine's Dock.

The impressive Alexandra Palace was used as the fictional Victory Square in Michael Radford's adaptation of George Orwell's *1984* (1984). The building had been fire-damaged in 1980, but since filming it has been restored as an exhibition hall and entertainment centre, and it has regained its status as a north London landmark.

Stanley Kubrick managed to film his Vietnam War film *Full Metal Jacket* (1987) in the UK, using the derelict Beckton Gas Works in Docklands, on the north side of the Thames, to double as a Vietnam war zone. Kubrick had tanks and palm trees in place for the powerful scene where Private Joker (Mathew Modine) and his GI buddies have to flush out Vietnamese soldiers from a crumbling town.

The much-loved British hit comedy *Four Weddings and a Funeral* (1994), starring the floppy-haired Hugh Grant along with Andie MacDowell, Kristin Scott Thomas and Simon Callow, was filmed at Greenwich Royal Naval College Chapel (a wedding), along the Embankment (the shot of the friends' Land Rover speeding along the road), Highbury Fields (the closing crying-in-the-rain scene), on the South Bank (the declaration of love via David Cassidy's song scene), in Wellington Street (the café discussion of how many lovers) and at St Bartholomew the Great church (another wedding). The film is discussed in greater detail on pages 51-3.

In his 1930s version of *Richard III* (1995) Ian McKellen can be seen riding a bicycle along Cheney Road. The film, directed by Richard Loncraine and starring Annette Bening, Kristin Scott Thomas, Jim Broadbent, Maggie Smith and Robert Downey Jr, was also shot in Battersea Power Station, Bankside, County Hall, St Pancras Chambers, Kensington Gore, the Royal Horticultural Hall and the Royal Geographical Society, as well as in Brighton and in Carnforth, Lancashire. Cheney Road had been used earlier in *The Ladykillers* (1955) and *Chaplin* (1992). Richard Attenborough's *Chaplin*, which has Robert Downey Jr in the lead, was also shot in Smithfield Market (which doubled as the old Covent Garden) and at the Hackney Empire theatre, in which Chaplin performed in his early years and which has subsequently been restored. *Chaplin* also used Putney Bridge to double as Waterloo Bridge.

Mike Leigh habitually sets his films in London. *High Hopes* (1988), starring Philip Davis, Ruth Sheen, Edna Dore and Philip Jackson, was shot partially in the streets behind King's Cross Station, while the Oscar-nominated *Secrets & Lies* (1996), starring Brenda Blethyn, Timothy Spall and Marianne Jean-Baptiste, filmed scenes outside Holborn Underground Station (where Blethyn and Jean-Baptiste meet for the first time) and in Quilter Street (Blethyn's house), The Green, Winchmore Hill (Spall's shop) and Whitehouse Way, Southgate (Spall's house). In many ways, Mike Leigh's more recent films encapsulate life in London, with films such as *Naked*, *Life is Sweet* and *Career Girls* all dealing with honest and everyday life in London. *Life is Sweet* focuses on the suburbs, while *Career Girls* pokes fun at estate agents and the Docklands.

The popular British film *Shooting Fish* (1997), directed by Stefan Schwartz and starring Kate Beckinsale, Stuart Townsend and Dan Futterman, was shot in various spots around London, including Mill Hill and Alexandra Palace (the scene of them rummaging through rubbish). The much-hyped Spice Girls' music movie *Spice World* (1997) is very much a London film, with the girls crisscrossing the city in their distinctive double-decker bus (which was Tardis-like in its interior) before the final concert at the Royal Albert Hall. The film was shot at The Mall, Canary Wharf, Embankment, King's Road, Tower Bridge and the Broadgate Arena. Also in 1997, but in distinct contrast, was actor Gary Oldman's directorial debut, the harsh drama *Nil By Mouth*, starring Ray Winstone and Kathy Burke, which was shot in South London. *The X-Files* movie (1998) – pretty much an extension of the TV series

London locations used to double for other places

Death Wish III Lambeth Hospital stood in for the New York Bronx, and Brixton doubled as The Bronx.

Evita RAF Halton, near Aylesbury, stood in for the Argentinian parliament building.

Eyes Wide Shut Shot in Hackney and Westminster with locations dressed to look like New York.

Full Metal Jacket Beckton Gas Works in Docklands was used to portray Vietnam.

GoldenEye Somerset House doubled as Moscow.

Highlander The Chirton Block, Finsbury Square, represented New York.

A Kiss for the Dying A bank in Long Acre, Covent Garden, was transformed into the Philadelphia Central Police headquarters.

The Misadventures of Margaret The Masonic Hall in Great Queen Street was used for a Manhattan interior.

The Mission Fort Amherst in Chatham was used as a dungeon in Colombia.

Mission: Impossible The foyer of County Hall, on the South Bank, stood in for the CIA headquarters, and Aldershot as Virginia.

but extremely well made – was largely shot in the US, but there is a scene using the backdrop of the Royal Albert Hall, where the UK-based conspirators meet to discuss how to get rid of Mulder and Sculley.

Stanley Kubrick's last film, *Eyes Wide Shut* (1999), starring Nicole Kidman and Tom Cruise, was nominally set in the US, but all the shooting was done in the UK. As Kubrick refused to fly, it was necessary for London to double for the US and, if you look closely in some scenes – especially where Cruise passes over a bridge – the distinctive architecture can be seen. Among the London locations that Kubrick used were Chelsea & Westminster Hospital, Hamleys toyshop on Regent Street, and Islington; out-of-London scenes were shot at Luton Hoo and Highclere Castle in Hampshire (scene of the orgy).

The attractive and enjoyable comedy-drama *This Year's Love* (1999), directed by David Kane, was filmed in and around Camden Town, making good use of the bars and shops at Camden Lock.

The broad comedy *Mad Cows* (1999), based on Kathy Lette's bestselling novel, stars Anna Friel as Maddy, a young Aussie mother trying to cope with her baby in an inhospitable London. Thrown into jail after borrowing a bag of frozen peas in Harrods to try to ease the ache of her lactating breasts, she entrusts her baby to her useless best pal Gillian (Joanna Lumley), who knows next to nothing about children. Directed by Sara Sugarman, the film was shot all over London. As well as Harrods (where they even had the store's boss Mohamed al-Fayed 'acting' as a doorman), filming took place at two Georgian Greenwich houses (acting as homes for Maddy's boyfriend and mother), Wandsworth Prison for the prison scenes, and Mentmore House in Hertfordshire, which was dressed for the party scene.

Neil Jordan's *The End of the Affair* (1999), based on Graham Greene's novel, is set in London during the Second World War and stars Ralph Fiennes, Julianne Moore and Stephen Rea as the three people caught in a love triangle. Much of the film was shot in Brighton, but the closing scene of the V-1 missile hitting a house was filmed at Kew Green.

selected films

84 Charing Cross Road (1987)
Despite the title giving away the whereabouts of the London antiquarian bookshop where Anthony Hopkins works, the actual site has been redeveloped several times since it was a bookshop in the 1950s. The film, elegantly directed by David Jones, is based on Helene Hanff's book, which had already been

adapted into stage and television productions. The story is about the pen-pal relationship between outspoken New Yorker Hanff (played by Anne Bancroft) and the mild-mannered Frank Doel (Hopkins), which lasts for 29 years. When eventually she comes to London and visits him, the shop has closed and he has died. The characters are beautifully played, and there is a fine supporting cast. Though most of the filming took place at Shepperton Studios, some of the exteriors were filmed in Richmond (convenient for the studios) and some in New York.

101 Dalmatians (1996)

A live-action remake of the much-loved Disney animated classic, based on Dodie Smith's book *The Hundred and One Dalmatians*, this film is played very much for broad laughs, and with the aid of digital effects you'd almost believe there *are* 101 Dalmatians. Jeff Daniels plays Roger, a computer artist who has a Dalmatian named Pongo, while Joely Richardson is Anita, a struggling clothes designer, also owner of a Dalmatian, this time a female. While riding their bikes in the park, at which they arrive after passing through virtually every key London landmark, the two lonely humans are brought together by the two dogs, and it is true love all round. The evil fly in the ointment is Richardson's evil aunt, the wonderful Cruela De Vil (Glenn Close in a perfectly hissable performance) who decides she must have a dalmatian-skin coat. The early scenes of Daniels and Richardson riding their bikes through London were shot in Leicester Square, Piccadilly Circus and Burlington Arcade, and their clash of bikes takes place in Battersea Park. Scenes were also shot at Kenwood House on Hampstead Heath and in Oxfordshire. A couple of errors slipped into the film. Roger's and Anita's flat is in South Kensington (north of the river), but in later scenes they can see Big Ben and the Thames from the south side of the river. Strange. Also, a skunk creeps into the police van with Cruela and her cronies, although skunks aren't native to the UK. A follow-up, *102 Dalmatians* (2000), has scenes of the puppies dashing over Westminster Bridge.

Alfie (1966)

From the opening-credits sequence filmed on Vauxhall Bridge it is clear that director Lewis Gilbert made *Alfie* very much a London film. From the bridge Michael Caine's smooth-talking Alfie is quickly off to a quiet area behind King's Cross Station for a little car-bound assignation with Siddie (Millicent Martin), the first of a series of women with whom we see the chirpy but deeply flawed Alfie dallying as he crisscrosses the capital. While Gilbert shot the majority of the interiors at Twickenham Studio, he also filmed in Notting Hill (where Julia Foster's and Shelley Winters's flats are located), Battersea and Ladbroke Grove; while the scenes of Alfie working as a street photographer see him outside landmarks such as Tower Bridge and the Houses of Parliament. Bill Naughton adapted his own stage play, and added the unusual device of having Caine speak directly to the camera. The impressive cast also included Shirley Anne Field, Jane Asher and Eleanor Bron.

An American Werewolf in London (1981)

John Landis achieved the remarkable feat with *An American Werewolf in London* of managing to convince the police to shut down Piccadilly Circus over two nights as he shot an ambitious series of scenes of a werewolf escaping into the street and numerous cars ploughing into each other. The film is a very much tongue-in-cheek tale of a couple of young American backpackers who are attacked by a werewolf. One (Griffin Dunne) is killed, but the other, David

△ Michael Caine, Shelley Winters and a friendly beefeater check out the London sights, in *Alfie*.

Kessler (played by David Naughton), survives, only to be visited in his hotel room by the ghost of his mutilated buddy, who warns him that something strange is going to happen. The first time David turns into a werewolf he kills some tramps near Tower Bridge and attacks someone else at Aldwych Underground Station, before waking up naked in London Zoo. It is the final scene in Piccadilly Circus, though, that is best remembered as the werewolf runs amok along the West End streets and cars smash into each other. The film, which also stars Jenny Agutter, is something of a cult classic, with excellent effects provided by Rick Baker.

Blow-Up (1966)

Michelangelo Antonioni's *Blow-Up* is one of those classic Swinging Sixties movies in which beads and long hair are par for the course. David Hemmings plays a top fashion photographer who wanders into a park wearing a snappy pair of white jeans and proceeds to take secretive photographs of a couple he sees kissing and holding hands. The park is actually Maryon Park off the Woolwich Road, while Antonioni also shot in West London and around Holland Park. The photographs taken by Hemmings lead him to a woman (Vanessa Redgrave) who wants the snaps, and when he thinks he has witnessed a murder in the park the body promptly disappears. The film, which also stars Sarah Miles, is very much about the difference between reality and fantasy, and was quite a success when it was released.

Production designer Assheton Gorton described making *Blow-Up* as 'complex'. He said: 'We started looking for locations based on a treatment, and as we found the locations we took the director round. He then wrote the script into the locations, and I think that is one of the reasons it works so well. We found this park out in Woolwich: Maryon Park. A very extraordinary park with a sort of hill in the middle surrounded by big tower blocks, right on a bend in the Thames. We also had to have somewhere that would service a scene with an antiques shop on the edge of the park, and we were lucky. There was a place there that we took over and converted into an antiques shop.'

He added: 'But there were certain aspects of the park that weren't in the original script, like the tennis courts. As we found the locations, the script was written into them. In this particular case it altered the structure of the film, because all the mime sequences at the end of the film – the tennis courts, and the mime artists picking up this imaginary ball and throwing it about – created a theme that they then wrote back, right to the very beginning.'

A Hard Day's Night (1964)

When it comes to pop movies you don't get much better than *A Hard Day's Night*. Directed by Richard Lester, it features The Beatles at their most charming and spontaneous, just as fame is truly about to descend on them. The film is shot in black and white in a social-realism, documentary style. The Beatles play themselves, Norman Rossington plays their manager (named Norm), and the excellent Wilfrid Brambell plays Paul McCartney's childlike grandfather, who escapes to cause havoc at any given opportunity. The Beatles head off on a train journey that takes in towns such as Minehead, Taunton and Newton Abbot before returning to London for a televised concert. Just before the concert an unhappy Ringo goes walkabout (encouraged by the mischievous Brambell) and ends up walking along the Thames near Kew Bridge. The concert itself was shot at the long-gone Scala Theatre on Charlotte Street (though the fire-escape scenes had to be filmed at the Hammersmith Odeon), while the chase scenes were filmed at Notting Hill Gate.

△ Gary and Martin Kemp and gang pose in the Greenwich streets, from *The Krays*.

Richard Lester later recalled that, with the Fab Four on the verge of international fame, filming was extremely problematic. Describing the London street scenes, he said: 'Basic logistics were impossible. As soon as I had them run to their marks and do a scene, 2,000 crazed fans would appear, popping up out of manhole covers. Then the police would crash down and say "Piss off!" We'd have to find another location and do take two. Then the whole bloody thing would start again.'

Interview With the Vampire: The Vampire Chronicles (1994)

Neil Jordan directed this epic and lush adaptation of Anne Rice's bestseller and boldly cast Tom Cruise as Rice's beloved vampire, Lestat de Lioncourt. This is a stunning piece of work, attempting to cover the centuries as well as the homoerotic subtext of vampirism. The film opens in contemporary New

Orleans with the vampire Louis de Pointe du Lac (an impressive Brad Pitt) being interviewed about his life by a reporter, played by Christian Slater. Louis sets about recalling his life over the past 200 years, his relationship with the vampire Lestat, who initiated him, and Claudia, the young girl (wonderfully played by Kirsten Dunst) they both fed on and created. Filming took place in Deptford, London, and in Wilton's Music Hall, Grace's Alley, Ensign Street, Whitechapel, as well as in San Francisco, Paris, New Orleans and Louisiana. Cruise was so adamant that his vampire makeup should not be seen by prying press eyes prior to the film's release, that covered walkways were erected between the location sets and his trailer/dressing room.

The Jokers (1967)

Michael Winner is in quite splendid form with *The Jokers*, an excellent comedy-caper based on a great script by Dick Clement and Ian La Frenais, and starring the youthful Michael Crawford and Oliver Reed. Reed and Crawford play brothers of highish society (remember, this was the 1960s, so that sort of thing didn't matter too much) who decide to steal the Crown Jewels. Not only do they get away with the playful scheme, they end up handing back the jewels by placing them in the Scales of Justice on top of the Old Bailey. It says much for Winner's powers of persuasion that he managed to get permission actually to film at the home of the Crown Jewels, the Tower of London, and the Old Bailey even agreed to his using the real Scales of Justice. He also shot in a Jermyn Street nightclub that would later become better known as Tramp.

The Krays (1990)

The shrewd casting of pop-star brothers Gary and Martin Kemp (now better known in the London soap *EastEnders*) as notorious East End gangsters Ronnie and Reggie Kray did much to bring attention to Peter Medak's film about the murderous duo. The film-makers chose to shoot the key scenes of the Krays' family house, where their mum (wonderfully played by Billie Whitelaw) still ruled, largely in Caradoc Street in Greenwich. Richmond Theatre also featured in the film, transformed into an East End club.

The Ladykillers (1955)

This enduring example of the great Ealing comedies, directed with flair and dark humour by Sandy Mackendrick, boasts a cast to cherish. A sweet old lady, Mrs Wilberforce (wonderful Katie Johnson), takes in a sinister lodger, Professor Marcus (Alec Guinness, sporting pantomime teeth in a role that was originally to be played by Alastair Sim), who then asks if his brutish string quartet can practise in one of the rooms. They are, of course, a gang of violent and deeply suspicious criminals who are planning a robbery. Ealing built her house at the end of Frederica Street, off Caledonian Road, which is close to – but not close enough for a proper view of – St Pancras Station. The back of the house supposedly looks out on to a tunnel from the station, though the actual tunnel was Copenhagen Tunnel. The gang stage a hold-up (filmed in Cheney Road at the back of King's Cross Station, and also used as a location in *Richard III* (1995) and *Chaplin* (1992) and bring back the loot to the house. When she discovers what the gang is up to they plot to kill her. Of course, though, their vicious ineptitude gets the better of them, and it is the sweet little old lady who is left holding the loot. Having disrupted the residents of Frederica Street for several weeks, Ealing Studios staged a street party hosted by cast and crew when they left.

The Lavender Hill Mob (1951)

Charles Crichton's *The Lavender Hill Mob* is one of the best Ealing comedies, and, though largely studio-shot, its film locations are very specific. Filming took place in Lavender Hill, just south of the Thames. It is a fantastic story. Alec Guinness plays the mild-mannered bank clerk whose job it is to accompany gold bullion in a guarded van. He finally decides to attempt to steal the money, and with the aid of Stanley Holloway (who runs a company producing metal memorabilia) and two professional crooks (the hilarious Sid James and Alfie Bass) they plan how to stage the robbery. They fashion a clever plan that involves Guinness being tied up and left in a warehouse by the river. He manages to stumble out and fall into the Thames just as the police arrive, and they manage to save him. As Guinness and Holloway make their getaway to Paris, they are filmed boarding a converted Dakota airliner at the old London Airport. Watch out for a young Audrey Hepburn as Chiquita in the opening scenes.

Lock, Stock and Two Smoking Barrels (1998)

The sharply structured and edited London crime-film proved to be a great success at the box office and heralded the arrival of some new talents both behind and in front of the camera. When a high-rolling card game turns out to have been fixed, a group of young Londoners need to raise some big money in double-quick time. Their hunt for cash takes them to the East End and entangles them with a gun-toting gang, some upper-class drug dealers and tough-as-nails enforcer Big Chris (played by former footballer Vinnie Jones). The boxing scene was shot at Repton Boys Club, while the bar run by J.D. (played by Sting) is in St John Street, close to Smithfield Market. Filming also took place at Bethnal Green Town Hall, Borough Market and in Camden.

Martha – Meet Frank, Daniel and Laurence (1998)

The charming comedy from debut film-maker Nick Hamm featured a cast of very much up-and-coming talent from both sides of the Atlantic. When Martha (Monica Potter) decides to head to the UK with her last $99, she finds herself drawn into the romantic machinations of three best friends, all of whom fall for her. First up is Daniel (Tom Hollander), who sees her at the airport in the US and connives a way to talk to her. Next is Frank (Rufus Sewell), who gets annoyed with Daniel; when he spots Monica he realizes she is the one his friend is obsessed with and sets about chatting to her. What neither realizes is that Laurence (Joseph Fiennes) has also fallen for her, after trying to link up with Laurence at the airport but bumping into Monica and ending up driving her into town. London is very much a character in the film, with eating and drinking important to the storyline. Shooting took place at venues such as Blakes Hotel in Roland Gardens (where Monica spends her first night in London), at Battersea Park Café and at a branch of Livebait, the chain of fish restaurants. The UK airport where Monica lands (and leaves from at the close of the film) is actually Stansted Airport, north-east of London. When Martha meets Frank, it is in Battersea Park. Nick Hamm has said he 'felt comfortable with material that is contemporary, satirical and comedic. I was also very keen to

London locations used to double for other places

Mrs Dalloway Cornhill, in the City, doubled as 1940s Bond Street, and Walthamstow Town Hall as an American building.

Patriot Games Greenwich Naval Hospital acted as The White House, Washington.

Quills The Royal Naval College became Napoleon's home.

Reds Crockers Folly pub, Maida Vale, doubled as the New York Writers' Club, while Somerset House doubled as a building stormed by Bolshevik revolutionaries.

The Saint Camden Town Hall acted as the American Embassy in Moscow, and Woolwich Arsenal stood in for a Russian palace.

Shining Through The Aldwych and Kingsway doubled as New York, St Pancras as Zurich, and the Royal Naval College as the Pentagon.

Sleepy Hollow Somerset House doubled as 1780s New York.

do a picture set in contemporary London. I think that there is a real renaissance happening in London, that it is a very positive and exciting place to be at the moment.'

Notting Hill (1999)

A massive hit internationally, this marvellously performed romantic comedy certainly put the London district of Notting Hill on the map. Fans of the film from around the world wander around Portobello Road and the surrounding streets, hunting for the doorway to Hugh Grant's house and to his fictional bookshop. Grant plays William Thacker, the owner of a pretty unsuccessful travel bookshop in – where else? – Notting Hill. One day international movie star Anna Scott (Julia Roberts) walks into his shop... and things are never quite the same again. The film traces their developing relationship, often hilariously and sometimes romantically, until they reach the point where they both have to make decisions. Roberts is completely at ease as the much-adored Anna Scott, and this is certainly one of her best performances. Hugh Grant does the bumbling, inept but charming Englishman better than anyone else, though the film's revelation was Grant's grungy flatmate Spike, played brilliantly by Rhys Ifans.

The screenwriter Richard Curtis recalls: 'When I was lying sleepless at night I would sometimes wonder what it would be like if I turned up at my friend's house, where I used to have dinner once a week, with the most famous person at that time, be it Madonna or Princess Diana. It all sprang from there. Notting Hill is an extraordinary mixture of cultures. It seemed like a proper and realistic place where two people from different worlds could actually meet and coexist – that Anna would be shopping there, that William would live there and that Spike might think it was a groovy place to dwell in. Notting Hill is a melting pot and the perfect place to set a film.'

For the production team, though, there was the practical reality of organizing a production in such a busy urban area. Location manager Sue

Quinn said: 'It's extraordinary how many people live in the Notting Hill area.' But the film-makers wanted to capture the flavour of Notting Hill, 'which meant filming in the most populated areas, the main area being Portobello Road, where William's bookshop was situated'.

△ Art imitates life. Hugh Grant faces the press from the step of the house with the blue door, in *Notting Hill*.

Although Notting Hill is the main location, there are also trips to the Ritz Hotel on Piccadilly (where Anna holds her press interviews), to the Savoy Hotel on the Strand (where Anna holds her final emotional press conference), and to Nobu, at the Metropolitan Hotel on Park Lane, where Anna and William have a meal. The film was also shot at Kenwood House on Hampstead Heath for the scene where Anna is making the Henry James film.

The house with the blue door (280 Westbourne Park Road), where Grant lives, was actually once owned by Richard Curtis, and in early 2000 that self-

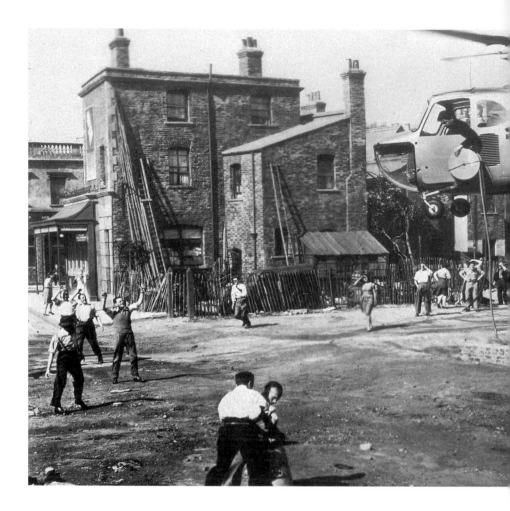

△ A helicopter hovers over the Lambeth location for *Passport to Pimlico*.

same blue door – just the door – was auctioned for £9,300. William's shop is really Nicholls Antique Arcade at 142 Portobello Road, which was redesigned to house the fictional bookshop. The original shop, on which the fictional one is based, is nearby, at 13 Blenheim Crescent. In the dinner-party scene where Roberts is asked how much she makes for her film roles, she replies $15 million – the exact amount she was paid for making *Notting Hill*.

Passport to Pimlico (1949)

In this enchanting and whimsical comedy set shortly after the Second World War, an old royal charter that cedes the London area of Pimlico to the Dukes of Burgundy is found in a shell hole, and the locals declare the area an independent state in the very heart of London. They decide they will have no

rationing restrictions and set up a border with the rest of the capital, where they enter into trade agreements with other Londoners. When the government tries to take action against the residents, they even stop the tube trains from running beneath them and start asking for passports. Although set in Pimlico, the location was across the river on a bombsite in Hercules Road, Lambeth, where the film-makers used some of the remaining houses. Screenwriter T.E.B. Clarke, who received an Oscar nomination, based the film on a real story, when the Canadian government presented to the Netherlands a room in which Princess Juliana was to bear a child.

Patriot Games (1992)

The early section of the Harrison Ford film *Patriot Games* is set in London, which CIA analyst Jack Ryan (Ford) is visiting with his family to give a lecture at a naval college. The film doesn't sit still, and as Ford walks away from his lecture to meet his family he interrupts an attempted IRA splinter-group assassination attempt on one Lord Holmes (James Fox). After shepherding his family to safety, our Jack leaps into action, bundling over one assassin and shooting another. Unfortunately, the one he shot is the brother of one of the other assassins (Sean Bean), who is captured but swears revenge. The scenes of both Lord Holmes's car leaving Buckingham Palace and Ford leaving his naval-academy lecture were shot at the Royal Naval College, close to the Thames at Greenwich. Greenwich Naval Hospital was also used to double as The White House. A later scene of a terrorist contact in a London bookshop was filmed in Burlington Arcade in Piccadilly, while scenes of a chase on the Underground were filmed at Aldwych Station. His good deed done, Ryan and his family head back to the US, but little do they know that Sean Bean is soon to be after them.

The Servant (1963)

A rich and ineffectual young man (played with consummate ease by James Fox) is gradually taken over and controlled in his own home by his manservant (Dirk Bogarde) and his sensual sister (Sarah Miles). Scripted by Harold Pinter (who also has a cameo role as 'Society Man') from Robin Maugham's novel, the film, expertly directed by Joseph Losey, caused something of a sensation when it was first released, perhaps because of the orgy scene towards the end of the film. Fox's Georgian house was actually a house in Royal Avenue, Chelsea. Bogarde, who also handled some of the directing while Losey was in hospital for two weeks, recalled the experience of the complex camera setups involved in filming in and around a single location: 'There was no elaborate set; it was simply the house, an actual house in Chelsea, and Joe used the house as the metaphor all the way through.'

Sliding Doors (1998)

A well-received romantic comedy, written and directed by Peter Howitt, the film offers the intriguing storyline of tracing two possible lives for a woman after she loses her job. Gwyneth Paltrow masters a British accent, playing Helen Quilley subtly differently in both possible versions of her life. At the start of the film Helen loses her job. Then in one storyline she catches the Tube and gets home to find her boyfriend (John Lynch) is having an affair, leaves him and starts building life afresh. In the other storyline she misses the train and carries on with her relationship, blissfully unaware that he is seeing someone else while her life gets worse and worse. This is very much a London film, though it does not play the game of showing lots of typically distinctive London sights. The Underground scene was shot on the Waterloo and City Line, while the bar where Paltrow drowns her sorrows (and later gets a job as a waitress), is actually Bertorelli's restaurant and bar on Charlotte Street. Filming also took place in Chelsea & Westminster Hospital, Fulham Road, on Hammersmith Bridge and at the Blue Anchor pub in Hammersmith. The final scene where Paltrow and John Hannah, the man she meets when she leaves her boyfriend, have an emotional moment in the rain was shot on the Albert Bridge.

Wonderland (1998)

Set over one weekend in South London, Michael Winterbottom's film is an intimate portrait of a family struggling to find love and fulfilment as they go about their daily lives.

Scripted by Laurence Coriat, it cleverly interweaves stories, allowing the characters to exist in the same area but only occasionally to touch each other's lives. Coriat said: 'I also really wanted to do a story about London, because I haven't seen a film yet that looks at all the different sides of the city.' After Winterbottom had decided on his actors (the excellent cast includes Gina McKee, John Simm, Shirley Henderson and Ian Hart), he decided to use unconventional methods of filming the city. These included taking locations around London pretty much as the crew found them, and filming real people instead of extras. The film was also largely shot with a hand-held camera and a much-reduced crew. It was made entirely on location in London, and, in keeping with the natural style of the film, production design was very minimal: locations such as Soho bars and cafés, football stadiums, pubs and bingo halls were filmed without the usual encumbrances of lighting, props and set-dressing.

Michael Winterbottom said: 'The film is set in very specific parts of London – a section of South London between Vauxhall, Elephant and Castle and Brixton, and in Soho. And because of the way we decided to film, we shot everything in what we felt was the "real" location. For example, in the script Nadia (Gina McKee) worked in a café in Soho. Now, often when you make a film you might shoot that café somewhere else just to make it easier. But on *Wonderland* we always shot in real places – so her café is on Old Compton Street.

'What's more, because we shot in real locations, without extras and when places were open, we had to shoot at the same time as the events were happening. For example, the opening scene of the film takes place in the Pitcher and Piano bar in Soho. Normally, a film would take over a location like that, close it down, fill it with extras and probably shoot a night scene at ten o'clock in the morning.

'For us to get that "end of the night" scene we had to wait until the end of the night, wait until everyone was drunk and getting ready to go home, before we could get the right atmosphere. So the film is incredibly specific in its setting. But hopefully the more accurate and true you are to one place, the more easily it will be recognized by people everywhere.'

London restaurants used as film locations

Bring Me the Head of Mavis Davis The Atlantic Bar and Grill, off Piccadilly Circus.
Eyes Wide Shut The Café Royal, Regent Street.
Four Weddings and a Funeral The Dome on Wellington Street (now a Café Rouge restaurant).
Help! The Dolphin on Blandford Street.
Howards End Simpson's-in-the-Strand.
Martha – Meet Frank, Daniel and Laurence Blakes Hotel, Roland Gardens, Battersea Park Café and one of the Livebait restaurants.
Mojo Alfredo's, Essex Road.
Nil By Mouth The Wimpey Bar, Southwark Park Road.
Notting Hill Nobu restaurant, Metropolitan Hotel, Park Lane.
Sleepers Odette's restaurant in Primrose Hill.
Sliding Doors Bertorelli's in Charlotte Street, The Blue Anchor pub in Hammersmith and Fat Boys Diner, Spitalfields.
Spiceworld – The Movie The Tower Hotel Café, St Katharine's Way.
Wonderland The Pitcher and Piano bar in Soho.

The World Is Not Enough (1999)

The nineteenth James Bond film also happens to be the one with the most footage actually shot in London. Bond has travelled around the world tackling bad guys, but when he gets back to London it is normally for another vital meeting with M or a bedroom assignation of some kind.

In this film – the first directed by Michael Apted and the third starring Pierce Brosnan as Bond – the exciting pre-credits sequence is largely made up of a hectic London chase via landmarks old and new. On M's instructions, Bond retrieves a ransom in Bilbao, then heads back to the MI6 headquarters without knowing that a bomb is implanted in the cash. In London at MI6 the cash is detonated killing its intended victim, an important friend of M's. Bond spots the assassin in a speedboat on the Thames and 'borrows' a highly powered experimental jet boat from Q Branch, flies out of the MI6 building and sets off past the Houses of Parliament in pursuit of the killer.

Bond's boat was launched from a slipway constructed to the lee of the real headquarters, starting the chase of the killer (the attractively-named Cigar Girl, played by Maria Grazia Cucinotta) in her twin-engine 36-foot Sunseeker Superhawk 34 with its healthy dose of hardware.

The thrilling chase takes them along the river past the Houses of Parliament, through the waterways next to Docklands apartments in Tobacco Wharf (the biggest cheer at any screening comes when two traffic wardens get drenched by water flung up from the speeding boats). Eventually they reach the Millennium Dome at Greenwich, where the lovely female killer is despatched. Cue the opening credits.

Brosnan himself took the opportunity to take the controls of the boat. He said: 'It's a good crack. It's great! How often do you get to do this? You know, go down the River Thames pumping along at 60 miles per hour with the theme music playing!'

Stunt coordinator Simon Crane said: 'It was a very exciting sequence. We tried to make it as difficult and original as possible. There have been lots of boat sequences before, but this is Bond, this is the opening sequence. It has to be the best ever. Bond chases a powerful and expensive Sunseeker speedboat driven by a mysterious female assassin. Bond is in a very fast prototype jet boat that travels across the water at 80 miles an hour and is extremely manoeuvrable. People won't have seen this sort of boat before. There are lots of exciting jumps, including an amazing barrel roll when Bond rides up the back of the Sunseeker and executes a 360-degree roll. In the process of doing that he knocks out her stern-mounted machine gun. Then he spins round and jumps over her again. It was a tricky and very difficult sequence to execute successfully and required a lot of rehearsing.'

Special-effects coordinator Chris Corbould said: 'The spectacular high-speed boat chase on the River Thames took a lot of preparation and close cooperation with Simon Crane's stunt team. We had a small and extremely powerful boat with an amazing rate of acceleration. I've never seen a boat like this, and on top of that you've got rockets, you've got guns, you've got parachutes, you've got all sorts. This probably has double the gadgets of the last film.

'There were a number of explosions on the river during the chase, and my primary concern was that we didn't blow the boat in the air. We carried out a lot of very big explosions in an area in which it is not easy to work. We were in the heart of London, all around Canary Wharf and Docklands. Logistically, it was a difficult place to work. We would have been in trouble if local inhabitants had complained about the noise and disruption, but they all seemed to have enjoyed the experience of having a Bond film in their back yard, so to speak.'

key london locations

Burlington Arcade

A shopping arcade built in 1819, with 72 small shops and its very own private police force, the Beadles. It has a striking glass roof and a grand entrance on Piccadilly with stone sculptures and mouldings.

Address: Between Piccadilly and Old Burlington Street, Westminster
Films: *101 Dalmatians, Incognito, Patriot Games*

Borough Market

One of London's oldest fruit markets, located under Victorian railway arches, which has become popular over recent years for atmospheric filming with that distinct London feel.

Address: entrance on Stoney Street, near London Bridge Station
Films: *Entrapment, Howards End, Keep the Aspidistra Flying, Lock, Stock and Two Smoking Barrels*

Cheney Road

Cheney Road and the surrounding streets of Battle Bridge Road and Wellers Court off Pancras Road contain atmospheric Victorian two-storey and four-storey brick terraces and warehouses. They back on to late-Victorian (now preserved) gasworks and gasholders.

Address: Cheney Road, King's Cross
Films: *Chaplin, The Ladykillers, Richard III*

County Hall

An impressive Edwardian office building with a 730-foot Thames frontage, formerly home to the Greater London Council. It has been converted to a hotel, restaurants, an amusement arcade and the London Aquarium, but parts are still available for filming. It's also situated next to the British Airways London Eye.

Address: Riverside Building, South Bank
Films: *Angels and Insects, Mission: Impossible, Richard III, Scandal*

MOVIE LOCATIONS *london*

Horticultural Halls and Conference Centre

Impressive halls and conference centre with cement arches in classic Danish style. Hall Two is Art Deco, while the site also features classic Edwardian style and the attactive ironwork supports a splendid glass ceiling.

Address: Vincent Square, Victoria

Films: *Indiana Jones and the Temple of Doom, Martha – Meet Frank, Daniel and Laurence, Richard III, The Saint*

Middle Temple

The famous Thames Embankment location for London's barristers and one of the four Inns of Court. It features a striking Elizabethan hall, sixteenth-century architecture and gardens and bears a striking resemblance to the cloister of the House of Commons. Its position in the centre of London makes it popular with film-makers.

Address: Middle Temple Lane

Films: *Shakespeare in Love, Wilde*

National Maritime Museum

The site incorporates the Queen's House (built 1616–35), the Royal Observatory (built 1675) and underground vaults. In 1999 the museum opened a new extension, Neptune Court, designed by Richard Mather, with a large glass-domed roof. There are lovely riverside views.

Address: Romney Road, Greenwich

Films: *101 Dalmatians, Sense and Sensibility*

Royal Naval College

The stunning Royal Naval College consists of four Georgian buildings with large inner courtyards. Of special note are the Painted Hall (1708), used as a dining room, the Chapel and the Lower Hall, once used as a senior officers' dining room.

Address: King William Walk, Greenwich

Films: *The Avengers, Four Weddings and a Funeral, An Ideal Husband, The Madness of King George, Patriot Games, Sense and Sensibility*

St Paul's Cathedral

Sir Christopher Wren's magnificent cathedral church, featuring crypt, marble floor, Whispering Gallery, triforium and two external galleries.

Address: St Paul's Churchyard, the City

Films: *Lawrence of Arabia* (opening memorial scenes), *The Madness of King George* (staircase leading to dome)

Somerset House

A fine eighteenth-century building with a river frontage. The house dates back to 1176, and Elizabeth I lived at a palace that stood on the site. The building has five wings, four of which surround a courtyard, around which is a dry moat. It is currently home to the Courtauld Institute.

Address: Strand

Films: *Black Beauty, GoldenEye, Portrait of a Lady, Sense and Sensibility, Sleepy Hollow*

Strawberry Hill House

Horace Walpole's Strawberry Hill House is one of the most influential Gothic Revival buildings in England. Hogarth bought the riverside property – set in 35 acres – in 1747 and made a series of additions to the structure. The house is currently St Mary's College, but available to film-makers for evening and night shoots.

Address: Waldegrave Road, Strawberry Hill, Twickenham

Film: *Richard III*

Tate Gallery

The main building of the impressive Tate art gallery was built between 1897 and 1906 and is a popular London attraction. The airy and grand location can be made available to film-makers out of gallery hours.

Address: Millbank

Films: *Love and Death in Long Island* (gallery scene interiors), *Mission: Impossible* (entrance represented the embassy)

Woolwich Arsenal

Also known as the Royal Arsenal, this ex-military property is set in more than 70 acres and contains various buildings ranging from warehouses to the officers' mess. The site includes two large sheds being converted to studio use, large warehouses, a network of roads and a large boiler room.

Address: Warren Lane, Greenwich

Films: *The Leading Man, Richard III, The Saint*

south and south-east england

WITH ITS ROLLING COUNTRYSIDE, STATELY HOMES, ATTRACTIVE forests and beaches and – of the greatest importance to any film-maker shooting on location – the lowest rainfall and the most sunshine in the UK, the South and South-East of England are among the most popular regions for film companies. Easy intercontinental travel via Gatwick and Heathrow airports also helps explain why the area is favoured by film-makers.

The fact that London is never more than a couple of hours or so away is another reason why films being shot on location are often filmed here, especially by companies using Shepperton Studios as a base. And its miles of coastline, varied rural landscapes and fine selection of country houses mean that many 'classic' movies have been shot in the South and South-East, including *A Room With a View, The Madness of King George, A Man For All Seasons* and *Four Weddings and a Funeral*.

Brighton, with its shingle beaches, Regency architecture and cosmopolitan town centre, is a special magnet for film-makers. Capitalizing on this, the town is developing its own film industry infrastructure and it has become a favoured place for members of the UK's creative community to live in. It is within easy reach of a plethora of attractive country houses, impressive countryside and a variety of other seafronts, ranging from desolate sand-dunes to traditional seaside towns.

Over recent years probably two films have done most to draw attention to the region and at the same time boost tourist interest. These are *The Madness of King George* (which made great use of beautiful Arundel Castle) and *Four Weddings and a Funeral* (especially the old coaching house at Amersham, which provided the famous four-poster bedroom scene). Television

productions have often favoured southern locations, too, mainly because they offer such a broad variety of locales in close proximity to each other.

There is a long and rich tradition of film-making in the region, with experiments with movies taking place as early as 1896. In that year film-maker Esme Collings was making short films, including reputedly the first blue movie, filmed in a garden in Hove and advertised in a catalogue as being suitable for 'Gentlemen's Smoking Concert Audiences Only'; while hypnotist, astronomer and magic lanternist George

The Crown Hotel, Amersham

The fictional Somerset inn, The Boatman, the pub where Charles and Carrie spend their first night of passion, is really the sixteenth-century coaching inn, the Crown Hotel in Amersham. After the release of the film the hotel received countless calls from customers wanting to stay in the same room – and use the same four-poster bed, seen above – as the movie couple stayed. The Boatman's exteriors were actually those of The King's Arms, also in Amersham.

Film: *Four Weddings and a Funeral*

Albert Smith was shooting films about everyday Brighton life in 1897.

Brighton is acknowledged as having played an important role in the development of early cinema. In 1898 Esme Collings made *The Broken Melody*, featuring the stage actor Mr Van Bien – notable because actors were not used in films until many years later, early film-makers preferring to feature ordinary folk rather than having to pay professionals. At the beginning of the new century Smith, Collings and others established the Brighton School, which would be devoted to film-making, while in 1910 reputedly the first purpose-built cinema, the Duke of York's, opened.

Because some film-makers were based in Brighton and there were support services around the town, the resort gradually acquired a reputation as a fine film location over the years. Sometimes, though, the film-makers didn't bother coming. The Hollywood film *The Gay Divorcee* (1934) stars Ginger Rogers as a would-be divorcee staying at a Brighton hotel, while Fred Astaire is the author who falls for her. It was the first major success for the two as a singing and dancing double-act – but it was not shot in Brighton.

The popular British film *Bank Holiday* (1938) is a comedy-drama about a group of varied characters in Brighton over a bank holiday weekend, while Margaret Lockwood starred in the US film *The Brighton Strangler* (1945) about an actor appearing in a play called *The Brighton Strangler* who is accidentally knocked on the head. He wakes up convinced he is a killer and heads to Brighton on a murder spree.

The much-loved comedy *Genevieve* (1953) is about love and laughs on the London to Brighton Vintage Car Rally; in *Playground Express* (1955), directed by John Irwin, a Brighton funfair manager recruits youngsters to help deal with a bully; in the thriller *Jigsaw* (1962), directed by Val Guest, Jack Warner (who gained fame in TV's *Dixon of Dock Green*) played a policeman on the trail of a serial killer; while David Hemmings appeared in *Be My Guest* (1965), about a young couple who set up a guesthouse in Brighton.

Richard Attenborough returned to the scene of his *Brighton Rock* triumph (discussed on pages 48-9) in 1969, but this time as director rather than actor. He made his directorial debut with the acclaimed anti-war musical *Oh! What a Lovely War*, set in the town, making great use of Brighton Pier and the Royal Pavilion. The film features a wondrous cast – including Ralph Richardson, John Gielgud, Maggie Smith and Ian Holm – brilliantly drawing attention to the arrogance and stupidities behind the First World War.

In 1979 a rather different type of musical descended on the town, when *Quadrophenia* recalled the seaside clashes of the mods and rockers. In the 1970s two *Carry On...* films used Brighton locations to add a little spice to the usual bawdy antics. Both *Carry On At Your Convenience* (1971) and

Carry On, Girls (1973) were filmed in the town. In 1986 the closing scenes of the Bob Hoskins crime film *Mona Lisa* were also shot there. Other films that have been shot in Brighton include *A Handful of Dust* (1988), *Tommy* (1975) and *Under Suspicion* (1992).

In West Sussex the Michael Caine thriller *The Black Windmill* (1974) was filmed at Black Tower Mill at Clayton; the wedding sequence of Stanley Kubrick's *Barry Lyndon* (1975), which starred Ryan O'Neal, was shot at Petworth House chapel; *Dance with a Stranger* (1985), with Miranda Richardson, was filmed at Goodwood and on Worthing beach; director Sidney Morgan made several short films on Shoreham beach in the 1920s, including *Little Dorrit* (1920); and Charles Jarrott's *Mary Queen of Scots* (1971) was shot at Parham House, Pulborough. In East Sussex the prologue on the White Cliffs for *Henry V* (1989), directed by and starring Kenneth Branagh, was shot at Birling Gap.

Also shot in Sussex was *The Innocents*, directed by Jack Clayton and based on the Henry James story *The Turn of the Screw*, and starring Deborah Kerr, Michael Redgrave, Peter Wyngarde and Megs Jenkins. The film was shot partly at Sheffield Park Gardens. Peter Collinson's *Up the Junction* (1967) was partly filmed at Worthing seafront; *The Punch and Judy Man* (1962), directed by Jeremy Summers and starring sad-faced comedy favourite Tony Hancock as the melancholy children's entertainer, was filmed on Bognor Regis seafront; and the classic British thriller *Hell Drivers* (1957), which stars Stanley Baker, Herbert Lom and a young Sean Connery, was shot at Ford Airfield.

> ### The Black Swan, Effingham
>
> When American backpackers Griffin Dunne and David Naughton stagger into the attractively named The Slaughtered Lamb pub in the middle of the misty Yorkshire moors they are looking for a friendly smile, a warm fire and a refreshing pint. Instead they get some aggressive locals, so they head back on to the moors, where something large and wolf-like is waiting for them. In spite of the Yorkshire setting, director John Landis filmed in Surrey, at The Black Swan, Effingham, near Leatherhead, a lovely traditional pub.
> **Film:** *An American Werewolf in london*

In Kent the variety of the coast – ranging from gentle seaside resorts to isolated beaches – combines with the county's working ports to offer fascinating location venues. The Historic Dockyard at Chatham, the birthplace of the Royal Navy, is renowned as the most complete Georgian dockyard in the world, and as well as offering a working museum it is also perfect for period maritime scenes. Some of the blockbuster hit *The Mummy* (1999) was filmed there, as well as at Frensham Great Pond in Surrey.

The attractive seaside towns of Broadstairs (where Charles Dickens once lived and worked), Whitstable and Folkestone offer much in terms of beauty,

MOVIE LOCATIONS *south and south-east england*

though Folkestone is now also home of the UK terminal for the Channel Tunnel. (Ironically, the blockbuster Tom Cruise hit *Mission: Impossible*, which had the Channel Tunnel as the setting for its closing-action sequences, had to shoot those scenes in Scotland.) Kent's countryside, too, is popular with film-makers – and was vital to the success of the TV series *The Darling Buds of May* – with venerable castles and estates, such as Hever Castle and Leeds Castle, enhancing the picturesque quality of the region. Distinctive of the area are the White Cliffs of Dover, which were memorably seen on the big screen in Ken Annakin's epic comedy *Those Magnificent Men in Their Flying Machines* (1965).

Kent has hosted an impressive roster of major productions. In 1965 alone, Chilham played host to projects as varied as the period romp *The Amorous Adventures of Moll Flanders*, directed by Terence Young and starring Kim Novak and Richard Johnson; and *The Collector*, an adaptation of John Fowles' story, which was made by the top Hollywood film-maker William Wyler and starred Terence Stamp and Samantha Eggar. Also shot there was the acclaimed Michael Powell film *A Canterbury Tale*.

Sean Connery took a period change of pace to star alongside Donald Sutherland in the Michael Crichton-written and -directed adventure *The First Great Train Robbery* (1978), filmed in the countryside between Ashford and Folkestone. The Tommy Steele musical *Half a Sixpence* was filmed in the historical Pantiles of Tunbridge Wells

Beautiful Hever Castle, near Sevenoaks, has acted as the setting for several films over the years, including *The Princess Bride* (1987), directed by Rob Reiner and based on William Goldman's book; Michael Winner's so-so remake of *The Wicked Lady* (1983), starring Faye Dunaway; *Lady Jane* (1986), which starred a young Helena Bonham Carter; and the John Goodman comedy *King Ralph* (1991).

Films making use of locations in Berkshire include *Three Men and a Little Lady* (1990), which was shot at the Douai Abbey School in Reading; rowing drama *True Blue* (1996), which was filmed at Eton College, as was *Chariots of Fire* (1981) and the 1993 version of *The Secret Garden* (also filmed at Allerton Park and Luton Hoo); cult musical *The Rocky Horror Picture Show* (1975), which was filmed at Oakley Court near Windsor; and the US-set military-academy drama *The Lords of Discipline* (1983), which was shot at Wellington College at Crowthorne in Berkshire.

Many films have used the beautiful locations of the university town of Oxford, though it has also gained an international reputation through the success of the TV detective series *Inspector Morse*. Close to Oxford is the stunning stately home of Blenheim Palace, which has featured in such films as *The Avengers* (1998), *Entrapment* (1999) and *Black Beauty* (1994).

The Merchant Ivory film *Howards End* (1992) was filmed in Magdalen College and Oxford Town Hall (where Helena Bonham Carter meets her lover at a lecture). The house that represented Howards End is in a village near Henley-on-Thames in Oxfordshire. Mansfield College was the setting for the opening sequences of the big-budget epic Western *Heaven's Gate* (1980), directed by Michael Cimino, starring Kris Kristofferson, John Hurt and Isabelle Huppert, and hailed as one of the great movie flops. Val Kilmer's action film *The Saint* was also shot in and around the city. *Oxford Blues* (1984) was filmed at Oriel and Christ Church Colleges and at the Oxford Union, and *White Mischief* (1987), featuring Charles Dance and Greta Scacchi, was shot at Magdalen College.

selected films

Anne of the Thousand Days (1969)
Though little seen nowadays, *Anne of the Thousand Days* is a fine example of the Tudor films popular at one time and recently enjoying a resurgence with the success of *Elizabeth* and *Shakespeare in Love*. Richard Burton played the youngish Henry VIII, while Genevieve Bujold played his love, Anne Boleyn. For added poignancy director Charles Jarrott filmed at Hever Castle, near Sevenoaks, which was the Boleyn family home and where the unhappy couple first courted. The impressive castle, lovingly restored by William Waldorf Astor, has also been used for the films *Princess Bride*, *Lady Jane* and *Bullseye*. The film was based on Maxwell Anderson's play, and Bujold gives a wonderful performance, though at times it seems as if Burton is acting by numbers. *Anne of the Thousand Days* was also shot at the Royal Naval College in London (which acted as Henry VIII's Greenwich Palace) and Penshurst Place, in Kent, which has also featured in *Young Sherlock Holmes* (1985) and the TV series *Love on a Branch Line*.

The Avengers (1998)
Though generally acknowledged to be a bit of a flop, there is in fact something fascinating about this uneven updating of the 1960s cult TV series. With Ralph Fiennes as the bowler-hatted John Steed and Uma Thurman as the leather-clad Mrs Peel, it should have been a massive hit, especially when you add Sean Connery as the mad bad guy into the plot. Unfortunately, it didn't work out, and you can tell from the desperate editing that things had

gone badly wrong. That being said, there are moments of pleasure – not least from the impressive locations. Great use is made of Blenheim Palace, near Oxford (used for the exteriors of Hallucinogen House), while other houses on show include Syon House in Middlesex, Stowe House, in Buckinghamshire and Hatfield House in Hertfordshire. The film-makers also shot at the Royal Naval College in Greenwich, and for Mrs Peel's flat enlisted architect Richard Rogers' Chelsea home.

Black Narcissus (1947)

This sumptuous adaptation of Rumer Godden's novel explores the great physical and emotional challenges faced by a group of nuns who struggle to establish a mission in a remote part of the Himalayas. Deborah Kerr gives a fine performance as the Sister Superior, and the film won Oscars for Alfred Junge's art direction and Jack Cardiff's colour cinematography.

In his book *Magic Hour* Jack Cardiff recalls the film: 'Naturally, we all expected to go on location to India and were greatly surprised when Micky [director Michael Powell] told us that the entire film would be made at Pinewood Studios, with the exception of just one day of exteriors at Horsham in Sussex, where there was a garden filled with subtropical plants and trees. It was a wise decision. It gave us greater control. With Junge's sets and backings and the magic of "Poppa" Day's [effects artist W. Percy Day] matte paintings, there were many more artistic opportunities unencumbered by the usual problems on a far-off location.'

Brighton Rock (1947)

A fresh-faced young Richard Attenborough played the nasty gang leader Pinkie Browne in *Brighton Rock*, an adaptation of Graham Greene's novel. It was a change of pace for the 'safe' Attenborough to be the vicious teen leader of a gang of slashers, and he took advantage of a meaty role to consolidate his growing reputation. The film was adapted by Greene himself, working with playwright Terence Rattigan, while direction was in the safe hands of John Boulting. The film is full of fine performances, and offered an early hint that Brighton wouldn't be filmed just as a pretty seaside resort but could offer a darker side for film-makers taking the trip to the south coast. Filming took place specifically at the Palace Pier and Brighton Railway Station.

Attenborough recalled that filming was problematic at times. He said: 'There was a lot of opposition because it was casting shame on the comfortable seaside town of Brighton and so on. But that was all dealt with. We had to have a caption saying "Of course, Brighton is not like this today."'

He added that much of the footage was 'stolen', meaning that it was shot on the streets without the public knowing they were being filmed.

A Canterbury Tale (1944)

A highly curious piece of drama from Michael Powell and Emeric Pressberger, this has little to do with Chaucer but remains highly intriguing – if hardly the wartime propaganda piece that might be expected. A young US serviceman (John Sweet) meets a Land Girl (Sheila Sim, who later married Richard Attenborough) and a British soldier (Dennis Price) at a small village station after mistakenly thinking he had arrived at Canterbury. The three band together to unmask the mysterious 'Glueman', a shadowy figure who is in the habit of pouring glue into girls' hair. Suspicion falls on the local squire (played by Eric Portman), whose lectures are well attended mainly because young girls are scared to be out on the streets because of the 'Glueman'. The squire's house is actually Wickhambreaux Court in Kent (though the interiors were shot at Denham Studios), while filming also took place in Canterbury. In the film the village where the characters meet is called Chillingbourne, but it is actually a montage of various Kent villages, including Shottenden, Selling, Fordwich and Wingham.

Carrington (1995)

Written and directed by Christopher Hampton, *Carrington* is based on the true story of the dazzling but doomed English painter Dora Carrington (played by Emma Thompson) and her unconventional relationship with writer Lytton Strachey (Jonathan Pryce). Location manager Nick Daubeny had to find houses in the spirit of the originals, Tidmarsh Hall and Ham Spray, where the two set up home and later formed a *ménage à trois* with Ralph Partridge (played by Steven Waddington). Daubeny found them in privately owned Turville Lodge in Henley-on-Thames and Bolebrooke Mill, a bed-and-breakfast in Hartfield, East Sussex. The houses were transformed, with Carrington's pictures re-created by artist Jane Gifford, with Pryce and Samuel West (who played Gerald Brenan) as models. The film was also shot at Robin Hood's Bay in North Yorkshire, which stood in for the Sussex Downs, and on the rugged Welsh coast.

Dirty Weekend (1993)

Michael Winner made a slight change of pace from his successful *Death Wish* films to offer this time a woman vigilante cleaning up the streets of Brighton rather than have Charles Bronson taking on New York. Based on Helen Zahavi's novel (she co-wrote the script with Winner), the film features the

△ A cigar-chomping Michael Winner points out the next shot to his star Lia Williams while on location in Brighton for *Dirty Weekend*.

impressive Lia Williams as Bella. Shortly after she moves into her own Brighton flat, she finds herself being spied on and later harassed by a man living near by. She sorts things out by resorting to judicious use of the hammer, but then realizes it isn't just one man who needs her attention. Though extremely rough around the edges, the film offers snippets of interest – especially in the form of Williams' performance. Winner shot in and around Brighton, and as usual his film is edited by one Arnold Crust Jr (also known as Michael Winner).

The Draughtsman's Contract (1982)

Peter Greenaway's first feature-length film was made on the scanty budget of just £3 million, but his inspired use of locations and skilful production design give it a look far beyond its budget. On the surface the story is a simple one. A draughtsman (Anthony Higgins) is hired to produce twelve drawings of a country house, Compton Anstey. But rather than being paid in hard cash, he asks the lady of the house, Mrs Herbert (well played by Janet Suzman), for 'the unrestricted freedom of her most intimate hospitality'. What develops is a film about sex, class and art, with the elements of a murder-mystery, for odd things begin to happen as the drawings progress. The owners of the country house originally asked for their property's location to be kept secret, but when ownership passed on it was revealed that the beautiful home is actually Groombridge Place, near Tunbridge Wells, built in the seventeenth century, with gardens designed by the diarist John Evelyn.

A Fish Called Wanda (1988)

One of the big hits of the 1980s, *A Fish Called Wanda* proved to be a perfect amalgam of two very British comedy styles – the classic Ealing comedies of the big screen with the off-beat television humour of the Monty Python team. The story was originated by John Cleese and veteran Ealing director Charles Crichton (who made *The Lavender Hill Mob*), and it was Crichton who took the directing credit. An American element came in the form of Jamie Lee Curtis (who until then had rarely displayed her comedic skills) and Kevin Kline as the duo who try to get hold of diamonds stolen in a robbery. Cleese is Archie Leach (the joke being that this was the real name of Cary Grant), a barrister representing the criminal boss behind the raid, and whom Curtis sets about seducing to try to find out where the diamonds are. The robbery sequence took place in Hatton Garden, London's diamond centre, while Cleese's law offices are in Lincoln's Inn Fields. The interior Old Bailey sequences were shot in a former courtroom that is part of Oxford Town Hall, while the prison scenes were filmed at Oxford Prison. The London flat that Cleese borrows for his assignation with Curtis is a converted warehouse apartment on the South Bank with views of Tower Bridge. The closing scenes of the attempted escape were shot at Heathrow Airport.

Four Weddings and a Funeral (1994)

There was little stopping this endearing British comedy when it arrived at the cinemas. It took the UK and the US by storm, and launched Hugh Grant (playing the endearing, bumbling Charles) into leading-man status. At the same time it brought to the screen a selection of wonderful locations and helped boost the business of a certain hotel in Amersham. Directed by Mike Newell, the film was made on a modest budget of £3 million but went on to become one of the biggest UK hits ever, only subsequently overshadowed by

△ Rowan Atkinson (the priest in the distance) presides over wedding two, shot in the chapel of the Royal Naval College at Greenwich, in *Four Weddings and a Funeral*.

its sort of follow-up, *Notting Hill* (1999). So, to run through those weddings and a funeral!

Wedding One: Filmed at St Michael's Church in Betchworth, near Dorking. In the film everyone wanders across fields to the reception, but in fact this was shot in the grounds of Goldingtons, a private manor house near Sarratt in Hertfordshire.

Wedding Two: Filmed in the chapel of the Royal Naval College at Greenwich, with the reception shot at Luton Hoo, the stately home at Luton, Bedfordshire.

Wedding Three: Though supposedly held in Scotland the production couldn't afford to head north of the border, so the wedding of Andie MacDowell's Carrie and Hamish (Corin Redgrave) was filmed at Albury Park, near

Guildford, Surrey, with the Scottish reception shot at the impressive Gothic house Rotherfield Park, at East Tisted, Hampshire.

The Funeral: The moving funeral of Gareth (an exuberant performance by Simon Callow) takes place shortly after Carrie's wedding, and was filmed at St Clement's Church in West Thurrock, on the Thames. The stark industrial background to the church offered a moving contrast to the joyous opulence of the previous weddings.

Wedding Four: With Charles due to be married to 'Duck Face' (aka Henrietta, played by Anna Chancellor), the wedding was shot at the Priory Church of St Bartholomew the Great, close to Smithfield Market in London.

Other locations include the Tower Hotel near Tower Bridge on the Thames, where the two lovers spend another night of passion; and the National Film Theatre on the South Bank, where Charles meets his brother. From the NFT he chases along the walkway outside the Royal Festival Hall, next to the Thames, where he declares his love for Carrie. For the French release Kristin Scott Thomas, who lives in France, dubbed her own voice.

Genevieve (1953)

This charming classic comedy is full of honest warmth, fine performances and some beautiful vintage cars. The background to the story is that two rival car owners challenge each other to a race on the return leg of the annual London to Brighton Vintage Car Rally. The drivers were Kenneth More and John Gregson (who couldn't drive prior to filming) and their passengers Dinah Sheridan (travelling with Gregson) and Kay Kendall as a trumpet-playing model. The director was Henry Cornelius. For convenience most of the filming was done on country roads close to Pinewood Studios rather than on the London to Brighton road, though filming did take place at The Jolly Woodman pub in Burnham, Berkshire, and a modest amount of pick-up

△ Kenneth More stands to encourage the London youngsters to cross, while John Gregson waits in car 27, *Genevieve*.

shooting, with the cars mounted on trailers, was done in the Brighton region. There was also filming on Westminster Bridge and in Hyde Park and the Strand as the race comes to a conclusion. A thoroughly enjoyable film, it was a fitting showcase for its two vintage stars: a 1904 Spyker and a 1904 Darracq (the actual Genevieve of the title).

Great Expectations (1946)

This truly remarkable early film from David Lean is full of wonderful performances that linger in the mind long after viewing. Based on Dickens' novel, the film also marked the first film performance by Alec Guinness, who plays Herbert Pocket opposite John Mills as the adult Pip. Though much of the film was shot in the studio, the frightening opening sequence where Pip first

△ John Mills as the adult Pip in David Lean's memorable *Great Expectations*.

encounters the escaped criminal Magwitch was shot in the atmospheric St Mary's Marshes, close to the mouth of the Thames. The forge where Pip lives as a young boy was also filmed there. Lean shot another – later – sequence close to the marshes, when Pip and Pocket are picked up in a rowing boat on the River Medway. For the scene in which Pip first arrives in London by coach Lean chose to film outside St Paul's Cathedral.

Howards End (1992)

Though much of the film is set in London, E.M. Forster's story revolves around the house of the title, for which the Merchant Ivory team used Peppard Cottage, near Henley-on-Thames in Oxfordshire. The story relates how the Wilcox family are shocked when the elderly Ruth Wilcox (Vanessa Redgrave) leaves the house to her friend Miss Schlegel (Emma Thompson),

△ Peppard Cottage, the setting for Merchant Ivory's *Howards End*.

who later develops an unlikely relationship with her late friend's husband Henry (Anthony Hopkins), and marries him. A subplot has Miss Schlegel's sister Helen (Helena Bonham Carter) falling for the working-class Mr Bast (Samuel West). For a local village the film-makers shot at Dorchester, on the Thames in Oxfordshire, while the London locations included the department store Fortnum & Mason, St James's Court Hotel, Victoria Square, Simpson's-in-the-Strand restaurant, Admiralty Arch and St Pancras Station.

Kind Hearts and Coronets (1949)

This wonderfully delicious dark Ealing comedy was recently voted number six in the British Film Institute's list of the top hundred British movies, and it is certainly one of the greatest films to emerge from the UK. It made a star

of Alec Guinness, who gives truly remarkable performances. 'Performances', plural, is correct, because he plays eight aristocratic members of the D'Ascoyne family – a general, a snob, a photographer, a suffragette, an admiral, a clergyman, a banker and the duke. But though he controls the film, it is actually Dennis Price who is the star, playing Louis Mazzini, the penniless ninth in line to inherit the D'Ascoyne dukedom, who sets about systematically murdering the eight between him and the title. The dukedom also includes Chalfont Castle, for which director Robert Hamer actually used Leeds Castle, near Maidstone in Kent. With its battlements and moat, it is clear why Mazzini wants to get his hands on it. The castle, dating from the ninth century, is in a beautiful location and is certainly well worth a visit. *Kind Hearts and Coronets* is full of fine performances and great quotations: from this film comes the line 'Revenge is the dish which people of taste prefer to eat cold'.

The Madness of King George (1994)

In this impressive big-screen adaptation of Alan Bennett's clever play Nigel Hawthorne reprises his excellent performance as England's eccentrically benevolent late-eighteenth-century king. The title of the play was *The Madness of George III*, but the film was re-titled in case audiences thought they had missed the first two films in a series. The fact that Hawthorne had honed his performance on stage is clear, for he is tremendous as George III, who gradually becomes ill and shows signs of mental instability. As his illness gets worse, the court and Parliament start their intrigues, while his son (Rupert Everett, in a performance that helped re-establish his reputation) makes plans to take the throne. Nicolas Hytner made his debut as director and brilliantly opened out the play through excellent use of a whole series of locations. Arundel Castle in Sussex was used as the exterior for Windsor Castle, while the Windsor interiors were filmed at Wilton House, near

Salisbury in Wiltshire. Also used was Thame Park, near Oxford, for the scenes in which George is sent to visit his doctor-cum-psychiatrist, Willis (Ian Holm), for treatment. Other locations include Eton College, Berkshire, acting as the Houses of Parliament (look out for playwright Alan Bennett as a Member of Parliament near the end of the film); St Paul's Cathedral in London; and the Royal Naval College at Greenwich. The film is memorable for its remarkable performances, Helen Mirren especially good as George's loyal wife, Queen Charlotte. While she and the Prince of Wales (Everett) are passing the crowds she whispers the classic line: 'Smile and wave. It's what you're paid for.'

A Man For All Seasons (1966)

This elegant adaptation of Robert Bolt's stage play is beautifully directed by Fred Zinnemann, and the film won six Oscars, including best picture, best director, best script (by Bolt) and best actor, presented to Paul Scofield. He plays the Catholic statesman Thomas More who clashed with Henry VIII (played with gusto by Robert Shaw) over the king's plans for the Church. The story calls for much of the film to be based at Hampton Court, but in fact sets at Pinewood Studios were used, with the studio's swimming pool standing in for the River Thames. Zinnemann did do some location filming, at a former Benedictine nunnery called Studley Priory at Horton-cum-Studley, near Oxford, while the scene where Henry leaps from his barge into the Thames mud was shot at a stretch of the Beaulieu River on the Beaulieu estate in Hampshire. This lovely estate, the home of the National Motor Museum, includes impressive grounds and Beaulieu Abbey.

Mona Lisa (1986)

This sharp and often brutal thriller opens in London as prostitutes tout their trade and gangsters struggle for power, but it is the closing sequences in Brighton that somehow linger in the mind, perhaps because only when the

△ Bob Hoskins and a very big hand from *Mona Lisa*.

characters reach the sunshine do they begin to believe that some sort of escape from the claustrophobic pressures of London might be possible. Directed by Neil Jordan, the film stars Bob Hoskins as ex-con George, just out of prison but immediately returning to the underworld, driving the high-priced call girl Simone (the excellent Cathy Tyson in her first film role) from job to job. The early scenes see them at work at top London hotels (like The Ritz), around the streets of Soho (seedier in the days when the film was made) and in wealthy Hampstead. Then the duo and Simone's young abused friend (played by Sammi Davis) try to escape the mobster boss Mortwell (a stunningly nasty performance by Michael Caine) by heading to the south coast. They hide in Brighton and finally seem to have found some sort of peace – until Mortwell's thugs find them on Brighton Pier.

The Mummy (1999)

Although the majority of the filming of the successful horror/thriller *The Mummy*, written and directed by Stephen Sommers, took place at Shepperton Studios and on location in Morocco, two key scenes were filmed away from the studio to depict the River Nile. The scene where the band of adventurers – Brendan Fraser, Rachel Weisz and John Hannah – board their steamer to set off to try to find the lost city of Hamunaptra was filmed at Chatham Docks. The film's location manager, Gilly Case, said: 'The art department did an incredible job of making the docks look like Giza in the 1920s.' While the river in the background is the Thames rather than the Nile, the special-effects magicians provided shots of pyramids and background buildings. The film also used Frensham Great Pond in Surrey for the sequence where that self-same steamer catches fire and sinks.

Onegin (1999)

Ralph Fiennes gives one of his best performances as Eugene Onegin in this beautifully structured adaptation of Alexander Pushkin's novel in verse, *Eugene Onegin*, directed by his sister Martha Fiennes. *Onegin*, set in 1820s Russia, tells the moving story of how disaffected young Onegin has to leave St Petersburg to inherit his uncle's estate and strikes up a delicate though warm friendship with a neighbour, Vladimir Lensky (Toby Stephens). He is also charmed by Lensky's love for his fiancée, Olga (Lena Headey), and intrigued and amused by Olga's young sister, Tatyana (Liv Tyler), a spirited beauty who surprises him with a passionate declaration of love. Disturbed by her directness, he coolly – and politely – rejects her love. He lives to regret his decision.

The crew started shooting in freezing temperatures and snow-covered streets in St Petersburg in early March 1998, then after a week's shooting moved back to the UK to sets in Shepperton Studios and local locations. Producer Simon Bosanquet said: 'We thought it would be wonderful to shoot the whole film in Russia, but, although we had a great support team there, it would have posed several practical problems, not least the fact that half of the film is set in the spring and Russia was still covered in snow during early April. The location manager Jim Clay and his team found some remarkable locations a few miles from Shepperton for the exterior shots of the Larin and Onegin estates, which look nothing like England and everything like Russia.' In total the film used four sound stages at Shepperton for the interiors, as well as several nearby exterior locations, including Thursley Common (which doubled for the birch and pine forests of the Russian countryside, where the team built Tatyana's folly), plus the

derelict Elizabethan country house called The Grange, in Winchester, which stood in for the Onegin country estate.

△ Alphonsia Emmanuel, Kenneth Branagh, Hugh Laurie, Imelda Staunton, Emma Thompson and Stephen Fry, in *Peter's Friends*.

Peter's Friends (1992)

In the early 1990s, when Kenneth Branagh and Emma Thompson were still married and regarded as the royal couple of the acting world, they gathered their thespian buddies together and headed off to a beautiful stately home to make a film. *Peter's Friends* can be regarded as a sort of British *The Big Chill* and features a fine cast of comedians and actors. The story is that the wealthy Peter (Stephen Fry) invites his old university chums to stay at his family home – partly so they can deal with old issues and current relationships, but mainly so he can tell them about his illness. The family home is actually Wrotham Park, at Barnet in Hertfordshire, and is the perfect backdrop to this warm-hearted comedy. Wrotham Park also played host to Ken Russell's fascinating but raunchy film *Gothic* (1986) about Byron and Shelley, and to *Princess Caraboo* (1994), a well-meaning period story about a young woman who pretends to be a princess.

Quadrophenia (1979)

A musical drama that has gathered increasing cult value as the years have gone by, this film offers a fascinating glimpse of an era and style long gone. With music from The Who, the film, directed by Franc Roddam, is essentially about the bitter rivalry between the scooter-riding and fashion-conscious mods and the leather-jacketed rockers as they fought it out around Brighton in 1964. Roddam filmed in and around Brighton, though the Brighton pub scene was actually filmed in London. He also filmed in Shepherd's Bush in London and in the distinctive 1960s-style café, Alfredo's, on Essex Road in Islington, London. A few gaffes slipped  into the film: some of the rockers are shown wearing Motorhead T-shirts long before the band was formed; and in a scene of the gangs fighting a poster for the film *Heaven Can Wait*, which came out in 1978, can be seen.

A Room With a View (1986)

Though the first part of *A Room With a View* unfolds in Italy (Florence in particular), the second part is very much set in England as we observe the Honeychurch family at play and are introduced to the stuffy Cecil Vyse (a fine performance by Daniel Day-Lewis). In the film young Lucy Honeychurch (Helena Bonham Carter, establishing her reputation as princess of such costume dramas) is travelling with her cousin Charlotte (Maggie Smith) in Italy, and there she meets Mr Emerson (Denholm Elliott)

and his son George (Julian Sands). While walking after a picnic George kisses her, throwing her feelings into confusion. She returns to England and her family home. The

△ Liam Neeson and Laura San Giacomo pose on Brighton beach, in *Under Suspicion*.

team of Merchant Ivory (producer Ismail Merchant and director James Ivory) used the private house Foxwold, near Brasted in Kent, as the Honeychurch residence. They acquired the house for the film through writer-critic John Pym, whose family has lived there since the 1880s and who happened to have written *The Wandering Company*, a book about Merchant Ivory. The stunningly beautiful, gabled house had the added value of being set in grounds in which further shooting could take place. It was there that Ivory shot the scene where Lucy, Lucy's mother and Cecil discover Sands, Simon

Callow (playing the Reverend Beebe) and Rupert Graves (playing Lucy's brother) romping naked in a pond. The film-makers also filmed in the nearby National Trust village of Chiddingstone, which appeared as the local village in the film, and at another nearby National Trust site, Emmets Garden, where a garden party sequence was shot.

The Secret Garden (1993)

A much-loved children's book by Frances Hodgson Burnett, *The Secret Garden* was first made into a film in 1949. Although the filming was very much studio-bound, this in fact lent much atmosphere to the gloomy house and the shrouded, misty and special garden. The story is about a lonely orphaned girl who is sent to live with her uncle and his invalid son. Initially difficult and confused, she grows to love the house, and when she discovers a hidden-away garden she helps bring joy back to the boy and his father. In the 1993 version, directed by Agnieszka Holland, a lot of effort was made to find the right garden. The result was an amalgam of several locations, plus judicious use of Pinewood Studios. The film was shot in the main at Luton Hoo, near Luton, at Allerton Park, near Knaresborough in Yorkshire, and at Fountains Hall, near Ripon, also in Yorkshire. Some scenes were shot at Eton College, Berkshire, Harrow School, Middlesex, and at St Pancras Station in London. In the newer version Kate Maberly takes on the role of the young Mary, sent to live in the stuffy family home, while the film provided memorable roles for Maggie Smith and Heydon Prowse.

Under Suspicion (1992)

A fine script from writer-director Simon Moore turned into this interesting, and highly atmospheric film set in 1959 in Brighton. Liam Neeson stars as Tony Aaron, an ex-cop turned seedy private eye who makes his money faking adultery cases to help clients get round the divorce laws. He suddenly finds himself the chief suspect in a murder inquiry and has to set about proving his innocence. Moore makes good use of the Brighton locations (though in one continuity gaffe a modern British Telecom telephone box can be seen in the opening sequence). He also shot in the Welsh village of Portmeirion, which gained fame as the location for the cult 1960s TV series *The Prisoner*. Some scenes were filmed in Miami.

Wilde (1997)

A handsomely mounted biopic about the life of playwright and wit Oscar Wilde, the film focuses on his love for Lord Alfred Douglas, which brought about his disgrace, jailing and eventual exile from Britain. Stephen Fry is excellent as Wilde, finding the perfect vehicle for his natural wit, while Jude Law makes a suitably attractive Lord Alfred 'Bosie' Douglas. The film does a fine job of telling a rounded story, dovetailing Wilde's declared homosexuality with his affection for his children, and is well staged by director Brian Gilbert. It was shot around London, but made good use of other locations, especially Magdalen College, Oxford. For the exile sequences they also popped over to Spain.

Wish You Were Here (1987)

One of the big British hits during the late 1980s, this propelled to fame the young Emily Lloyd (whose father, Roger Lloyd Pack, is a regular on British television in *Only Fools and Horses* and *The Vicar of Dibley*). *Wish You Were Here* was written and directed by David Leland, who admitted that the story was very much based on the younger years of the madam Cynthia Payne, whom he came to know when writing the script of *Personal Services* about her later career. Set in the 1950s, the film stars Emily Lloyd as a foul-mouthed teenager growing up in a seaside town. Leland used locations in the Sussex resorts of Worthing and Bognor Regis, while the bowling scenes were shot at Brighton. The Dome cinema, where Lloyd meets her older lover (played by Tom Bell) is a real cinema in Worthing, an elegant listed building built at the beginning of the twentieth century.

south-west and west england

THE WEST COUNTRY HAS LONG BEEN A FAVOURITE HOLIDAY DESTINATION for the British when it comes to taking advantage of those few weeks of summer sunshine. The area has also been the inspiration for writers, poets and creative folk over the centuries, and books written by authors like Daphne du Maurier, John Fowles and Thomas Hardy have given evocative descriptions of the beauty of the landscape and coastline.

The West Country covers an extensive area, from the tip of Land's End to the elegant maritime port of Bristol, taking in Cornwall, Devon, Somerset, Dorset and Wiltshire. These counties have long been used in films, especially when it comes to literary adaptations that call for the descriptive powers of authors to be translated to the big screen.

The effect the area has had on authors is legendary. Daphne du Maurier is for ever associated with Cornwall, having penned stories set in such distinctive places as Bodmin Moor (backdrop for the classic *Jamaica Inn*) and beautiful Helford Passage (the setting for the pirate romance *Frenchman's Creek*). Dorset will always be linked with Thomas Hardy, who revived the ancient region of Wessex, and set novels including *Tess of the D'Urbervilles* and *Far From the Madding Crowd* there. Other writers inspired by the area include Ruth Rendell, John Fowles, Jane Austen and Henry Fielding.

Hardy had links with Cornwall as well. He lived there for a while, and when he was staying on the coast at St Juliot, where he was working as a stonemason restoring the local church, he met his future wife, Florence Emily. Their meeting and his time in Cornwall inspired him to write *A Pair of Blue Eyes*. Agatha Christie put Devon on the literary map, for she lived in Torquay for many years and used the town as the setting for several of her books.

From the enduring image of Meryl Streep walking along the seafront promontory of The Cobb at Lyme Regis in the adaptation of *The French Lieutenant's Woman* (1981), or the impressive use of elegant country houses in Oscar-winning *Sense and Sensibility* (1995), to the lush rural settings of John Schlesinger's *Far From the Madding Crowd* (1967), or the crashing Cornish waves in the surfing film *Blue Juice* (1995), the region's beauty makes a massive impact on the screen.

The entire coastline of Cornwall has been designated an Area of Outstanding Natural Beauty, and the county is one of the most popular holiday spots in the UK. The Atlantic crashes on to its shores on three sides, and, while Cornwall certainly has its share of sunshine in summer, in the winter it can be lashed by storms. The county's profile changes as you travel from west to east. The stark beauty of the sea-swept cliffs of Land's End blends into elegant beaches, peaceful inlets and picturesque hidden villages. Inland is the barren beauty of Bodmin Moor, while in north Cornwall rocky Tintagel is reputed to be the birthplace of King Arthur. However, only one of the many films about Arthur was shot at Tintagel. That was *Knights of the Round Table* (1953), starring Robert Taylor and Ava Gardner, some scenes of which were filmed there.

Films shot in Cornwall include *Never Let Me Go* (1953), featuring Clark Gable and Gene Tierney, filmed at Mullion harbour, Newquay and Mevagissey (though director Delmer Davies went elsewhere for a double for Tallinn in Estonia); the comedy *Yellow Sands* (1938), starring a young Robert Newton and Marie Tempest, filmed at Sennen Cove; the 1940 version of *The Thief of Baghdad*, which featured Conrad Veidt and Sabu and was filmed at Gunwalloe; and the classic *Ghost Train*, shot at Liskeard in 1941.

> 'A friend who had started going down to Cornwall said we had got to come down, that it is a really vibrant scene down here with surfing, and all the parties going on. We went down, had a look, had a go in the water and thought, yeah – this is just the place.'
>
> Peter Salmi, producer of *Blue Juice*

The beautiful Minack Theatre at Porthcurne (a stunning Greek-style outdoor theatre overlooking the sea) was the location for *Love Story* (1944), which starred Margaret Lockwood as a dying pianist who finds true love with a pilot (Stewart Granger) whose eyesight is failing. Disney has made trips to Cornwall, too. Its 1949 version of *Treasure Island*, starring Robert Newton, was filmed at the Carrick Roads estuary, on the rivers Fal and Helford and at Gull Rock, while its version of *The Three Musketeers* (1993) offers the sight of young thespians Charlie Sheen, Kiefer Sutherland, Oliver Platt and Chris

O'Donnell wielding their swords in places that include Charlestown, Boconnoc Estate, Lanhydrock, Pentire and Rumps Point.

The comedy *Crooks in Cloisters* (1963), starring Ronald Fraser, Barbara Windsor and Bernard Cribbins, about a gang of forgers posing as monks, was filmed at St Mawes; the enchanting comedy *Miranda* (1947), directed by Ken Annakin and starring Glynis Johns as a mermaid caught by a doctor on holiday in Cornwall, was shot partly at Polperro and Looe; and the period adventure *Dangerous Exile* (1957), about the young would-be Louis XVII brought to Pembrokeshire after the French Revolution and hidden from attack, was shot in Porthluney Cove, Carrick Roads, Falmouth bay and harbour and Caerhays Castle.

Nicolas Roeg shot scenes of his enchanting children's film *The Witches* (1990), based on Roald Dahl's story, at the Headland Hotel in Newquay, with the remainder of the work filmed at Bray Studios. Starring Angelica Huston, Mai Zetterling and Rowan Atkinson, it is about a young boy who is turned into a mouse by witches staying at his hotel. With the aid of his grandmother he conspires to thwart the witches, who plan to poison all the children in Britain. Huston is perfect as the witches' leader.

Also filmed to great effect in Cornwall were the excellent surfing film *Blue Juice*, Ang Lee's exquisite version of *Sense and Sensibility* (1995), and *All the Little Animals* (1998), the directorial debut of top British producer Jeremy Thomas. Francis Ford Coppola was in the county to shoot scenes for his vampire film *Bram Stoker's Dracula* (1992), starring Gary Oldman, Winona Ryder and Anthony Hopkins, which he filmed at Tintagel and St Michael's Mount; while an earlier horror film, *The Final Conflict* (1981) – the third of the *Omen* films – starring Sam Neill as the Devil on Earth, was filmed at Penrice, St Austell, Luxulyan and Prideaux Place, Padstow.

Recently, two major-budget films were shooting at the same time in north Cornwall and using neighbouring locations. At one point the two films, *Amy Foster* (1997) and *Oscar & Lucinda* (1997), the latter starring Ralph Fiennes and Cate Blanchett, even used the same beach. *Oscar & Lucinda* was also shot at Boscastle (where houses were repainted for the film), Port Isaac, Bossiney, Crackington Haven, Morwenstow and Trebarwith. Trevor Nunn's *Twelfth Night* (1996), which starred Helena Bonham Carter and Imogen Stubbs, was shot at Lanhydrock (Olivia's house, garden and estate), St Michael's Mount (Orsino's castle), Trerice (Olivia's estate), Trebarwith (the shipwreck scene) and Prideaux Place, Padstow. Prideaux was the main location, chosen by Nunn because it offered everything 'from the formal prose of gracious gardens to the high drama of its coastal landscape'.

Somerset – which has a reputation for cider, cheese and more cider – is known as the 'county of contrast', and its lush rolling countryside is resonant with its ancient history. Glastonbury Tor in particular was important to the Ancient Britons and it continues to attract contemporary travellers wanting to forge a link with the ancient past. In another link with Arthurian legend, monks at Glastonbury Abbey claim to have found there the remains of King Arthur and Queen Guinevere.

Devon is a mixture of beautiful coastal scenery and rich agricultural country. Towns such as Brixham, Paignton and Torquay (the last the setting for the television classic *Fawlty Towers*) are popular tourist spots, while larger towns like Plymouth and Exeter are rich with reminders of their historic past. Films shot in the county are as different as *Carry On – Follow That Camel* (1967) and *A Matter of Life and Death* (1946).

Carry On – Follow That Camel stars Phil Silvers, Kenneth Williams, Jim Dale and Joan Sims and is a tale of cricket and the Foreign Legion. It was filmed around Devon as well as (re-creating the sand-dunes of North Africa) at Camber Sands in East Sussex. Michael Powell made one of his earliest films in Devon, shooting *Phantom Light* (1935) both at Eddystone Lighthouse and at Hartland Point, as well as in Wales (the film is about a haunted Welsh lighthouse), and returned to the county in 1946 to make the much-loved classic *A Matter of Life and Death*. Other films shot in Devon include the Norman Wisdom comedy *Press for Time* (1966), which was filmed at Teignmouth, and the disturbing but compelling supernatural drama *The Shout*, directed by Jerzy Skolimowski and starring Alan Bates, Susannah York and John Hurt.

'Far From the Madding Crowd *was shot in Dorset, a most beautiful place and very important to my life I lived in a little cottage, and I remember driving to work very early each morning, seeing the dew in the trees... it was a wonderful experience, after which I decided I was going to live in the country.'*
Julie Christie

Dorset has naturally been the location for many film and television versions of Thomas Hardy novels. Films of Hardy novels shot in the county include *Far From the Madding Crowd* (1967), *The Woodlanders* (1997) and *The Scarlet Tunic* (1998). Other works made in Dorset include *Wilde* (1997), starring Stephen Fry; *Emma* (1996), which featured Gwyneth Paltrow and Toni Collette, and the classic crime two-hander *Sleuth* (1972), starring Michael Caine and Laurence Olivier.

Wiltshire, quite apart from its natural attractions, benefits from the fact that it is only an hour or so from London and therefore all the more

△ The beautiful Wilton House, near Salisbury, the setting for a variety of films including *Sense and Sensibility* and *The End of the Affair*.

popular with film-makers hesitant to venture too far from the capital. Continuing the Arthurian connections, legend has it that Merlin, King Arthur's magician, is buried at Marlborough. No Arthurian film has been made in the county, but many of the Hardy adaptations have strayed into Wiltshire to take advantage of the rolling landscape, and some of Ang Lee's *Sense and Sensibility* was also filmed there. So, too, was *Doctor Dolittle* (1967), starring Rex Harrison, Samantha Eggar and Anthony Newley, which was filmed at Castle Combe (proclaimed England's Most Beautiful Village in 1966), which was transformed into Puddleby-on-the-Marsh; the Merchant Ivory film *Maurice* (1987); and the Beatles romp *Help!*, part of which was filmed on Salisbury Plain.

Wilton House near Salisbury is a popular venue for filming. Over the years a large number of films have been shot there, including *Barry Lyndon* (1975), *The Madness of King George* (1994), some sequences of the Richard Harris Western *Return of a Man Called Horse* (1976), *Scandal* (1989) and the Mel Gibson version of *The Bounty* (1983). In the same area near Salisbury is Old Wardour Castle, where one of the scenes in the Kevin Costner adventure *Robin Hood: Prince of Thieves* (1991) was filmed. Jane Campion's *The Portrait of a Lady* (1996), starring Nicole Kidman, was filmed at Heale House as well as at Wilton House.

The two major cities of the region are Bath and Bristol, both of which have featured in several major films and have developed thriving media support-industries. Val Guest shot *80,000 Suspects* (1963), starring Claire Bloom and Richard Johnson, in Bath, and Bryan Forbes directed *The Wrong Box* (1966), with Ralph Richardson and John Mills, there. Other films made in Bath include the tough British drama *Hollow Reed* (1996), directed by Angela Pope and starring Joely Richardson and Martin Donovan; *King of the Wind* (1989), with Richard Harris, Glenda Jackson and Nigel Hawthorne; and the BBC version of *Persuasion* (1995).

In the nearby seaside resort of Weston-super-Mare, Frank Launder made his satirical comedy *Lady Godiva Rides Again* (1951), which stars Pauline Stroud, Stanley Holloway, Diana Dors and Alastair Sim. The closing sequences of *The Remains of the Day* (1993) were filmed there, too.

Bristol was used partly for the location of the supernatural thriller *The Medusa Touch* (1978), starring Richard Burton as a novelist who thinks he can cause disasters; while rock musician Sting made his film debut in Chris Petit's *Radio On* (1979), an art-house hit about a man travelling from London to Bristol. On a much smaller scale, Kate Winslet turned from her big-budget success in *Titanic* to feature in the low-budget short film *Plunge* (1997), about a group of Bristol roadsweepers who discover a surfboard in a bin and take off to Cornwall to try their hand at surfing. Winslet plays a female roadsweeper they meet on their travels.

Wilton House

This lovely country house (see opposite) near Salisbury is frequently used by film-makers, who are drawn by stunning interiors (the Double Cube Room and the Cloisters are often filmed) and beautiful and extensive grounds, which contain woods, gardens and water gardens. The mansion is notable for its south front, designed by Inigo Jones. During the Second World War the property was used for military purposes, and the Normandy invasion was planned in the Double Cube Room. For some scenes in *The End of the Affair*, the house had to be made to look more dilapidated.

Films: *Barry Lyndon, The Bounty, The End of the Affair, The Madness of King George, Mrs Brown, The Portrait of a Lady, Scandal, Sense and Sensibility*

MOVIE LOCATIONS *south-west and west england*

selected films

Amy Foster (aka Swept From the Sea 1997)

Based on a story by Joseph Conrad and with a script by acclaimed writer Tim Willocks, *Amy Foster* had all the credentials for a romantic movie hit. But despite its attractive looks and strong performances, the film made little impact at the box office. Rachel Weisz (later to star in the effects-laden *The Mummy*) is the servant girl who falls for a shipwrecked Russian in Cornwall but discovers that the course of true love is never smooth. The film-makers shot at Pentire Head overlooking Rumps Point (Amy's cottage); Port Quin (where the crew built a church, shop, pub and fishermen's sheds to add to the village's few cottages); Bodmin and Crackington Haven in Cornwall. They also headed north to Keighley in West Yorkshire.

Blue Juice (1995)

This fascinating attempt at a British surfing movie that made little impact at the time of its release but, thanks to shrewd casting, is now being reviewed and re-evaluated. Catherine Zeta-Jones stars, alongside Sean Pertwee and Ewan McGregor, in this warm-hearted and amusing story of a Cornish-based surf bum (Pertwee) who has to choose between the waves and his long-suffering girlfriend (Zeta-Jones). The Cornwall on show is beautiful – a mixture of beaches, villages and tiny winding lanes – and the film-makers do a good job of contrasting the Cornwall of tradition with the contemporary version, replete with cool surf dudes and raves. Filming took place in Newquay, St Ives, Mousehole, Chapel Porth and Godrevy, though some of the more blue-skied surfing sequences were shot in the Canary Islands.

Producer Peter Salmi said: 'What Carl [the director] and I were really looking for was a venue in which to set a film about four characters at a

particular time of their lives, coming up to the
end of their twenties. A friend who had
started going down to Cornwall said we had
got to come down, that it is a really vibrant

△ Catherine Zeta-Jones and
Sean Pertwee pose at the surf's
edge, in *Blue Juice*.

scene down here with surfing and all the parties going on. We went down,
had a look, had a go in the water and thought, yeah – this is just the place.'

Director Carl Prechezer added: 'Not only have you got surfing, you have
everything it brings with it, the countryside, the scenery – so we brought
London to the country and let it develop from there.'

The Browning Version (1951 and 1994)

The Browning Version, directed by Mike Figgis and starring Albert
Finney, Greta Scacchi and Matthew Modine, was filmed in Dorset. In fact,
two versions of this film have been shot in the county: the first in 1951,

△ Gwyneth Paltrow and horse are carefully led across water in an off-camera moment from *Emma*.

starring Michael Redgrave, and the second the 1994 Figgis version. Both used Sherborne School. Other films that used the impressive school, which can date its history from the eighth century, include the musical version of *Goodbye Mr Chips* (1969), which stars Peter O'Toole, and the 1948 drama *The Guinea Pig*, starring Richard Attenborough.

Emma (1996)

An elegant and amusing adaptation of Jane Austen's novel, this film is the first in which Gwyneth Paltrow displayed her skill with a British accent. She is excellent as the young Emma Woodhouse, whose

matchmaking skills are not quite as good as she thinks, and who finds happiness when she least expects it. Written and directed by Douglas McGrath, this is excellent entertainment, with a fine supporting cast. The film was shot around Dorset, making special use of Stafford House, in West Stafford, with the ballroom scenes filmed at Claydon House, Buckinghamshire.

Far From the Madding Crowd (1967)

An impressive and much-loved adaptation of Thomas Hardy's classic, this made exceptional use of numerous locations in Wiltshire and Dorset. Director John Schlesinger recruited a terrific cast – Alan Bates as Gabriel Oak, Julie Christie as Bathsheba Everdene, Peter Finch as wealthy farmer William Boldwood and Terence Stamp as Sergeant Troy – and had the script written by Frederic Raphael. Devizes in Wiltshire was called upon to act as Hardy's fictional market town of Casterbridge, with Schlesinger shooting in the Market Place, the Corn Exchange and in the twelfth-century St John's Church. The classic scene where the pregnant Fanny (Prunella Ransome) walks up the cobbled hill to the poorhouse was shot at Gold Hill in Shaftesbury, which gained still greater fame in the famous Hovis advertisement. The film was also shot partly at the intriguingly named Scratchy Bottom in Dorset (the scene where Oak's sheep tumble over a cliff), while the scene where Troy shows off his skills with a blade was filmed at the pre-Roman fortress of Maiden Castle. The impressive – and poignant – scene where rainwater pours through the mouth of a church gargoyle on to Fanny's grave was filmed at the church in Sydling St Nicholas in Dorset.

Actress Julie Christie warmly recalls her time making the film, saying: '*Far From the Madding Crowd* was shot in Dorset, a most beautiful place and very important to my life. I lived in a little cottage, and I remember driving to

work very early each morning, seeing dew in the trees... it was a wonderful experience, after which I decided I was going to live in the country.'

The French Lieutenant's Woman (1981)

John Fowles's complex novel *The French Lieutenant's Woman* was long thought to be unfilmable. John Frankenheimer, one director who had a go, said: 'There is no way you can film the book. You can tell the same story in a movie, of course, but not in the same way. And how Fowles tells his story is what makes the book so good.' But when acclaimed writer Harold Pinter teamed up with director Karel Reisz they managed to work out a film structure that worked. The film tells two parallel stories. In one, set in Victorian times, Sarah Woodruff (Meryl Streep) keeps her vigil for the French lieutenant she hopes will yet return to her, while also dallying with the obsessed Charles (Jeremy Irons) who falls for her. In the other, contemporary story, two actors named Anna and Mike who are playing Sarah and Charles are also having a forbidden affair. Fowles's story is set in the elegant Dorset town of Lyme Regis, and he makes great use of specific locations in the area. Most famous is the sequence where Streep as Sarah walks along The Cobb, the town's harbour wall, as the waves crash against

◁ Julie Christie is overshadowed by camera equipment during filming of *Far From the Madding Crowd*.

the walkway. Reisz also shot in the Undercliff, a stunningly beautiful area between Axmouth and Lyme Regis, in the sequence where Charles searches for fossils. The family hotel where Sarah stayed was actually the Steampacket Inn in Lyme Regis, while Reisz also dressed Broad Street, the main street through the town. The closing sequences, where Charles searches for Sarah in the Lake District, were shot at Lake Windermere for authenticity.

Land Girls (1998)

Land Girls proved to be an extremely popular release for FilmFour. It is a moving re-creation of rural Britain during the Second World War when women from all walks of life and parts of the country 'did their bit' by working on farms. Based on Angela Huth's novel, the film struck a nostalgic chord (especially with older audiences) and managed to combine romance with drama and was full of fine performances. During the war three very different girls – played by Anna Friel, Catherine McCormack and Rachel Weisz – are sent to work together on a Dorset farm and encounter friendship and experiences that will change their lives for ever. Director David Leland shot largely in Somerset, partly in Devon. He made great use of Dulverton town centre (for the Spitfire Parade with the Home Guard and Land Girls),

Bury Bridge (the scene where the three girls return from church) and Bossington beach near Porlock. The railway sequences were shot at Crowcombe Heathfield Station, part of the West Somerset Railway.

Producer Simon Relph said: 'The film has a very romantic feel, and it is an entertainment. One of the qualities we seem to have achieved is that there is not a sense of having dressed them up [the locations] – that is something to do with the area we filmed, which is in the very west part of Somerset. It is not intensely farmed, and the clock seems to have stopped here. We did look very hard at Dorset, where the book's storyline is actually located, but time had moved on.'

For Dulverton locals the arrival of the film crew was a great experience, and several were recruited as extras. Local councillor Keith Ross liaised with the producers and the local community, and also had a part in the film. 'I got a uniform and a gun and marched around a bit – I even got paid well,' he said. The film company also donated £5,000 to the town council in recognition of any inconvenience caused.

Another local man, Major Humphrey Bradshaw of Dunster, was recruited to play an officer who shows a Land Girl how to use a rifle. 'They were looking for someone who knew something about a Lee Enfield rifle – and I know an awful lot about a Lee Enfield,' he said.

A Matter of Life and Death (1946)

This remarkable and impressive film from the team of Michael Powell and Emeric Pressberger, shot during the end of the Second World War, is part-mystical fantasy and part-patriotic romanticism. A pilot (played with easy charm by David Niven) jumps from his damaged aircraft and is stunned to find he has survived the fall. He also falls for the American woman (Kim Hunter) who was the last person he spoke to on the radio. The mystical element comes when a 'negotiator' is sent from heaven to tell Niven he should have died and must go there; on earth the airman has to have an operation to sever the link with the other world. The magical early scene where Niven emerges from the sea and walks through the sand-dunes was filmed at Saunton Sands in Devon.

The Remains of the Day (1993)

Based on the Booker Prize-winning novel by Kazuo Ishiguro, *The Remains of the Day* is an elegant and moving film, full of fine performances and visual beauty. It is probably the perfect Merchant Ivory project: if there is one thing director James Ivory and producer Ismail Merchant know how to do, it is to make films that reflect the oddities and quirks of the English while at the same time rejoicing in the lush period settings. The story deals with honour, manners, love and duty in the years before and during the Second World War.

Anthony Hopkins is the core of the film, playing Mr Stevens, longtime butler of Darlington Hall. Stevens takes pride in the ordered running of the house, even ignoring the needs of family and those close to him to make sure that things run smoothly. Darlington Hall itself is actually four English stately homes, all of which offer different elements to suit the film. The exteriors are those of Dyrham Park, near Bath (see page 238), owned by the National Trust, while Darlington's library and dining room are actually in Corsham Court, near Chippenham in Wiltshire. The servants' quarter scenes were filmed at Badminton House in Gloucestershire, but several other key scenes were shot at Powderham Castle, near Exeter. In the closing sequences Stevens visits Mrs Kenton (the hall's housekeeper, played by Emma Thompson) at her guesthouse; these were filmed at the seaside resort of Weston-super-Mare.

Scandal (1989)

In the late 1980s *Scandal* was one of the few British films that made much of an impact on the press and the box office. Why it received press attention is easy to see: it retold the story of the seedy 1960s revelations that government minister John Profumo was unknowingly sharing the sexual attentions of showgirl Christine Keeler with a Soviet naval attaché. The film stars Joanne Whalley-Kilmer (as Keeler) and Bridget Fonda (playing Mandy Rice-Davies), which helped guarantee plenty of photographs in newspapers. Director Michael Caton-Jones filmed at Wilton House, near Salisbury in Wiltshire, which acted as Lord Astor's former estate Cliveden, the stately home where Keeler first met Profumo (played by Ian McKellen sporting an ill-fitting bald wig). Another key location was the mews flat where Keeler stayed with her friend Stephen Ward (John Hurt), which in real life was at Bathurst Mews, Paddington, but in the film was off Wimpole Street.

Sense and Sensibility (1995)

Taiwanese director Ang Lee achieved a *tour de force* in bringing Jane Austen's novel to the big screen, assisted in no small measure by leading lady Emma Thompson's fine Oscar-winning script. The story is set in eighteenth-century England, where newly impoverished sisters – one, played by Kate Winslet, spirited and flirtatious, another, Thompson, sensible and restrained – have to do their best in dealing with society and men. The film was shot around the West Country. Venues included Saltram House, near Plympton, which doubled as the Dashwood family home, Norland Park; Trafalgar House, near Salisbury, which was used as Sir John Middleton's home, Barton Park, and also for the game of lawn bowling by the Dashwood sisters and for Marianne's first meeting with Colonel Brandon; Flete Estate, at Holbeston, south Devon;

Montacute House, near Yeovil in Somerset, which featured in scenes where Marianne walks by the misshapen hedge; Wilton House, near Salisbury, scene of the ball attended by the Dashwood sisters; Mompesson House, in Salisbury, which acted as Mrs Jennings' London town house; and Mothecombe House, which doubled as the drawing room of Mrs Jennings' house as well as the backdrop to Edward's confrontation with Lucy and Elinor. The story of the making of *Sense and Sensibility* is beautifully – and often hilariously – told in Emma Thompson's compelling book, *Sense and Sensibility: The Diaries*.

Recalling the time spent filming at Montacute House, Thompson wrote that the National Trust was strict about hours but had 'very nice people who actually seemed quite pleased to see us'. She recalled that Lee was enchanted with the gardens, and especially the topiary of a hedge that appeared to be misshapen. She wrote: 'Apparently it snowed one year and the snow froze the hedge. When the thaw came, they cut away the dead bits and continued to grow the hedge. It looks like a brain. "Sensibility," said Ang, pointing at it triumphantly. "And sense," he continued, pointing in the other direction towards a very neat line of carefully trimmed flowerpot-shaped bushes. The stone lines of Montacute – grand, almost too grand though they are – give this part of the story a Gothic and mysterious flavour.'

Sleuth (1972)

One of the great battle-of-wits films, this has a wonderful script by Anthony Shaffer, who adapted his own successful stage production. Both Laurence Olivier and Michael Caine received Oscar nominations for their performances as the two men who struggle – mentally and physically – against each other. Olivier is crime-writer Andrew Wyke, whose wife Marguerite is having an affair with hair-salon owner Milo Tindle (Caine). Wyke hatches a complicated plot whereby he offers to help Tindle financially by allowing him to steal his

△ Kate Winslet and Emma Thompson take tea on the lawn in Ang Lee's *Sense and Sensibility*.

wife's jewels, so that Wyke can claim the insurance and Milo can sell the jewels. There are bagloads of twists and turns as the pair struggle to gain the upper hand, with nothing ever quite as it seems. The exterior of Wyke's fine country house is actually Athelhampton House near Dorchester, Dorset, but the interiors were all created at Pinewood Studios.

Straw Dogs (1971)

Sam Peckinpah's controversial *Straw Dogs* was set in a Cornish village where a mild-mannered American university researcher, David Sumner (Dustin Hoffman), turns to violence when taunted by villagers, who later attack him and rape his wife, Amy (Susan George). Peckinpah and the cast and crew arrived in Cornwall in January 1971 to shoot the exteriors in the village of St Buryan on the south-western tip of the peninsula. A farmhouse near the village was used as the Sumners' residence, and to prepare for their roles Dustin Hoffman and Susan George wandered the village, talking to locals, with a crew member following them around jotting down the exchanges (some of which made their way into the final film).

Peckinpah organized 'improvisations' – essentially drinking sessions – to help other cast members, such as Peter Vaughan, Ken Hutchinson and Del Henney, get into character. These were so lively that actor T.P. McKenna broke his arm in an incident at one of the parties and wore it in a sling for the shooting of the film.

Peckinpah was drinking heavily throughout filming, and during one night he woke Ken Hutchinson at 3.30 a.m., brandishing a bottle of tequila, and said they had to go and see the sea. They drove to Land's End and walked to the cliff's edge as the rain poured down. Hutchinson said: 'We sat down, listened to the sea, drank tequila, and he taught me the lyrics to a song called "Butterfly Mornings". I found out later that it was from *The Ballad of Cable Hogue* [another Peckinpah film]. Pissed as two farts, wet, cold, in the middle of winter – never been so happy in all my life.'

The Titfield Thunderbolt (1953)

One of the great Ealing comedies – also the first in colour – *The Titfield Thunderbolt* remains a thoroughly charming piece of whimsy directed by one of the greatest comedy film-makers to emerge from the UK, Charles Crichton. The film is also a favourite for fans of steam engines, and it wonderfully evokes an England of years gone by when rail travel was by steam. The plot is simple: the local railway line is under threat, so the Titfield villagers get together to try to run things themselves. The fictional Titfield Station was Monkton Combe Station (now long gone) at Monkton Combe near Bath, while Mallingford Station (the end of the Titfield line) was actually Bristol Temple Meads. The film also had a scene shot in London: the memorable sequence where the villagers sneak the Titfield Thunderbolt from a local museum was filmed at the old Imperial Institute, Exhibition Road, now the site of Imperial College.

Tom Jones (1963)

The film of Henry Fielding's comic romp, which starred a young Albert Finney, was a massive box-office success around the world and received a hefty ten Oscar nominations. It ended up winning four – best film, best director (Tony Richardson), best-adapted screenplay (John Osborne) and best
music (John Addison) – and despite its period setting it remains the perfect

1960s movie in terms of its joyfulness and passion. Nettlecombe Court in Somerset provided bedrooms and a hall for the film, while Richardson also filmed at Cranborne

△ Michael Maloney and Juliet Stevenson on London's South Bank, in *Truly Madly Deeply*.

Manor House in Dorset. Exteriors were shot on the lovely Exmoor moorland and in the Somerset town of Bridgwater.

Truly Madly Deeply (1990)

Writer-director Anthony Minghella wrote the script with actress Juliet Stevenson in mind, and she certainly fulfils his confidence, turning in a flawless performance in this unusual tale of spiritual romance. Minghella (later responsible for *The English Patient* and *The Talented Mr Ripley*) made a film that really clicked at the box office and provided a sublime combination of talents – the wonderful Stevenson playing a woman trying to get over the death of her husband, and Alan Rickman as the cello-playing husband (the original title was *Cello*) who returns from death to try to help her. The film is as funny as it is moving, and full of ironic charm. It was shot in and around Bristol, making good use of the city's Goldney Hall (for a concert scene), and also in London, specifically on the South Bank alongside the Thames.

The War Zone (1999)

This powerful and moving drama, based on the novel by Alexander Stuart, was the directorial debut of British actor Tim Roth, who starred in films such as *Reservoir Dogs*. A seemingly middle-class family move from London to Devon, and fifteen-year-old Tom learns that the war zone is at the heart of his family. He finds his new life boring but is little prepared for the secret shared by his father and sister, eighteen-year-old Jessie. Even more isolated and consumed by anger, he is determined to reveal the truth, and a harrowing story of how incest can destroy families unfolds. Beautifully filmed in a deliberately dark and gloomy style by cinematographer Seamus McGarvey, Roth used rain-drenched locations in the town of Torridge and around the north Devon coast.

For production designer Michael Carlin, the challenge was re-creating real sets. 'Tim was very concerned that we shoot in real spaces, that there were no fake façades or scaffolding, so it would feel real to the two younger actors. It would have been considerably easier to shoot a lot of the Devon house interiors on a sound stage, but Tim insisted on a real working house.'

After an extensive search in north Devon, Carlin found a house that, with the owner's permission, could be altered considerably. Keen to create an environment that would never spell home to the young characters of Tom (Freddie Cunliffe) and Jessie (Lara Belmont), Carlin had the house furnished with a mixture of old, inhospitable pieces that would have been left there by the previous owner and newer items the family would have brought with them from London. Carlin's proudest achievement was an isolated bunker, where Tom witnesses his father's assault on his sister, which had to be built from scratch. Carlin found a spot overlooking the jagged coastline, with rock formations providing the perfect dramatic backdrop. He designed a typical wartime bunker jutting out over the sea, which was taken away after filming.

Additional filming took place in three locations in Bideford, as well as pub and hotel locations in London, where the contrast between the timeless and the contemporary is most evident. Carlin said: 'We were keen to give the Devon sets and locations an unidentifiable quality, as though you've drifted back into a non-specific era of the past, which is how Tom sees it.'

The Woodlanders (1997)

Another adaptation of a Thomas Hardy classic, this marked the fiction-film debut of acclaimed documentary film-maker Phil Agland. It is a well-staged and solid retelling of the story of a Victorian timber merchant who decides to marry his daughter to a new doctor, despite having promised her to a local woodsman. Rufus Sewell is the swarthy woodsman and Emily Woof the daughter who loves him. Agland displays a fine eye for exteriors and does a good job of using attractive rural Dorset locations as well as filming at Breamore Estate in Hampshire.

Agland and producer Barney Reisz approached the Breamore Estate, a working estate near Salisbury, that has been in the Hulse family for ten generations and has remained largely unchanged for 400 years. The crew shot the majority of the outdoor woodland scenes on the estate, as well as using the interior and exterior of the Elizabethan manor house and the family's private Saxon church, whose vicar appeared in the film, conducting the marriage ceremony between Grace and FitzPiers. Other locations included the interior of Winchester Cathedral, the streets of Winchester, and a manor house and stables in nearby Alvediston.

Barney Reisz said: 'The cooperation of the estate was vitally important to us. As a former location manager I understand the disruption that a film crew can cause to members of the public, but Edward Hulse allowed us the freedom of his estate, often offering invaluable advice on practical problems.'

Central to the story is the fictional village of Little Hintock. Although some authentic woodland survives, no useable intact villages of the period remain, so designer Andy Harris and his team, which included local craftsmen, built a village of seven thatched houses beneath a chestnut and oak wood in the middle of the estate. And as they needed to remain in place from autumn to spring to cover the seasonal changes for the shoot, the film-makers had to get planning permission.

Filming outdoors during the changing British seasons brought special problems, recalled Reisz. Filming under a canopy of chestnut trees in autumn proved dangerous, with many near-casualties from plummeting chestnuts. 'Then in the spring, as a result of an unusually mild winter, the vital bluebell wood came into flower one anxious week later than the previous year. On the other hand, having the whole estate as our stage meant we could take advantage of any unexpected natural beauty to change the backdrop of our scenes.'

selected beaches

Beaches around the UK and Ireland have been shown to dramatic effect in films, and there is nothing like the sight of beautiful yellow sands and a bright blue sea on the screen to make you long for fresh sea breezes.

The films *Local Hero*, *Hilary and Jackie*, *A Matter of Life and Death* and *Shakespeare in Love* all featured beaches, but imagine the problems faced by a film crew on location on a beach. The principal thing that any film-maker wants on location is control. The problem with beaches is there is so much that is uncontrollable – the tide, the wind blowing sand into the cameras, the annoyance of a seagull dipping into camera shot or the arrival of an inappropriate boat on the distant horizon. And if the cameraman is not using a steadicam, the operator has the problem of trying to balance a heavy camera on shifting sands.

Because any production has to try to avoid including hordes of people, very often filming will take place in the colder months (the cinematographer will make the sky and sea much bluer and the sand much more yellow), meaning that often the actors have to smile and act as if they are enjoying summer sunshine when, more often than not, they are experiencing the opposite. Yet you still can't beat a beautiful beach on the silver screen to make an audience yearn for a holiday.

1 **Local Hero** Camusdarrach in Morar, Scotland.
2 **Chariots of Fire** West Sands Beach at St Andrews, Scotland.
3 **Elizabeth** Bamburgh, England.
4 **Get Carter** Seaham, England.
5 **Little Voice** Scarborough, England.
6 **Shakespeare in Love** Holkham, England.
7 **Drowning by Numbers** Lowestoft, England.
8 **Brighton Rock** Brighton, England.
9 **Wish You Were Here** Bognor Regis, England.
10 **Wilde** Lulworth and Studland, England.
11 **A Matter of Life and Death** Saunton Sands, England.
12 **Land Girls** Bossington, England.
13 **Blue Juice** St Ives, England.

14 **Lawrence of Arabia** Merthyr Mawr sand-dunes, Wales.

15 **Hilary and Jackie** Formby, England.

16 **Bhaji on the Beach** Blackpool, England.

17 **Highlander** Refuge Bay, Cuartaig, Morar, Scotland.

18 **With or Without You** Magilligan Strand, Northern Ireland.

19 **The Quiet Man** Tully Strand, Connemara, Ireland.

20 **Ryan's Daughter** Inch Strand and Coumeenoole Strand, Ireland.

central england

CENTRAL ENGLAND IS FULL OF PROMISE FOR FILM-MAKERS IN TERMS of its variety of locations, wealth of history and strong base of film-making talent. From the east coast, through the counties north of London and across to the Welsh border, the region perhaps lacks the more obvious cinematic locales of the south coast's beaches and coastline, or the dramatic landscapes of Scotland or Wales but compensates with its unusual beauty and wealth of fine rural regions, inner cities and stately homes.

The fact that Elstree Studios are in Hertfordshire – the base for films such as *Star Wars*, *Who Framed Roger Rabbit?* and the *Indiana Jones* trilogy – means that directors often film pick-up shots (scenes inserted into a film) in the area. In Birmingham, Norwich and Nottingham there are busy television production studios, so it is no surprise that many of the top costume-drama television series – including *Vanity Fair*, *Middlemarch*, *Sharpe*, *The Buccaneers*, *Pride and Prejudice* and *Brother Cadfael* – have been filmed in the region.

Film-makers basing themselves at Elstree have easy access to the counties of Essex, Suffolk, Norfolk, Cambridgeshire, Bedfordshire and Hertfordshire, and if they are looking for coastal sites – especially ones less populated than those in the South – then the East of England offers many options. The final beach scene of Oscar-winning *Shakespeare in Love* was filmed at Holkham beach in north Norfolk, although director John Madden and his team also shot at a number of other locations in London and in Oxfordshire.

Apart from deserted beaches, the historical towns of Norfolk offer much to film-makers, while adjacent Suffolk's medieval towns, gentle countryside and elegant country houses are strong attractions. Stanley Kubrick used a variety of UK locations for filming *Eyes Wide Shut*, two being the Anglo-Indian palace of Elvedon Hall in Suffolk, and Thetford Forest in Norfolk. Director Joseph Losey filmed his period film *The Go-Between* (1971) in Norfolk, largely using Melton Constable Hall, an impressive seventeenth-century country house. The film, which stars Julie Christie, Edward Fox and Alan Bates, features a classic cricket game that was filmed on the green at Thornage, a small village between Holt and Melton Constable.

Norfolk and Suffolk locations feature again in the well-appreciated *Singleton's Pluck* (1984), directed by Richard Eyre. The film is about a Norfolk farmer who decides to walk his fattened geese to market in London. Suffolk was also the location for the wonderfully enigmatic Peter Greenaway film *Drowning By Numbers* (1988). The popular TV series *The Practice* was shot in this area, too. Several Norfolk spots have doubled for foreign parts. Sydney Pollock filmed his Oscar-winning *Out of Africa* (1985), starring Robert Redford and Meryl Streep, in the region, with the opening shots (supposedly of Denmark) actually filmed at Castle Rising; while in Fred Zinnemann's *Julia* (1977), featuring Jane Fonda and Vanessa Redgrave, Winterton in Norfolk doubled as Cape Cod in the 1930s.

Marlon Brando and Stephanie Beacham star in Michael Winner's steamy drama *The Nightcomers* (1972), which was inspired by the Henry James novella *The Turn of the Screw*. The film was shot at Swanton Hall in Cambridgeshire, a historical building that is mentioned in the Domesday Book of 1086 and was taken over by the RAF during the Second World War.

Essex, with its proximity to London, has been another popular filming location over the years, though it will also probably acquire notoriety with the release of the violent crime-film *Essex Boys* (1999), directed by Terry Winsor and starring Sean Bean. In 1957 Val Guest filmed part of the science-fiction movie *Quatermass II* (the US title was *Enemy from Space*) at the Shell Haven Refinery in the county. In 1969 director Guy Hamilton used RAF bases for filming his wartime epic *Battle of Britain*, with an all-star cast that includes Laurence Olivier, Robert Shaw, Michael Caine, Christopher Plummer and Kenneth More. The film was shot at Northweald Aerodrome in Essex as well as at RAF Duxford and RAF Hawkinge, in

Hatfield House

Hatfield House in Hertfordshire, the home of the Cecil family for some 400 years, was built on the site of a mansion where Elizabeth I spent much of her childhood. The current building contains Elizabethan artifacts as well as many other attractions. Surrounding the house are magnificent parklands and gardens. The bomb-damaged village featured in the climax of Steven Spielberg's *Saving Private Ryan* was built at nearby Hatfield Aerodrome.
Films: *Batman* (the interiors of Wayne Manor), *Greystoke: The Legend of Tarzan, Lord of the Apes*, *Shakespeare in Love* (doubled as Greenwich Palace)

△ Michael Keaton as Bruce Wayne outside Wayne Manor (in reality Knebworth House), in *Batman*.

Knebworth House

Much used in film production, Knebworth House in Hertfordshire was originally a modest brick Tudor manor but was transformed in the 1840s into a Gothic-style Victorian building. The addition of gargoyles, battlements and towers created a striking exterior, making it a popular spot for film-makers and television crews.

Films: *Batman, Eyes Wide Shut, Haunted Honeymoon, Jane Eyre*

London at St Katharine's Dock, and overseas in France and Spain.

Knebworth House in Hertfordshire has been home to several films. It was the exterior of Wayne Manor (interiors were filmed at Hatfield House) for the Tim Burton updating of *Batman* (1989), starring Michael Keaton, and was also used in the cult classic *Sir Henry at Rawlinson's End* (1980), starring Trevor Howard, Patrick McGee and Vivian Stanshall (creator of the project). Also shot at Knebworth was comedy-thriller *Haunted Honeymoon* (1986), starring Gene Wilder, Gilda Radner

and Dom DeLuise; Michael Winner's 1977 remake of *The Big Sleep*, starring Robert Mitchum, Sarah Miles and Richard Boone; Ken Russell's vampire-worm tale *Lair of the White Worm* (1988); and even – incongruously – the dire Diana Dors sex-farce *Keep It Up Downstairs* (1976), directed by Robert Young.

Award-winning British director Mike Leigh shot scenes in *Topsy-Turvy* (1999), his film about Gilbert and Sullivan starring Jim Broadbent, Allan Corduner, Timothy Spall and Lesley Manville, at Langleybury Mansion in Hertfordshire. The red-brick Georgian house with Victorian additions contains a school complex in its grounds, which Leigh also used after it closed in early 1998.

Robert Bolt, the acclaimed screenwriter, tried his hand at directing with *Lady Caroline Lamb* (1972), casting his wife Sarah Miles as Lady Caroline; she appeared alongside Laurence Olivier, Jon Finch, Ralph Richardson and John Mills. The film was shot at Chatsworth House in Derbyshire, a stately home that has among its many treasures a portrait of the real Lady Caroline.

An interesting link to many films shot in Derbyshire is the popular Red House Stables Museum, close to Matlock. The horses and carriages provided by the museum have regularly worked in films over the years, with credits including *Women in Love*, *Jane Eyre*, *Chitty Chitty Bang Bang*, *Far From the Madding Crowd* and *The Princess Bride*. Jodie Foster visited nearby Warwickshire to film *Candleshoe* (1977), directed by Norman Tokar and also starring Helen Hayes, Leo McKern and David Niven (who took on four roles). The film was shot at Compton Wynyates, which was used for both the exterior and interior of the main house, and at Tysoe for the hospital scenes, in actual fact filmed in the local village school.

Nottingham is the home town of British director Shane Meadows. He filmed his first feature, *TwentyFourSeven* (1997), starring Bob Hoskins, in and around the city, as he did with his more recent *A Room for Romeo Brass*

(1999). No beautiful vistas here, though: these are tough stories of life on inner-city estates. In some ways films like these look back to Karel Reisz's *Saturday Night and Sunday Morning* (1960), shot in a (then) new realistic style and telling the story of ordinary factory workers, played by Albert Finney, Shirley Anne Field and Rachel Roberts.

Leicestershire, a county that straddles the rolling hills and farmland of Rutland to the east and the industrial cities to the west, provides the backdrop for films such as Christopher Hampton's *The Secret Agent* (1996), starring Bob Hoskins, Patricia Arquette, Robin Williams and Gerard Départieu. Like Richard Attenborough's *Shadowlands* (1993) and the caper film *Buster* (1988), directed by David Green and starring Phil Collins and Julie Walters, *The Secret Agent* made use of the impressive restored Loughborough Great Central Railway, which runs steam locomotives along its line and glories in a restored platform in Loughborough.

Early scenes from the much-loved John Cleese comedy *Clockwise* (1986), directed by Christopher Morahan from a script by Michael Frayn, was filmed at the Guild of Students at the University of Birmingham in Edgbaston as well as in West Bromwich, while the famous scene in which Cleese demolishes a telephone box in anger was shot at Much Wenlock in Shropshire.

Also filmed in Shropshire was the Michael Powell and Emeric Pressberger film *Gone to Earth* (1950), which features Jennifer Jones, David Farrer and Cyril Cusack. Some parts were filmed at Much Wenlock, at Longnor Hall near Shrewsbury (Squire Reddin's house) and on the Shropshire–Wales border. The film gained unwanted notoriety when it was re-edited after a disagreement and court case between Powell and producer David O. Selznick. Selznick discarded all but 35 minutes of Powell's original and shot extra scenes, added a spoken prologue and released the film in 1952 under the title of *The Wild Heart*.

selected films

△ Pete Postlethwaite takes in the view from the top of an electricity pylon, in *Among Giants*.

Among Giants (1998)

Directed by Sam Miller, this endearing romantic drama was scripted by Simon Beaufoy, who is perhaps better known for scripting the international hit *The Full Monty*. The film stars Pete Postlethwaite as an unemployed labourer and keen amateur climber who is offered a job painting fifteen miles of electricity pylons in three months. He gathers a team together, one of whom is a backpacking young Australian (Rachel Griffiths) with whom Postlethwaite falls in love. This is new British cinema, so, of course, it has to end in tears, but along the way there is a lot of enjoyment to be had, especially when it comes to Miller's sweeping camera movements as he tracks the pylons across the countryside. The film was shot at Burbage Rocks and Millstone Edge in Derbyshire and at The Vine pub, Cemetery Road, Sheffield, in South Yorkshire. The latter county was also the source of settings at Thorpe Marsh Power Station, Doncaster, and Gleadless Valley, Sheffield.

A Clockwork Orange (1971)

After the death of director Stanley Kubrick in 1999 *A Clockwork Orange* was finally re-released in the UK. It had been withdrawn on Kubrick's insistence shortly after he made the film, but despite – or perhaps because of – that, it remained an underground cult hit. The film traces the antisocial behaviour of Alex (a compulsive Malcolm McDowell) and his gang as they make their violent way around their neighbourhood. Eventually, Alex is captured and made 'safe': a clockwork orange. Kubrick's film, based on Anthony Burgess's celebrated novel, still makes for harrowing viewing despite the passage of time and it is full of remarkable performances. The film was shot at Brunel University, Uxbridge, Middlesex; Shenley Lodge, Shenley, Hertfordshire; Thamesmead South Estate in London; Aylesbury, Buckinghamshire; the South Bank near the Royal Festival Hall, London; and at Joyden's Wood, Bexley, Kent (where Alex is beaten up by the police).

Drowning By Numbers (1988)

Writer-director Peter Greenaway was at his most playful (not something critics generally associate with him) with the charming *Drowning By Numbers*. Filmed on location near Southwold on the Suffolk coast, the film stars Joan Plowright, Juliet Stevenson and Joely Richardson as three women, all named Cissie Colpitts, who each happen to find ways of drowning their husbands. They get away with their crimes because each has a relationship with the local coroner (played by Bernard Hill), who would rather stay in bed than get involved in an investigation. A conceit in the film is that the numbers one to a hundred appear in sequence throughout, encouraging viewers to try to spot them, sometimes in the oddest places – on two dead cows in a field, for example.

The Haunting (1999)

This big-budget horror film used exteriors of two impressive English stately homes to create the horrific house where a band of unfortunates gather for an experiment with the supernatural. The $70 million-budget film used Harlaxton Manor and Belvoir Castle, both near Grantham. The film was an updating of the 1963 film *The Haunting*, based on Shirley Jackson's 1959 novel, *The Haunting of Hill House*.

Director Jan de Bont was adamant that the house itself was the main star of the film. 'I had two things in mind. The hall in *Citizen Kane* and the hotel in Kubrick's *The Shining*. Both are so huge that by the sheer scope of them you feel terrorized.'

If... (1986)

Lindsay Anderson's highly acclaimed film caused controversy when released, with its tale of pupils at a public school who resort to violence. But this is no simple story, and Anderson mixes surrealism with realism and draws out an extraordinary performance from lead actor Malcolm McDowell. The film was scripted by David Sherwin (and originally entitled *Crusaders*), although Anderson had a big impact on the project when he came on board. Sherwin, McDowell and Anderson went on to make two more films together (*O Lucky Man!* and *Britannia Hospital*) and were working on a fourth before Anderson's death. *If...* is a complex and often cruel exposé of an English public school, focusing on three pupils in particular who rebel and eventually set about shooting teachers and fellow students. The scenes of McDowell and his gang shooting from the rooftops are unforgettable, and the film is a powerful experience. Anderson shot the school scenes at Cheltenham College in Gloucestershire, the boarding-school he had actually attended as a pupil.

Anderson recalled the governors as quite amenable to the school being used, especially when he first pitched the script to them. 'They were very cooperative, really. Mind you, I don't think any of them took films all that seriously, and I think that I was also a bit dishonest, certainly as regards Cheltenham, in playing down the anarchic, critical side of the script. But I don't know that they would have been bothered anyway, though it isn't a flattering picture of English education.'

Jane Eyre (1995)

Italian director Franco Zeffirelli pinpointed Haddon Hall, near Matlock in Derbyshire, as the location he wanted to use for his impressive adaptation of the much-loved Charlotte Brontë tale of Jane Eyre (played by Charlotte Gainsbourg) and the passionate Mr Rochester (William Hurt). He shot there for three weeks and made great use of the stunning manor house and its gardens, brilliantly transforming them into the fictional Thornfield Hall, Rochester's home. The final scenes of the burning hall were shot on a studio stage, though Wingfield Manor, between Alfreton and Matlock, was used for the aftermath of the Thornfield fire. Other locations included the National Trust's Brimham Rocks in North Yorkshire. The horses and carriages were provided by the Red House Stables and Carriage Museum, near Matlock.

Lady Jane (1985)

Helena Bonham Carter had her first lead role in *Lady Jane*, the fascinating story of tragic Lady Jane Grey, installed as monarch of England for just nine days while around her politicians plot the future of the country. Acclaimed theatre director Trevor Nunn made his debut as a film director, making great use of locations around the country to tell the story of Jane and her marriage of convenience to Guildford Dudley (played by Cary Elwes). The home of the Grey family is now in ruins amid the bracken and rocks of Bradgate Park in Leicestershire, and some exteriors were shot at the site. Other venues included Dover Castle (used for the Tower of London); Leeds and Hever Castles in Kent; Haddon Hall and the grounds of Chatsworth House in Derbyshire; and Compton Wyngates, near Stratford-upon-Avon. Chastleton House, near Chipping Norton in Oxfordshire, represented Princess Mary's home, and Little Moreton Hall in Cheshire made an appearance as a brothel.

Lair of the White Worm (1988)

Ken Russell took a wonderfully over-the-top approach with this tongue-in-cheek adaptation of the little-known Bram Stoker story about a massive snake-like worm that has a nasty habit of nipping out of its cave and nibbling people. An archaeologist unearths the skull of a worm-like creature that seems to spark off deaths at an estate. Russell filmed *Lair of the White Worm* at Knebworth House in Hertfordshire and in the Peak District National Park in Derbyshire. Russell himself has a cameo at the start of the film when he wanders by a house and calls out 'Hello, Mary' to actress Sammi Davis.

◁ Malcolm McDowell and director Lindsay Anderson, on location shooting *If...*

Mansfield Park (1999)

Patricia Rozema's ambitious and impressive adaptation of *Mansfield Park* is a witty, romantic and enjoyable take on Jane Austen's story. The book, Austen's third and perhaps most controversial, tells the story of Fanny Price (Frances O'Connor) who, when she is ten, is sent from her dingy Portsmouth home to live with her wealthy relatives, the Bertrams, in Mansfield Park. She is raised as the family's poor relation and is constantly reminded of the debt of gratitude she owes to the family. But she grows to be a strong-willed character and becomes a writer, attracting the attention of a charming Londoner, Henry Crawford (played by Alessandro Novice) as well as her sensitive cousin, Edmund (Jonny Lee Miller). The evils of the slave trade provide a backdrop as Fanny must start making decisions, throwing Mansfield Park into disarray.

As well as adapting the novel, Rozema worked with Austen's letters and early journals. She handed production designer Christopher Hobbs (who designed the sets for *Velvet Goldmine*) the challenge of establishing the right look for the film. He found the perfect stand-in for Mansfield Park in Kirby Hall, an empty Elizabethan house in Northamptonshire. Inside the hall Hobbs designed a world for the Bertrams that reflected a lean, spare sense of design. 'In Georgian houses the furniture was actually very sparse and kept back against the walls,' he said. 'You'd have lots of servants, so instead of cluttering your rooms you'd have the servants carry tables and chairs in as necessary.' Hobbs also adopted a more realistic design approach for Fanny's home in Portsmouth, bringing out its dank, bleak atmosphere.

Rozema said: 'From the beginning, I didn't want to do another Jane Austen garden party. I wanted to show the passion of Jane Austen, her fierce humanity, her devastating wit and her deep-seated belief in the power of love between two people. The more I read about Jane herself, the more I wanted to bring her incredible spirit into the story and give some of that dynamism back to Fanny. It is often said that *Mansfield Park* is Jane Austen's most autobiographical novel. I found myself speculating on how far that could go.'

Maurice (1987)

This boasts a pre-stardom role for Hugh Grant, this time as Clive Durham, who helps awaken the sexuality of Maurice (James Wilby), a fellow student at King's College, Cambridge. The Merchant Ivory film is based on E.M. Forster's novel, written in 1913 but not published until after his death. The film rights were owned by King's College, and the Merchant Ivory team not only managed to convince the college to allow the film to be made but also persuaded it that shooting should take place at the university itself. Also in the cast are Rupert Graves (who plays Scudder, the man with whom Maurice

finally experiences physical love), Denholm Elliott and Simon Callow.

Memphis Belle (1990)

In 1944 American director William Wyler made a documentary called *The Memphis Belle* about a B-17 Flying Fortress bomber based at RAF Bassingbourn in Cambridgeshire going on its twenty-fifth and last mission towards the end of the Second World War. The documentary served as the inspiration for this feature version of the final flight of the B-17 and its young crew. Director Michael Caton-Jones and producer David Puttnam had to gather still-functioning B-17s as well as Mustang support aircraft and the enemy Messerschmitt ME-109s. Aerial photography took place over Duxford in Cambridgeshire, where the Imperial War Museum's collection of aircraft is kept, while an empty airbase at Binbrook in Lincolnshire was transformed

△ Matthew Modine drives a jeep packed with US airmen in a scene from *Memphis Belle*.

into a hectic bomber station during the war.

To prepare the young Hollywood cast Caton-Jones put them through their paces prior to filming. He said: 'We sent them to the SAS training ground for eight days before shooting. We had them going on night patrols, crawling under barbed wire and digging latrines – things that Hollywood actors don't ordinarily do. It had the desired effect in getting them to act like a group who had to be able to depend on each other.'

Revolution (1983)

It is probably true to say that *Revolution* played its part in toppling the local film industry, but if there had been a revival in the early 1980s – as some commentators of the time claimed – it was a pretty flimsy one to be so easily knocked off its stride. Full of scale and ambition, *Revolution* probably looked

great on paper, but somehow the elements never properly gelled, and Al Pacino looks terribly out of his method-acting depth as the trapper who becomes involved in the American

△ Singer Annie Lennox shouts with revolutionary zeal, in *Revolution*.

War of Independence. What work best are the locations! King's Lynn doubled as New York, and the film was also shot in Thetford, on Dartmoor and in Cambridgeshire.

Saturday Night and Sunday Morning (1960)

When Alan Sillitoe's novel *Saturday Night and Sunday Morning* was published in 1958 he (along with playwright John Osborne) was hailed as one of the key angry young voices of British literature, taking stories into the workplace of ordinary people. Sillitoe, who wrote the screenplay, worked closely with director Karel Reisz to bring out the honesty of the Nottingham neighbourhood where he had grown up and worked in a factory. The film stars Albert Finney (in his first major role) as Arthur Seaton, a worker in a bicycle factory (in fact the same one that Sillitoe had worked in as a young man) and railing against his dead-end job. The film also deals with the impact his frustrations have on the women in his life, played by Shirley Anne Field and Rachel Roberts. The street sequences were shot in the Nottingham suburb of Radford, and while the film makes for often-grim viewing it is extremely powerful and at times moving.

Shadowlands (1993)

This is the director Richard Attenborough at his best. *Shadowlands* combines beautifully subtle performances, fine writing and lovely locations, and the film is even more moving because it is based on a true story. It lovingly details the relationship between the writer C.S. Lewis (who wrote the Narnia books) and the poet Joy Gresham. They meet when Lewis (played sublimely by Anthony Hopkins) is a bachelor fellow at Magdalen College, Oxford, and she visits with her young son (played by Jospeh Mazzello). Lewis finally admits that he is in love with Gresham (Debra Winger) after she is diagnosed as having cancer, and when they take their honeymoon shortly before her death they visit the Golden Valley in Herefordshire. When it came to filming the Golden Valley scenes Attenborough and his team found that the valley – on the border with Wales – wasn't as unspoiled as it had been in the 1950s, when the couple had honeymooned there. Instead they filmed at Symonds Yat, close to the River Wye near Goodrich. A lot of the filming took place in Oxford, at locations including Magdalen College, the Randolph Hotel (for the scene where the two first meet), Christ Church Meadow and the Sheldonian Theatre. The restored Great Central Railway Station at Loughborough in Leicestershire was used, too (Attenborough was brought up in Leicester), while Pengethley Manor Hotel near Ross-on-Wye became the hotel where Lewis and Gresham stay before visiting the Golden Valley.

Shakespeare in Love (1998)

This part-comedy, part-drama and part-romance proved to be a massive hit, and rightly so. The film is a thoroughly enjoyable tale of a young Shakespeare (Joseph Fiennes) suffering from writer's block while setting out to write his new play, tentatively entitled *Romeo and Ethel, the Pirate's Daughter*. He falls for beautiful Viola De Lesseps (Gwyneth Paltrow), who disguises herself as a man to take a part in the new play. The film won eight Academy Awards – including best film, best actress (Paltrow) and best supporting actress

(which went to Judi Dench for her brief turn as Queen Elizabeth) – and was popularly received around the world. In the latest British Tourist Authority 'Movie Map', director John Madden

△ Director Richard Attenborough stands before the Golden Valley location for *Shadowlands*.

(who also made *Mrs Brown*), writes: 'Although much of a production can be studio-based with meticulously designed sets, it is the authentic locations, from spectacular countryside to ancient castles, that really set a film alight. I am very fortunate to have Britain as a backdrop. I have to take into account the number of people involved in any particular film sequence, so convenience and accessibility of the location are important – and everywhere is reasonably accessible, however remote. The contrasting scenery within this small country is breathtaking. You can't better the wide-open skies and landscapes of the north Norfolk coastline, where we filmed *Shakespeare in Love*, or the rugged but verdant Scottish mountains in *Mrs Brown*.'

△ Director John Madden takes to the stage to prepare the cast for a scene in *Shakespeare in Love*.

The film's London of 1592 was built in a former garden nursery behind Shepperton Studios, and it took 115 men eight weeks to construct the seventeen buildings, among them a brothel, a tavern, a marketplace and two theatres. According to reports, Judi Dench begged that the three-storey replica of The Rose Theatre should not be destroyed, and it is now packed away in a warehouse waiting to see if an institution might be able to make use of it.

The final scenes, in which Viola is seen walking from the sea on to a stunning beach, were shot at Holkham beach, on the Holkham Estate in north Norfolk. The Holkham Estate beach is one of the most unspoiled in the country; the foreshore is about five miles long, and on the day of the shoot the weather behaved perfectly. Another vital scene, the sequence where Viola finally declares her love for Will, was shot on a meadow at the estate.

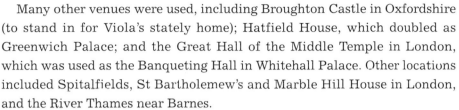

There were obviously hopes that the film would help put Norfolk firmly on the world movie map. Julian Campbell of Eastern Screen said: 'We are always striving for what is known as the *Braveheart* phenomenon, where a film is instantly associated with a particular area and the tourism spin-off will be quite large. That is the Holy Grail for that sort of thing.'

Many other venues were used, including Broughton Castle in Oxfordshire (to stand in for Viola's stately home); Hatfield House, which doubled as Greenwich Palace; and the Great Hall of the Middle Temple in London, which was used as the Banqueting Hall in Whitehall Palace. Other locations included Spitalfields, St Bartholemew's and Marble Hill House in London, and the River Thames near Barnes.

Sleepy Hollow (1999)

Set in 1799 in a fictional Dutch community in upstate New York, Tim Burton's *Sleepy Hollow* is based on Washington Irving's classic tale *The Legend of Sleepy Hollow*. Johnny Depp plays an ambitious New York police investigator named Ichabod Crane, a follower of new scientific ways who is delighted to be sent to rural Sleepy Hollow, where a series of citizens have been beheaded by a mysterious headless horseman. He finds himself involved in a mystery that mixes the supernatural with commonplace crime, and eventually solves the terrible mystery of the awful headless horseman. Tim Burton said: 'I'm a big fan of all the Hammer horror films of the 1950s and 1960s, and this script had a lot of classic, beautiful horror images. What I liked about the script is that it's respectful of the original story but takes it into new territory.'

After scouting a number of Dutch communities in upstate New York and the Hudson Valley, where the real town of Sleepy Hollow is located, the film-makers agreed that Burton's vision could best be achieved by shooting primarily on stages. Additionally, they decided to build their own town of Sleepy Hollow in a contained environment. Partly because of Tim Burton's love of the old Hammer horror films, they decided to come to the UK.

Production designer Rick Heinrichs and his team built the grand Van Tassel Manor House at Leavesden Studios, while they created the impressive Western Woods at Shepperton Studios. The crew built a foreboding set made up of 30-foot-tall trees constructed of fibreglass and steel fashioned from moulds of oak trees in Windsor Great Park.

But the most elaborate and ambitious set is Sleepy Hollow, built on private property in the Lime Valley, about an hour's drive west of London near Marlow. The collection of period buildings includes a church, bridge, blacksmith's, bank, tavern and hayloft, general store, notary public, mill house, livery stable, Mr Killan's Farm and Philips's residence. Another location was Somerset House in London, which stood in for 1780s New York.

TwentyFourSeven (1997)

A powerful low-budget drama, this heralded the arrival of a sparky new talent in British cinema: writer-director Shane Meadows. Nottingham-based Meadows (who co-wrote the film with his childhood friend Paul Fraser) made several short films with friends before moving up to *TwentyFourSeven* (entitled *24:7* in some places) and a slightly larger budget. He still cast many of his pals – and used locations similar to where he lives – but also managed to recruit that excellent British actor Bob Hoskins to take on the lead role. Hoskins plays Alan Darcy, a trainer of a kids' football team fallen on hard times, who manages to pull himself together to try to encourage a group of youngsters to learn to box and set up a

gym. A mixture of drama and well-observed humour, the story is very much Nottingham-centred, and Meadows brings out the highs and lows of living on inner-city estates. He also allows a trip to the countryside, when the youngsters go to the empty hills (in fact the nearby Peak District in Derbyshire).

Meadows made the ambitious decision for a feature first-timer of shooting the film in black and white, setting it clearly apart from other recent British movies. Meadows said at the time: 'There are so many UK films coming out at the moment. I wanted a more personal film so it could stand out. I've always seen it in black and white. I like classic British Ealing black-and-white movies, and the way people were represented in those films. You can identify people by their clothes. Visually, it is the shape that counts, so you identify people in black and white in a better way.'

Women in Love (1969)

Another Ken Russell work, this is a critically well-received adaptation of D.H. Lawrence's novel, perhaps most famous for the fireside nude-wrestling scene involving Alan Bates (as Rupert Birkin) and Oliver Reed (as Gerald Crich). Glenda Jackson won her first Academy Award for best actress for her performance as the forthright Gudrun Brangwen, while Jennie Linden played her more timid sister. Russell shot the film in Nottinghamshire (Lawrence's home county) as well as in Derbyshire, County Durham, Northumberland and Yorkshire, with a brief shoot in Zermatt, Switzerland.

△ The elaborate and atmospheric village of *Sleepy Hollow*, constructed near Marlow.

MOVIE LOCATIONS central england

british islands

isle of man

JUST A FEW YEARS AGO THE ISLE OF MAN (ONLY 221 SQUARE MILES in area and with a population in 1991 of just over 69,000) would hardly have rated a mention when it came to any discussion about film locations in Britain. In fact, it is a fair bet that if you had a conversation with an overseas producer – perhaps even a British one - in the early 1990s, they would have had little or no idea where the Isle of Man actually was.

Things all changed in the mid-1990s with the establishment of the Isle of Man Film and Television Fund, which was set up to make available equity investment to film and television productions shooting on the island. All well and good, but the big difference compared with other regions of the UK was that any production that adhered to a specific list of conditions would be eligible for up to £350,000 per production: an extremely useful amount by any stretch of the imagination. This was possible because the Isle of Man has its own form of government and its own tax system.

Not surprisingly, over the past few years film and television productions have rushed to take advantage of the financial and practical assistance on offer, and likewise the Isle of Man has gone out of its way to try to establish itself as one of the most helpful locations in the UK. There was a time, a few years ago, when the UK was regularly losing productions to Ireland before the preferential deals were offered. Since 1995, it has been Ireland that has sometimes been losing films, this time to the Isle of Man, which as well as its financial considerations is also easily able to double for Ireland.

That being said, naturally enough it has taken the island some time to win recognition as a location base, and some of the early films shot there have received little or no publicity, apart from occasional film festival exposure or a video release. It wasn't until the spectacular success of the whimsical comedy *Waking Ned* (aka *Waking Ned Devine* in the US) that location shooting on the Isle of Man truly came of age.

The first film to be shot on the island was *The Brylcreem Boys* in 1995, directed by Terence Ryan and with an impressive cast headed by Gabriel Byrne, Bill Campbell, John Gordon Sinclair, Angus MacFadyen and Riverdance star Jean Butler. Set during the Second World War, the film was about the strange situation facing Allied and enemy soldiers who found themselves captured and interned in prison camps in Ireland. Since the country was neutral during the war, prisoners found themselves in the unusual situation of sharing a prison camp. The POW camp was re-created on a disused airfield.

The Brylcreem Boys was first shown at the Cannes Film Festival in 1996 at a special screening (not part of the main competition, but aimed squarely at the industry) whose chief purpose was to hype the attractions of the Isle of Man to film-makers. Unfortunately, the film didn't go down too well, with quite a few laughs reserved for a sequence of the film featuring the red-headed Jean Butler launching into a Riverdance-style dance sequence in a local pub. The film was subsequently shown at the London Film Festival and at other overseas festivals, but its ambition was not fully realized and it made little impact.

The same could not be said for the Isle of Man and its attractive incentives. One thing that film-makers are good at is spotting an opportunity, and over the following years films flooded to this little island.

In 1996 two more films were shot there: the little-seen *The Harpist*, directed by Hansjorg Thurn and starring Christien Anholt, with the Isle of Man doubling as Hamburg and Dublin; and the inventive comedy *Stiff Upper Lips*, directed by Gary Sinyor and starring Peter Ustinov, Prunella Scales, Samuel West, Sean Pertwee, Frank Finlay and Georgina Cates. The latter is a very tongue-in-cheek play on the traditional costume drama adaptations of the likes of E.M. Forster, with the Isle of Man this time doubling as a rural English estate. The film was a moderate success, and again helped to focus more attention on the burgeoning ambitions of the Isle of Man.

More titles followed in 1997, chief among them *The Tichborne Claimant*, directed by David Yates and starring John Gielgud, Robert Hardy, Barry Humphries and Anita Dobson; and producer Jeremy Thomas's directorial debut of *All the Little Animals*, which featured Christian Bale, John Hurt and Daniel Benzali, though it was the filming in August and September that year of the apparently modest *Waking Ned* that was to be the key production.

Waking Ned (1997)

Waking Ned was the debut film of British writer-director Kirk Jones, who was inspired when he read a newspaper story about a postmistress in a tiny village who won a large cash prize but tried to keep it a secret from her fellow villagers. Jones developed the tale into a script about what happens to a small fictional Irish village named Tully More when it is discovered that one of the villagers has won a massive lottery prize.

Jones said: 'The whole story just snowballed, but it all started with the idea of someone in a very small community winning a very large sum of money. Once I began writing I took a trip to southern Ireland, where I spent time in a small village not unlike Tully More. I just sat in a corner of a pub watching people and observing their humour, joy for life and how they behaved.

'I think international audiences often love the charm and character of British films but can be put off by their pace,' he added. 'I saw the story in the tradition of *Local Hero*, because it's a big, modern fairytale set in a small village, but the difference is that I upped the pace quite a bit.'

Cast in the lead role of the boisterous Jackie O'Shea was the late Ian Bannen, while David Kelly played the more reserved Michael O'Sullivan. These two formed the centre of the film, two elderly heroes who set about tracking down the mysterious lottery-winner and who are caught up in a spiralling set of circumstances as they struggle to keep the money in the village. The next key casting task, though, was to find a real village to double for the enchanting fictional Tully More.

Despite the story's Irish setting, the production team opted for the rugged shores of the Isle of Man. Although not part of Ireland, ancient legend has it

△ The wily locals of Tully More plot how to spend their lottery win, in *Waking Ned*.

that in the early days of the world a great Irish giant scooped out part of Ireland and tossed it back into the sea. This scoop of land was to become the Isle of Man.

In fact, the production team of *Waking Ned* found that the Isle of Man looked a lot more like Ireland than did Ireland itself. 'We looked all over Ireland for a village like Tully More,' said Jones, 'but so many Irish farming communities now have contemporary buildings that just don't work. Also, many of the villages are spread out along a road instead of set in a cluster at the top of a hill, as I had always envisioned this little hamlet. I finally found a place I fell in love with.'

The place he fell in love with was a small village called Cregneash, and not only was it set on a hill above the sea, but luckily enough it was also a government-owned historical village with no modern buildings. The production team were convinced they had exactly the right place, and struck a deal with the authorities to take over the whole village. Next, though, they had to convince the villagers.

To try to win their support and confidence Jones staged a public meeting to introduce the film crew. 'I stood up to talk to them and saw the most incredible group of faces, all of them extraordinary characters,' Jones recalled. 'But they weren't smiling. I tried to tell a few jokes, but no one flinched. Finally, I just launched into the story of the film, and they began to laugh and they began to warm up and by the end of my speech they were clapping. After that, they really welcomed us and were incredibly helpful at every turn. Many of the villagers ended up in the film as extras.'

The notoriously fickle weather also decided to lend a hand, with producer Richard Holmes noting: 'It was a very blessed production. At one point we covered a big red postbox with a Virgin Mary grotto, and just as we were about to shoot the sun focused in on Mary and her face lit up with a halo of light. Another time it was raining all over the island except for the one little spit of beach where we were shooting. Those sorts of things kept happening. There seemed to be an unseen force at work.'

What perhaps wasn't such an unseen force was the involvement of major Hollywood studio Twentieth Century Fox, which led to the international success of *Waking Ned*. Buoyed by its successful (which can also be read as blockbusting) acquisition of that other very British comedy *The Full Monty*, Fox's speciality division Fox Searchlight made the move to pick up this seemingly modest and perhaps old-fashioned comedy for $5 million for the English-language territories, while making the film cost about $1 million. When the film was screened at Cannes in 1998 there was a real buzz around it. Fox moved quickly to turn that buzz into something more substantial – impressive critical acclaim and, just as important, talk of Oscar nominations.

When the film was released in the US – as *Waking Ned Devine* – in late 1998, that acclaim came hand in hand with impressive box-office returns. Isle of Man Film Minister David North was also quick to point out what the film's success could mean to the island, not only in terms of improving the island's reputation as a film-making venue but also in terms of its tourist trade. 'We have been lucky to have, so early, a world success with *Waking Ned*,' he said. 'A critical hit like this sometimes comes along just once in a lifetime for somewhere like the Isle of Man, and we have to make sure we now build on this.'

And build on the island's reputation as a film-making centre the Isle of Man Film Commission certainly has, with a virtually constant churn of productions keeping the island busy. Recent films shot there have included *Dreaming of Joseph Lees*, an impressive period drama starring Samantha Morton, Rupert Graves, Holly Aird and Frank Finlay; *Everybody Loves Sunshine*, with David Bowie and new Bond villain Goldie; *Best*, the biopic about the legendary Manchester United and Eire striker George Best, starring Patsy Kensit and Jon Lynch; and even a combination live action/animated version of *Thomas the Tank Engine* – entitled *Thomas and the Magic Railroad* – starring (of all people) Alec Baldwin and Jon Voight.

In fact, the success of the island has prompted Ireland, its nearest rival in terms of availability of financial incentives, to make moves to regain its lead. Having lost a number of productions to the Isle of Man, Ireland has restructured its own tax-breaks scheme and worked on further promotion of the availability of its local crews, locations and studio facilities. As yet, the Isle of Man doesn't have studio space... but give it time. It is understood that the Isle of Man Film Commission is considering plans for a medium-sized sound stage.

isle of wight

The Isle of Wight has regularly been used for television productions, although it was the success of *Mrs Brown* in 1997 that brought this attractive island into sharp focus. The film made exceptional use of Osborne House, which was owned by Queen Victoria and which served as virtually her permanent home in the later years of her life.

Other films shot on the island include the comedy *Guest House Paradiso* (1999), which starred Rik Mayall and Ade Edmonson; the David Essex musical *That'll Be the Day* (1973); and the last of the much-loved *St Trinian's* series of comedy films, *Wildcats of St Trinians*

Osborne House

Following the wonderful critical acclaim and worldwide box office success of *Mrs Brown* (or *Her Majesty, Mrs Brown* as it was titled in the US) the beautiful Osborne House experienced a stunning 25 per cent increase in visitors. The film starred an Oscar-nominated Judi Dench as Queen Victoria in mourning for the death of her beloved husband Prince Albert, and Billy Connolly as her loyal servant John Brown. Directed by John Madden (who went on to make the even more successful *Shakespeare In Love*) it was also filmed in Scotland – at Duns Castle, west of Berwick-Upon-Tweed – while Wilton House near Salisbury doubled as Windsor Castle.

It is the distinctive Osborne House, though, with its fountains, intricate gardens and Italian-style towers, that seemed to strike a deeper chord with viewers. In the film the loyal Brown walks through the garden with Queen Victoria down towards the sea, allowing the peaceful ambience to take hold. In the earlier Scottish-set scenes the Queen is in deep mourning, while as she approaches death at Osborne there is a greater sense of her coming to terms with grief.

At Osborne House itself there is a real awareness of the value of publicity it has generated from *Mrs Brown*. On weekdays there is a daily video-showing of *Mrs Brown* in the splendid former Royal Apartments of Princess Beatrice.
Film: *Mrs Brown*

△ Billy Connolly and Judi Dench in *Mrs Brown*, partly shot on the Isle of Wight.

(1980), directed by Frank Launder. A few scenes of *Julia* (1973), starring Jane Fonda and Vanessa Redgrave and the film debut of Meryl Streep, were also shot there.

channel islands

The Channel Islands, closer to France than to the UK, have been little used as a location setting, perhaps quite simply because of that distance and the complications involved in shipping equipment and personnel all the way to these small islands.

Jersey, just nine miles long and better known as a holiday spot, has been the location for several features over the years, and its profile was boosted in the 1980s when the BBC detective series *Bergerac*, starring John Nettles as

the Triumph Roadster-driving Sergeant Jim Bergerac, made the island its base for a number of years.

Films shot on Jersey include *Neither the Sea Nor the Sand* (1972), directed by Fred Burnley from a script by former television newsreader Gordon Honeycombe and starring Susan Hampshire and Frank Finlay and the wartime adventure film *Force 10 From Navarone* (1978), directed by Guy Hamilton and starring Robert Shaw, Harrison Ford and Barbara Bach. *Force 10* was a poorly received tale of Allied agents trying to blow up a German bridge during the Second World War, and was filmed at Malta and Yugoslavia as well as on Jersey.

Sequences from the sort-of follow-up to *A Fish Called Wanda*, *Fierce Creatures* (1997), directed by Fred Schepisi and Robert Young and again starring John Cleese, Jamie Lee Curtis, Michael Palin and Kevin Kline, were also shot on Jersey. Major scenes of the zoo-set comedy, though, were filmed at Marwell Zoological Park in Hampshire.

The nearby island of Guernsey was the setting for the French film *L'Histoire d'Adèle H* (1975), directed by François Truffaut and starring Isabelle Adjani and Bruce Robinson. The scenes of Victor Hugo's house were shot in St Peter Port, but other scenes were filmed on location in Barbados.

Sark was the setting for the delightful wartime comedy *Appointment With Venus* (1951) (entitled *Island Rescue* in the US), directed by Ralph Thomas and starring David Niven, Glynis Johns and Kenneth More. Niven plays an army officer who has to rescue a prize cow – named Venus - from the German-occupied island during the Second World War.

Also shot in and around the Channel Islands – as well as on the north coast of France – was the 1953 adventure tale *Sea Devils*, directed by Raoul Walsh. The film stars Rock Hudson as a smuggler who becomes involved with a British spy (Yvonne de Carlo) during the Napoleonic era.

northern england

THE NORTH OF ENGLAND BOASTS SOME OF THE MOST STUNNING FILM locations in the UK, and it also has two of Britain's most film-friendly cities in Liverpool and Manchester. These two cities – as well as other industrial and cultural centres such as Newcastle and Sheffield – offer a contrast to the undoubted natural beauty of such areas as the Lake District, the Yorkshire Moors and the Durham Dales.

Film-making in the North of England has chopped and changed over the years. At one point Liverpool, Manchester and Newcastle were wealthy, vibrant and powerful cities with strong personalities that were reflected in film and on television. In the 1960s kitchen-sink drama (such as *Billy Liar*) impacted greatly on film-makers, and suddenly those northern industrial towns were shown in their gritty reality. Often with an underlying humour – though sometimes just warts and all – these films offered a view of contemporary northern life, and not a simplistic vision of cobbled streets and cheery working folk. Things would – and could – never quite be the same again.

For a glorious period the best of British cinema was made in the North of England, with all the top talent – writers, directors and actors – flocking to the region and making films such as *This Sporting Life, Room at The Top* and *The Loneliness of The Long Distance Runner*. But the arrival of the Swinging Sixties drew things back to London, and, for a period, films that focused on the North seemed to dip away, with the supposed glamour of London a key item on the film-making agenda.

The area's rural landscapes, including their castles and stately homes, as well as its cities have long been popular with film-makers, on television especially, although programmes based in the North, such as *The Liver Birds*,

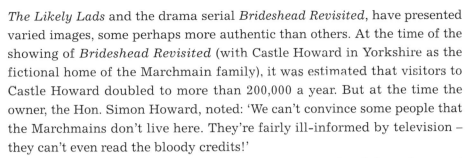

The Likely Lads and the drama serial *Brideshead Revisited*, have presented varied images, some perhaps more authentic than others. At the time of the showing of *Brideshead Revisited* (with Castle Howard in Yorkshire as the fictional home of the Marchmain family), it was estimated that visitors to Castle Howard doubled to more than 200,000 a year. But at the time the owner, the Hon. Simon Howard, noted: 'We can't convince some people that the Marchmains don't live here. They're fairly ill-informed by television – they can't even read the bloody credits!'

That being said, the success of *Brideshead Revisited* and the subsequent boost in tourism (aka additional revenue) meant that the Howard family was able to complete the renovation of the Garden Hall on the estate, which had been severely damaged by fire in 1940.

With the coming of the 1990s and a gradual increase in British film production (mainly thanks to the influence of Channel 4's funding policy and greater activity in BBC film production), more and more films started to be based in the North. Film-makers such as Peter Chelsom, Mark Herman and Terence Davies set their films very clearly in the areas they were brought up in. Films like *The Full Monty*, *Brassed Off* and *Little Voice* have consolidated the reputation for film-making in the North, while more classical costume dramas such as *Elizabeth* have revelled in the availability of appropriate locations.

The Film Office at Liverpool was the first dedicated office in the UK aimed at helping and enabling film-makers to visit the region. Liverpool has always had a strong sense of its own identity (from The Beatles to Liverpool Football Club), and also has a strong and vibrant media base to give film-makers practical and creative support. The city contains diverse architecture – from Roman to Art Deco – and with its proximity to the sea and countryside it offers plenty of options. It has frequently been called on to impersonate other cites, from London to Moscow and St Petersburg.

An early film (well, film serial) shot in Liverpool was the eighteen-episode adventure serial *The Vanishing Dagger* (1920), directed by Edward A. Kull and John F. Magowan, and starring Thelma Percy and Eddie Polo. Even earlier, in 1914, Southport Sands and Ainsdale beach, near Liverpool, stood in for the American prairie in G.B. Samuelson's Sherlock Holmes story

St George's Hall

An impressive Liverpudlian landmark, this offers much to film-makers looking for a unique contemporary atmosphere. The building features the world's largest organ as well as a concert hall, pillars, cells and catacombs, plus a courtroom that has a striking similarity to the Old Bailey. The frontage has also been transformed into Moscow for one film (*The Hunt for Red October*).

Films: *Hilary and Jackie*, *The Hunt for Red October*, *In the Name of the Father*, *Let Him Have It*

A Study in Scarlet. The same beach was used as a backdrop for an African village in *The Blue Peter* (1928), while more recently it was used in the closing scenes of *Hilary and Jackie*.

In 1972 Stephen Frears directed Albert Finney in *Gumshoe*. The film, which also stars Billie Whitelaw and Frank Finlay, was shot in Liverpool and London. Terence Davies shot both *Distant Voices, Still Lives* (1988) and *The Long Day Closes* (1992) in the city; while in 1985 *Letter to Brezhnev*, directed by Chris Bernard, drew attention to the city as the story of two Russian sailors who fall for local girls proved a breakthrough hit. Hugh Hudson's Oscar-laden *Chariots of Fire* (1981) was shot at locations in Liverpool as well as in Scotland and Cambridgeshire.

Playwright and screenwriter Willy Russell usually sets his stories in Liverpool, although Oscar-winning *Educating Rita*, set in Liverpool, was actually filmed in Ireland. *Dancin' Thru the Dark* (1990), the directorial debut of Mike Ockrent and starring Angela Clarke and Con O'Neill, was scripted by Russell and filmed in Liverpool, as was *Shirley Valentine*, directed by Lewis Gilbert and starring Pauline Collins. *Shirley Valentine*, though, was also filmed in London and on location in Greece.

Also shot in Liverpool was the crime-drama *Let Him Have It* (1991), based on the true story of nineteen-year-old Derek Bentley, who was hanged for a murder committed by his sixteen-year-old accomplice. Though the background to the story was London of the early 1950s, director Peter Medak shot the film largely on Merseyside, while the resort of New Brighton doubled for Croydon. Medak shot scenes at Liverpool Docks; St George's Hall doubled as the Old Bailey, and there was also filming in Falkner Square, where the two sleep on a park bench. The same location was used in *In the Name of the Father* (1993), as was St George's Hall.

Liverpool also provided the setting for *Hilary and Jackie* (1998), starring Emily Watson and Rachel Griffiths and directed by Anand Tucker; and the football drama *Best* (1999), about the life of the legendary Manchester United footballer George Best. The latter, directed by Mary McGuikin, was also filmed on the Isle of Man and stars John Lynch (McGuikin's husband), Patsy Kensit and Ian Bannen. Sections of Iain Softley's pre-fame-Beatles film *Backbeat* (1994), starring Stephen Dorff and Ian Hart, was shot in the city, the obvious place, though the thrust of the story was about the group's time playing in Hamburg.

Downtime (1997), a British thriller starring Paul McGann, was filmed entirely in Liverpool (though the setting is actually Manchester), mainly in a tower block, St George's Heights. The film is about a couple who get caught in a lift while a gang cause trouble on the floors above, and the location was used for three days for the opening sequence in which a woman prepares to throw herself from the twenty-first floor. Other filming was done at a disused sports centre in Warrington.

Sheffield in South Yorkshire suffered terrible hardship when the steel industry shrank, but it remains a tremendous city. It gained much glory from the international success of the comedy *The Full Monty* (1997), which was shot at various locations around the city. Even a Sylvester Stallone film has a Sheffield connection. His teamsters' film *F.I.S.T.* (1978), directed by Norman Jewison, which was shot in California, Iowa and Wisconsin, had its opening-credits steelworks sequence filmed at Carbrook Street in Attercliffe, Orgreave Coke Ovens and Hadfield Steelworks, and on the River Don. No sign, though, of Sly himself visiting the city. The football drama *When Saturday Comes* (1996) was shot at various places in the city as well as at the Balti King Indian Restaurant in Broomhill.

Newcastle upon Tyne is rightly described as the capital of the North-East. Near the mouth of the Tyne, the city has a history stretching back to Roman times, although it is best known for engineering and shipbuilding. In 1951 Ralph Thomas shot the spy thriller *The Clouded Yellow* there, with a script by Eric Ambler and starring Jean Simmons and Trevor Howard. In 1976 Michael Tuchner made a film version of the popular Newcastle-set TV series *The Likely Lads* (the film sported the same title), again scripted by Dick Clement and Ian La Frenais and as usual starring James Bolam and Rodney Bewes as those likely lads.

In 1971 writer-director Mike Hodges took Michael Caine to Newcastle to make the cult thriller *Get Carter*, a film that continues to receive critical acclaim and was recently re-released; and writer-director Mike Figgis used Newcastle as the location for his crime-thriller *Stormy Monday* (1988).

The impressive castles of Bamburgh and Lindisfarne are popular film and television locations in Northumberland, and over the years have been exceptionally well used by film-makers. In 1964 Peter Glenville shot *Becket* at both Alnwick and Bamburgh Castles as well as on Bamburgh beach. The film features Richard Burton, Peter O'Toole, John Gielgud and Sian Phillips. Ken Russell also used Bamburgh Castle and beach for the setting of his

Alnwick Castle

Northumberland's impressive Alnwick Castle is probably the finest example of a castle that has developed into a stately home, and in Victorian times it was described as 'the Windsor of the North'. The interiors are ornate and lavish, and much of the exterior stonework dates from the early fourteenth century. It was rebuilt in the late eighteenth century and then altered again for a more medieval atmosphere in the early nineteenth.
Films: *Becket, Elizabeth, King Arthur and the Spaceman, Mary Queen of Scots, Robin Hood: Prince of Thieves*

controversial *The Devils* (1971), which features Vanessa Redgrave and Oliver Reed. Even the medieval epic *El Cid* (1961), starring Charlton Heston as the Spanish hero, was shot at Bamburgh beach as well as at sunnier locations in Spain and Italy.

The beautiful county of Cumbria, described by Ruskin, who lived on Coniston Water, as the loveliest place in all of England, is best known for the Lake District National Park, and its lakes and fells have inspired writers as varied as William Wordsworth, Beatrix Potter and Melvyn Bragg. Karel Reisz shot the closing scenes of *The French Lieutenant's Woman* (1981) in the Lake District – for the sequences where the older Jeremy Irons steams across the lake – using Windermere, Rydal Water and Glen Rothay, Rydal, as well as Crag Wood House Hotel at Windermere (as the guesthouse run by Meryl Streep). Michael Anderson shot sequences of *The Dam Busters* (1955) at Thirlmere, while in 1974 director Claude Whatham filmed the children's classic *Swallows and Amazons* at Coniston Water, Windermere and Derwent Water.

Blackpool Pleasure Beach

Blackpool's seafront offers bright neon lights, waterside amusements and rides and fast-food shops galore. The distinctive Tower is the striking centrepoint of a town that has entertainment at its core and remains very much a typical English seaside resort.
Films: *Bhaji on the Beach, Funny Bones, Whatever Happened to Harold Smith?*

Ken Russell filmed *Mahler* (1974), starring Robert Powell and Georgina Hale, in Keswick and Borrowdale as well as at Black Park Country Park in Buckinghamshire, returning in 1989 to the same two Cumbrian locations to film scenes in *The Rainbow* (1989), starring Sammi Davis, Paul McGann and Amanda Donohoe. Russell also shot a few scenes of the rock musical *Tommy* (1975) in Cumbria, as well as in Brighton, Portsmouth and Hayling Island. He returned to the North-West in 1977 – this time to Blackpool – to shoot scenes for his opulently staged *Valentino*, about the life of the silent-movie star. The scenes, with Rudolph Nureyev in the title role, were shot at the Blackpool Tower Ballroom, though most of the filming took place in Spain.

Julie Walters stars in *She'll Be Wearing Pink Pyjamas* (1984), directed by John Goldschmidt, about a woman on an adventure-training course, which was filmed at Eskdale and Hall Flat Farm near Holmrook in Cumbria. Michael Caine played an inept Sherlock Holmes in *Without a Clue* (1988), which was filmed variously at Windermere, Derwent Water, Lakeside and Haverthwaite, as well as at Blenheim Palace in Oxfordshire and in Gloucestershire.

Blackpool, with its Tower and glittering illuminations, remains the prime resort of the North-West. The Tower was probably best used in a film in Peter

Chelsom's excellent *Funny Bones* (1995), which stars Lee Evans, Jerry Lewis, Oliver Platt and even Oliver Reed. The opening scenes see Evans atop the Blackpool Tower, and although the film was also shot in London and Las Vegas, Blackpool is most memorable. In 1941 John Baxter filmed scenes from *Love on the Dole* in the town, the film starring Deborah Kerr and Clifford Evans. Director Tony Richardson also visited Blackpool to film scenes for the well-received *A Taste of Honey* (1961), starring Rita Tushingham, Murray Melvin and Dora Bryan, though the film was largely shot in Manchester.

Gracie Fields stars in the Blackpool-set film *Sing As We Go* (1934), directed by Basil Dean and scripted by J.B. Priestley and Gordon Wellesley, while years later writer-director Gurinder Chadha used the beach and town as the backdrop for her film *Bhaji on the Beach* (1993). A Japanese film crew also visited Blackpool to shoot scenes for the much-praised film *Shall We Dance?* (aka *Shall We Dansu?*) (1995), about a Japanese man drawn into ballroom dancing when trying to meet the lovely dancer Mai, and who finds himself at the world championships, held in Blackpool. The opening scenes of *Whatever Happened to Harold Smith?* (2000) were shot on the big dipper at Blackpool, while the rest of the film, which stars Tom Courtenay and Lulu, was filmed in Sheffield.

Castle Howard, perhaps best known for being Brideshead, has featured as a backdrop for several films, including *Lady L* (1965), directed by Peter Ustinov and starring Sophia Loren, Paul Newman and David Niven, in which both exteriors and interiors were filmed; *The Spy with a Cold Nose* (1966), directed by Daniel Petrie and starring Laurence Harvey and Daliah Lavi (and a bulldog named Churchill), in which it was used to double as the Kremlin in Moscow; and Stanley Kubrick's *Barry Lyndon* (1975), starring Ryan O'Neal and Marisa Berenson, in which exteriors of the impressive house were shot.

John Schlesinger made one of the great films of the 1960s on location in Bradford, West Yorkshire, and helped cement Tom Courtenay's reputation as a fine young actor. He filmed *Billy Liar* (1963) there, with a cast also including Julie Christie, Wilfrid Pickles and Mona Washbourne. *Billy Liar* used locations including Baildon (on the hills overlooking Bradford and Billy's house), Victoria Square, Undercliffe Cemetery, Bolton Woods Quarries and the Mecca on Manningham Lane. At around the same time Lindsay Anderson filmed *This Sporting Life* (1963), starring Richard Harris as the single-minded rugby player, along with Rachel Roberts and Alan Badel. The film was shot at Wakefield Trinity Rugby Club, Wakefield in Yorkshire, and also at Bolton Abbey near Skipton, Yorkshire. Meanwhile Schlesinger also filmed at the Dons Rugby League ground at Tattersfield in Doncaster, using it as a location in *Sunday, Bloody Sunday*

(1971), which stars Glenda Jackson, Peter Finch and Murray Head.

Schlesinger returned to the region to film *Yanks* (1979), which stars Richard Gere, Vanessa Redgrave and Lisa Eichorn, shooting scenes in Stockport, Greater Manchester, Sleeton and Keighley, West Yorkshire. Liza Minnelli made her acting debut in *Charlie Bubbles* (1968), directed by and starring Albert Finney. The film, which also stars Billie Whitelaw, has many scenes in Manchester, and features the Manchester United football stadium, Old Trafford.

Tom Courtenay returned to Bradford to make the much-acclaimed *The Dresser* (1983), starring as the devoted dresser to an exhausted Shakespearean actor-manager (played by Albert Finney), who has a somewhat wild last day. Directed by Peter Yates, the film was shot at the Alhambra Theatre (the interiors), the entrance to Windsor Baths, Morley Street (used as the stage door) and at the Cork & Bottle pub in Barker Street.

Several films have been shot in the Openshaw area of Manchester, including *Elephant Walk* (1954), *Ghosts Do It* (1991) and *Indiana Jones and the Temple of Doom* (1984), along with the recent British hit *East is East* (1999). Perhaps a lesser-known Manchester-shot film is the Spanish zombie-horror film *Fin de semana para los muertos* (1974), also known under a number of other titles, including *Breakfast at the Manchester Morgue* and even *The Living Dead at Manchester Morgue*. Directed by Jordi Grau, the film stars Ray Lovelock, Cristina Galbo and Arthur Kennedy, and as well as being filmed in Manchester it contains scenes shot in Rome and Madrid.

'We found the right place in Openshaw, Manchester, where most exteriors were shot. The people on the street were astoundingly patient and warm. We trapped them inside their houses for two weeks, and they were wonderful. The real problem turned out to be the weather – the wettest October on record!'

Leslee Udwin, producer
East is East

At virtually the same time that Kevin Costner was donning his leggings to play Robin Hood in the big-budget *Robin Hood: Prince of Thieves*, another – more modest – version was being shot in the UK. Director John Irvin made *Robin Hood* (1991) with a low-key cast and selected as the principal location Peckforton Castle near Chester, which acted as the home of the Baron Daguerre. Nearby Beeston Caves were also used for filming, as was Tatton Park, Cheshire, and locations around the Welsh village of Betws-y-Coed.

Scarborough, on North Yorkshire's east coast, was the location for *Little Voice* (1998). Also aptly shot in Alan Ayckbourn's town was Michael Winner's adaptation of the Ayckbourn play *A Chorus of Disapproval* (1988). The film features an impressive cast, including Anthony Hopkins, Jeremy Irons, Richard Briers, Barbara Ferris and Jenny Seagrove. Scenes from the Spanish film *Beltenbros* (aka *Prince of Shadows*) (1991), directed by Pilar Miro and starring Terence Stamp, Patsy Kensit and Jose Luiz Gomez, were also shot in Scarborough, as well as in Madrid, Spain and Poland.

Mark Herman remained in the North of England to shoot *Purely Better* (2000), set in Newcastle and even featuring a cameo performance by the Newcastle and England soccer captain Alan Shearer. The film is a bittersweet comedy about two young football fans who dream about getting to see their beloved Newcastle United football team. The film also features stunning shots of the acclaimed Angel of the North sculpture in Newcastle.

The popular comedy *A Private Function* (1985), directed by Malcolm Mowbray from a script by Alan Bennett, was shot in Bradford (S.M. Furniss butcher's shop, Bolling Road, and Ben Rhydding, formerly Barracloughs butcher's shop) and Ilkley (the former Rosenthals butcher's shop, Church Street), with some scenes taken at the Regal Cinema in Henley-on-Thames, Oxfordshire, and in London. The film stars Michael Palin, Maggie Smith, Denholm Elliott and Richard Griffiths. *Kes* (1970), directed by Ken Loach and based on the book by Barry Hines, was filmed at Hoyland and Athersley, near Barnsley, and remains a popular film-going experience.

> ### York Minster
>
> Spectacular York Minster provides a convincing alternative to Westminster Abbey. Its construction started in 1229, with several towers built in the late fifteenth century. It is England's largest Gothic building and features a cavernous interior culminating in a 90-foot-high vaulted nave.
>
> **Film:** *Elizabeth*

Bryan Forbes filmed his allegorical drama *Whistle Down the Wind* (1961) at Burnley and Bacup. The film is about a girl (played by Hayley Mills) who finds in her family's barn a man (Alan Bates) wanted for murder and becomes convinced that he is actually Jesus Christ. Director Charles Sturridge used the impressive Carlton Towers in Yorkshire as Hetton, the family home of Tony Last (James Wilby) and his wife Brenda (Kristin Scott Thomas) in his adaptation of Evelyn Waugh's *A Handful of Dust* (1988). The film was also shot at the Café de Paris, close to Leicester Square in London, once a fashionable nightclub and now a trendy disco.

Yorkshire – or rather the romantic ideal of the more rugged parts of Yorkshire – was celebrated in *Wuthering Heights* (1992) (or to give it its full US release title, *Emily Brontë's Wuthering Heights*), directed by Peter Kosminsky and starring Ralph Fiennes, Juliette Binoche, Janet McTeer and Sophie Ward.

selected films

Alien³ (1992)

The third of the *Alien* films didn't manage the critical and audience success of the first two, but it remains a fascinating, if austere, addition to the series. As with the first two films (*Alien*, directed by Ridley Scott, and *Aliens*, directed by James Cameron), the production was UK-based. The film has a dark, brutal edge. Ripley (again played by Sigourney Weaver) is found in the wreckage of a crashed spaceship by residents of the prison world of Fiorina 161. As the film develops the Aliens gradually emerge and proceed to terrorize the inmates in the dank tunnels of the prison. The closing sequences are almost biblical as Ripley plays host-mother-killer to a new Alien by throwing herself into a furnace. As well as using studio sets *Alien* ³ took a trip north to shoot at Blyth Power Station in Northumberland, and to Dawdon beach, County Durham. Director David Fincher used the locations for early shots of the prison area and for exteriors. A spokesman for the Northern Media Forum that helped to find the locations commented: 'The director discovered a beach that had been blackened by coal over the years, making it look really weird.' The film also stars Charles Dance (as Ripley's doctor-lover), Charles Dutton and Paul McGann.

Backbeat (1994)

It would be difficult to imagine shooting any film that involved a Beatles storyline without filming in Liverpool. And while the story of *Backbeat* is about the so-called fifth Beatle, Stuart Sutcliffe, and the time the Beatles spent playing in Hamburg, *Backbeat* still makes good use of Liverpool locations. Directed by Iain Softley, the film stars Stephen Dorff as Sutcliffe and Ian Hart as John Lennon (he had already played Lennon in *The Days and Hours*), and the start of the film is very much about their relationship. The rest of The Beatles (it was still pre-Ringo days when the film takes place) don't think much of Sutcliffe's musical ability. When they go to play in Hamburg, Sutcliffe meets photographer Astrid Kirchher (played by Sheryl Lee). Eventually he leaves the band to paint and to be with her, though sadly he died of a brain haemorrhage aged just twenty. The film was shot in Gambier Terrace, Liverpool, the actual street where Lennon and Sutcliffe shared a flat, and the band's departure for Germany was filmed on an Isle of Man ferry at Victoria Dock, Birkenhead. The sequence where Kirchher tells Lennon that she loves Sutcliffe was filmed at Point of Ayr Lighthouse in north Wales and at nearby Talacre beach.

Bhaji on the Beach (1993)

The holiday charms of Blackpool are on display in Gurinder Chadha's wonderful comedy-drama *Bhaji on the Beach*, starring Kim Vithana, Jimmi Harkishin and Sarita Khayuria, about a group of Indian women of various ages who go on a daytrip up the M6 motorway from Birmingham and head for the beach at Blackpool. The film proved a great success and broke new ground in the warm way that it deals with different communities, sensitively showing the bond between them. Chadha has great fun with her story, and the scenes of the women eating, talking and playing on Blackpool beach and in the town's arcades are memorable.

Brassed Off (1996)

In this truly wondrous tale of a mining community facing possible closure of the local pit everyone has their money problems, but despite everything Pete Postlethwaite, the leader of the colliery's brass band, is determined to keep the band going and to reach the national finals. The film was slightly in the shadow of *The Full Monty*, which had a similar theme of men dealing with unemployment, but *Brassed Off* has a sharper political edge, with the closing scenes very much anti-government and a final message detailing the facts of mine closures in the UK. Written and directed by Mark Herman (who went on to make *Little Voice*), the film also stars Ewan McGregor and Stephen Tompkinson as band members and Tara Fitzgerald as the newcomer who forces her way into the band. The film was shot in the Yorkshire towns of Barnsley, Doncaster, Rotherham and Halifax and, for the closing concert scenes, at the Royal Albert Hall in London.

Mark Herman said: 'The original idea came from a radio report I heard in the North-East, Newcastle way, of a colliery band that had to close down when the pit closed... I had been wanting to write a story about pit closures but couldn't think of a good upfront story to turn it into cinema.'

Ironically enough, the only fly in the ointment came from the weather. Producer Steve Abbott commented: 'Now this really is unbelievable. We were filming in late autumn, and there was a certain "cold" look that we wanted. The weather, however, was as nice as it could have been – positively balmy, in fact. When we really wanted a bit of rain or drizzle, we actually got beautiful sunsets and crisp, clear mornings!'

Abbott was keenly aware of the impact that film crews can have on a community and he was keen to respect the communities being filmed. 'When we started filming in Grimethorpe, Doncaster and Halifax, the cooperation from the communities was fantastic. I think the communities we

△ Stephen Tompkinson (left) and
Pete Postlethwaite in the shadow
of the pits, in *Brassed Off*.

"invaded" realized that what we were doing, we were doing with honesty.' Mark Herman added: 'Once people had grasped the fact that we were there to film a very valid and honest story, and not to exploit them in any way, the cooperation was astounding and very gratifying. I think the local people realized that we were very much on their side.'

Certainly there was no sign of stretched limos cruising around the streets of Grimethorpe. 'Mark and I used to drive to the location every day in my old car, and during the journey we would discuss all sorts of things about the project that had to be addressed. There was no time, and, more important, no need for any table-thumping.'

Brief Encounter (1945)

This classic British movie was voted second in the top hundred British films by the British Film Institute poll of industry professionals. It is a wonderful movie rightly celebrated as a tear-jerker that movingly re-creates a little England on a railway platform. It is, of course, about very English repressed love, all the more intense because it is largely unspoken. David Lean directed this unforgettable expansion of Noël Coward's one-act play *Still Life*, and Celia Johnson and Trevor Howard are the respectable middle-class couple who fall in love but know ultimately they cannot be together and must return to their real lives. The film is shot in an elegant circle. The opening scene shows what appears to be a casual parting by two people, although it transpires that it is in fact an awful separation for both. The couple first meet when Laura Jesson (Johnson) has a speck of dirt in her eye, and Alec Harvey (Howard), a doctor, gets the dirt out.

Their relationship gradually develops from cups of tea to meals and visits to the cinema, until finally they realize they are in love, but cannot be together. The meetings are centred around Milford Station, where their respective trains arrive and depart. But because the film was shot during the war years Lean could not film too close to London because of air raids, and instead filmed at Carnforth Station in Lancashire. Slightly more worn now, the station is still there, although that classic little buffet (complete with railwayman Stanley Holloway and his love, the elegant Joyce Carey) has long gone. How long the station will remain is in the balance at the time of writing, with reports that it may be pulled down. Occasionally fans make a sentimental visit to the station, but it is not yet deemed a landmark worth celebrating and retaining because of *Brief Encounter*. Lean also shot some of the train scenes at Watford Junction, but it is Carnforth, with its sloping walkway and clock, that remains memorable. Howard and Johnson

△ Celia Johnson and Trevor Howard make a change from hanging about at railway stations by going boating, in *Brief Encounter*.

give their characters such dignity and restraint that when the film arrives back where it started – with their separation – it is all the more moving.

East is East (1999)

East is East first saw life as a sell-out play by Ayub Khan Din at the Royal Court Theatre in London. The script was developed and eventually commissioned for production by FilmFour and went into pre-production in August 1998 when the search started for the right locations. It is set in Salford in the early 1970s and is about youngsters in Asian families adjusting to life and facing up to the possibility of an arranged marriage.

Producer Leslee Udwin said: 'I did a massive search in London to find some suitable houses, but there was absolutely nothing! It became clear that we

△ Some heady fashions out on the city streets, in *East is East*.

would have to go north, which was quite a drain on the budget. So then we went to recce the area where Ayub grew up, but the streets he lived on weren't there any more! There were shadows of the past, but nothing we could use. We had to find a very specific H formation of roads to give the camera maximum room for movement. Eventually we found the right place in Openshaw, Manchester, where most exteriors were shot. The people on the street were astoundingly patient and warm. We trapped them inside their houses for two weeks, and they were wonderful. The real problem turned out to be the weather – the wettest October on record!

'We converted an old grocery into the Khans' chip shop. It was quite eerie – when Ayub walked in he said the hairs on the back of his neck stood up because the fish fryer was exactly the same colour and model as the one at his parents' chip shop, as was the multicoloured slash curtain. We had somehow instinctively captured the look and feel of the original.'

The film, directed by Damien O'Donnell, proved to be a great success in the UK, gradually building its box-office take week after week and being voted Best British Film in the 2000 *Evening Standard* Film Awards.

Elizabeth (1998)

With Queen Mary I, a zealous Catholic bent on Protestant repression, close to death in 1558, England is racked with financial and religious instability. Mary (Kathy Burke) even tries to have her sister, and heir apparent, executed for treason, but her plan fails. Within days Mary is dead and Elizabeth (Cate Blanchett) is crowned Queen of England, but just as quickly she has to deal with enemies from outside and rebellion in her own council. She retaliates, grows stronger and eventually becomes the legendary Virgin Queen of England. Shekhar Kapur's marvellously directed telling of the story of Elizabeth is a magnificent achievement, brilliantly acted and filmed in a luxuriant and dramatic

manner. The powerful film was shot at numerous locations around the country, including York Minster; Warkworth Castle, Alnwick Castle and Bamburgh beach in Northumberland; Haddon Hall near Bakewell, Derbyshire; the Tower of London; and Durham Cathedral.

Kapur said: 'The reason we went to so many locations was that there was a particular look I was looking for in the design of the film – and that look was dominated by my need to show that destiny is bigger than man... that destiny is even bigger than Elizabeth I. And because this was the story of a woman who pushed herself to this point, it was her destiny to come to this point, I needed a palette that was larger than man. And so I picked stone! I went to this cathedral built in the twelfth century. It was a shock to me that so many generations of people came and died in this cathedral, and after me there will be many more generations who will come and die. But this cathedral, this stone structure, will still

stand. And so I used it to signify the ultimate power of destiny.'

△ Director Shekhar Kapur discusses a scene with Cate Blanchett, in *Elizabeth*.

Fairytale – A True Story (1997)

Two young Yorkshire girls cause a sensation in 1917 when they claim to have taken photographs of fairies. Based on the true story of the Cottingley Fairies, this sentimental Victorian drama is never less than interesting and has a fabulous cast that includes Peter O'Toole as Arthur Conan Doyle, Harvey Keitel as Houdini – and even Mel Gibson in an uncredited appearance (well, his production company made the film), while the two little girls are well played by Florence Hoath and Elizabeth Earl. The film was shot in many authentic locations. Filming was done at Cottingley itself (for the school scenes), while Keighley Station in West Yorkshire was the stand-in for Cottingley Station and the magical beck was actually at

Ramsgill in North Yorkshire. Filming also took place at Pirbright in Surrey (the scenes of Windelsham Manor) and in the Hackney Empire theatre in North London. The story provided the basis of another film, *Photographing Fairies* (1997), which director Nick Willing shot mainly in London.

The Full Monty (1997)

One of the great surprise films of the 1990s, and one that managed to work all around the world, this is a wonderful blend of humour and drama set around the concept of a group of out-of-work men who decide to try to raise money by becoming strippers. The way in which the Sheffield steelworkers go about trying to earn money while also retaining their self-respect struck a chord. The film, directed by Peter Cattaneo, cost just $3.5 million to make yet grossed more than $35 million at the US box office alone, and helped make stars of Robert Carlyle, Tom Wilkinson and Mark Addy. The men try various schemes before hatching the idea to try stripping. The hilarious scenes of them in training are perfectly staged, as is the final uplifting scene at the club when they strip in front of 400 extras... and do the Full Monty (i.e. take everything off). The film was shot in and around Sheffield, and despite the fact that the backbone of the story is about the desperation of a group of out-of-work men, there is something strangely uplifting about both the city and the way it is shown on film. The opening canal scene where Carlyle is seen balancing on an abandoned car in the middle of the water was filmed at Bacon Lane, Sheffield, while the Job Club was actually Langsett School, Burton Street, and the graveyard scene was filmed at Crookes Cemetery. The final stripping scene was filmed at Shiregreen Working Men's Club, and Gerald's house was actually in Whirlow Park Road. The success of the film is evident in the fact that the local authority operates a tour around locations featured in the film (see page 249).

Get Carter (1971)

Over the years director Mike Hodges' *Get Carter* has developed into something of a cult classic, and it is perhaps a tribute to its popularity that Sylvester Stallone is starring in a US-set remake. In the gritty and brutal original version, Michael Caine plays Jack Carter, a London-based villain who returns to his native Newcastle to bury his brother and who sets about antagonizing the local gangsters as he tries to find out who the killer was. Caine is cold, calculating and very sexy, but then this is a film full of quite nasty people, most of whom get their just deserts. Playwright John Osborne appears as a camp Newcastle gang boss, while the late Bryan Mosley (*Coronation Street*'s Alf Roberts) plays a dodgy businessman. The film was shot in and around Newcastle, while the multi-storey car park chase scene was shot in Gateshead, Tyne & Wear, and the

△ Christopher Eccleston walks the muddy route into town, in *Jude*.

final beach shooting scenes were filmed at Seaham, County Durham. Whether the new version's Seattle locations can make suitable stand-ins for Newcastle remains to be seen.

Hilary and Jackie (1998)

Hilary and Jackie tells the remarkable story of one of the world's greatest cellists, the late Jacqueline du Pré, allowing Jackie's playing to provide a magnificent background to a story of volatile passions, thwarted ambitions and sibling rivalry. Directed by Anand Tucker, the film stars Emily Watson as Jackie and Rachel Griffiths as her sister Hilary. *The Sunday Times* described the film as 'one of the best British films of the decade', and the performances are certainly powerful and involving. The climax of this real-life story is the well-known fact that Jackie eventually died, aged 42, of

multiple sclerosis. Many of the film's scenes were shot in Liverpool, including concert scenes at St George's Hall, while the moving beach scenes were filmed at Formby. The film's Moscow sequences were shot in George's Dock in Liverpool.

Jude (1996)

This powerful adaptation of Thomas Hardy's harrowing story, beautifully filmed by Michael Winterbottom contains very impressive central performances by Kate Winslet and Christopher Eccleston. After his wife leaves him, a simple rural labourer (Eccleston) decides to follow his ambitions to become a teacher and moves to a university town, where eventually he falls deeply in love with his cousin, played by Winslet. Winterbottom films with gritty style and uses almost metallic tones (superbly shot by cinematographer Eduardo Serra) to portray the hardship and suffering of his characters. At the centre of the film is pure tragedy. It was shot in Richmond, North Yorkshire, Durham, Surrey and Edinburgh, at the Beamish Museum in County Durham and at Blanchford village in Northumberland.

Little Voice (1998)

Based on the successful stage play *The Rise and Fall of Little Voice* by Jim Cartwright, this film version, directed by Mark Herman (who made *Brassed Off*), features impressive performances by Michael Caine and Brenda Blethyn, but, more important, allows Jane Horrocks (who played L.V. on stage) truly to shine. Only Horrocks could have taken on the film role, as the character is called on to sing in the voices of numerous recording stars, something she did brilliantly on stage and superbly replicates on film. Brenda Blethyn plays L.V.'s sluttish mother who does everything to put her daughter down, while Caine is the dodgy agent who sees the shy talent as his way into the big time. Also in the cast is Ewan McGregor as the shy pigeon-loving telephone engineer who falls for L.V., the only one to offer her real support. The film is set totally in the attractive resort of Scarborough and makes great use of the seafront and local venues. Scarborough Spa Sun Court, the site of musical performances since the 1830s, is the location of the final scenes, when Horrocks and McGregor finally get to talk.

The original play was naturally stage-bound, offering Herman many challenges when it came to making the decision to take on the project. 'I loved the play,' he said. 'But this was the hardest writing job I've ever done, because in essence *The Rise and Fall of Little Voice* was about a girl who rarely leaves her room, and that's not very cinematic.' So Herman introduced new locations to widen the film visually and developed characters that were only referred to in the play.

One thing that didn't change, though, was the fact that Horrocks' singing was very real. 'Half of the play's impact was being in the same room as someone doing those imitations,' explained Herman. 'But with cinema, people can often subliminally tell if things are dubbed.' To counter this, most of the scenes where Little Voice sings were shot live. Jane Horrocks added: 'This is a very rare thing in a film, but the audience have got to absolutely believe I am doing it. And if they think for a second that I'm not, then you've lost the whole piece.'

Macbeth (1971)

When Roman Polanski's version of *Macbeth* was released, critics were left wondering why he had done it. Just fifteen months after his pregnant wife Sharon Tate was murdered by the followers of Charles Manson, he arrived in Northumberland to film his very brutal and bloody version of Shakespeare's play. At the film's release, the critic Roger Ebert wrote: 'I might as well be honest and say it is impossible to watch certain scenes without thinking of the Charles Manson case. It is impossible to watch a film directed by Roman Polanski and not react on more than one level to such images as a baby being "untimely ripped from his mother's womb"... Polanski's characters resemble Charles Manson. They are anti-intellectual and driven by deep, shameful wells of lust and violence.' The film is indeed a bloody masterpiece, with a powerful script by Polanski and theatre critic Kenneth Tynan. The casting was interesting, with relatively unknown British actors Jon Finch (Macbeth) and Francesca Annis (Lady Macbeth) in the leading roles. The opening shots were filmed at Morfa Bychan near Porthmadog, Talsarnau near Harlech, Ffestiniog and Black Rock Sands in Wales, before the crew moved to Northumberland to shoot at the visually impressive Lindisfarne Castle on Holy Island, the location where Polanski had made *Cul-de-Sac* in 1966. Lindisfarne stood in for Macbeth's Glamis

Castle, though Polanski also shot at Bamburgh Castle, just five miles away from Lindisfarne, for the king's palace.

The Railway Children (1970)

A true children's classic, this much-loved adaptation of E. Nesbit's novel is about three Edwardian children forced to move with their mother from London to the Yorkshire countryside after their father has been sent to prison charged with espionage. They are determined to clear his name, but at the same time become obsessed with the local steam railway, befriending a porter, Perks (Bernard Cribbins), and eventually helping to prevent an accident. The film was written and directed by Lionel Jeffries (perhaps better known as an actor), who managed to discover the perfect location for the film in the Keighley & Worth Valley Railway and its station at Oakworth, in the middle of the five-mile line. The house of the three railway children (played by Jenny Agutter, Sally Thomsett and Gary Warren) was actually a private farmhouse near Oxenhope, while Haworth (famous as the village where the Brontës lived) was used for street scenes. In fact, the Brontës' home, now the Brontë Parsonage Museum, was used as the home of the local doctor. The climax of the film has the children warning a traindriver of a landslide that is blocking a tunnel, in reality the Mytholmes tunnel, between Haworth and Oakworth.

Raining Stones (1993)

A wonderful combination of drama and humour from Ken Loach, this is a realistic film about the northern working classes and is certainly one of the best British films of recent years. Bruce Jones plays an unemployed Catholic father who tries to find the money to buy his seven-year-old daughter a Communion dress. The wonderful opening scenes see him and pal Ricky Tomlinson chasing a sheep, and further honest and insightful humour follows as Jones sinks deeper into desperation trying to keep himself and his family afloat. Scripted by Jim Allen and based on the community in which he lives, the film was shot in and around Middleton, Greater Manchester.

Robin Hood: Prince of Thieves (1991)

When Kevin Costner came to the UK to shoot the big-budget *Robin Hood: Prince of Thieves* it was clear that this was going to be no simple single-location/studio shoot. No, Costner and his director Kevin Reynolds crisscrossed the country for their locations, though not even stopping once in poor old Sherwood Forest, the legendary home of Robin and his pals. To this updating the film-makers added a black character to fight alongside Robin

– a Moor named Azeem (played quite delightfully by Morgan Freeman), who ends up giving the film a much-needed sense of gravitas. The rest of the film is a mixture of styles: Costner plays Robin as intense and pretty humourless; Mary Elizabeth Mastrantonio, cast late in the day as Maid Marian, doesn't have any chemistry with Costner and seems much too tough for him; while Alan Rickman as the Sheriff of Nottingham is in almost a different film, having great fun with some daft lines. But the film does look good! When Robin and Azeem return to England, it is beneath the white cliffs of Seven Sisters near Eastbourne. Robin then battles with some of the sheriff's men at Hadrian's Wall, at Sycamore Gap, near Housesteads in Northumberland, and is then off to the old family home of Locksley Castle, played in the film by Old Wardour Castle in Wiltshire. For Sherwood Forest the film-makers used a mixture of Burnham Beeches near London (where the outlaw camp was built), the Yorkshire Dales National Park and Hampshire's New Forest, while the

memorable scene where Robin fights Little John (Nick Brimble) with wooden staffs on a river bridge was filmed at Aysgarth Falls in the Yorkshire Dales National Park. Hulne Priory at Alnwick in Northumberland was used as Maid Marian's home, while the interior of the Priory Church of St Bartholomew the Great at Smithfield in London (where some of *Four Weddings and a Funeral* was also shot) was used to represent Nottingham Cathedral. The exteriors of Nottingham Castle were in reality the walled city of Carcassonne in southern France.

On the first day of shooting, Costner and his merry men stood in Sherwood Forest (on that day Burnham Beeches) and found that bad weather meant that aircraft had been diverted directly over the area – a day ruined and a lot of money wasted. The great British weather caused a number of problems for Reynolds, too: 'When we started shooting there were a number of key parts that hadn't even been cast. But we wanted the English look, we wanted the

drizzle. And we paid the price for it. One of the problems of making pictures today is that there is just so much pressure – so much money.'

△ Morgan Freeman and Kevin Costner atop Hadrian's Wall, in *Robin Hood: Prince of Thieves*.

Room at the Top (1958)

Laurence Harvey stars in one off his best roles as Joe Lampton, an ambitious young local government worker who causes the death of his real love but still continues to climb to the top by marrying into a rich family. Directed by Jack Clayton and based on John Braine's bestseller, the film – as did the book – showed the industrial North as it really was, and helped to change the face of British cinema. The film, which also stars Simone Signoret, Heather Sears, Donald Wolfit and Donald Houston, was shot extensively in Bradford, using Bradford City Hall (interior office scenes and the Council Chamber), Cartwright Memorial Hall, the Bankfield Hotel, Bingley (for the dance scene),

Gilstead Moor and Canal Road Mills. A sequel, *Life at the Top* (1965), also starring Harvey, showed Joe ten years later, as both he and his wife unhappily have affairs. The film was again shot in Bradford, using Bradford City Hall, the Wool Exchange, Wingfield House, Bingley (the garden-party scene), Ilkley Station and Ilkley Moor.

Stormy Monday (1988)

Director Mike Figgis – perhaps best known for his Oscar-winning *Leaving Las Vegas* and his cop-drama *Internal Affairs* – made his first major film in Newcastle, with a high-profile cast that includes Melanie Griffith, Tommy Lee Jones, Sting and Sean Bean. Granted, when he made the film none was yet a major star, and at that time his chosen filming area, Newcastle's waterfront, was hardly the most popular spot in the city. Tommy Lee Jones plays a tough American gangster named Cosmo, who wants to buy up properties, including the jazz club run by Finney (played well by local boy Sting). Sean Bean plays a drifter who helps Finney out, while Griffith is the waitress he falls for. Figgis does a wonderful job of creating a stylish look for the city, using locations near the waterfront under the Tyne Bridge. In fact, the city's bridges are exceptionally well used in the film, with the final showdown taking place on the impressive High Level Bridge. Filming also took place at Newcastle's Royal Station Hotel.

Swallows and Amazons (1974)

This mild children's film is based on the much-loved book by Arthur Ransome about four children growing up in the Lake District of the 1920s. The feeling might be slightly old-fashioned, but the magnificent Lake District locations are memorable. Directed by Claude Whatham, the film stars Virginia McKenna, Ronald Fraser, Simon West, Sophie Neville and Zanna Hamilton. In his book *Fire over England* Ken Russell wrote: 'I have never read the Arthur Ransome classic but if it is as dull as the film, I doubt I ever will… Everyone is frightfully prissy and well behaved.' The film was shot at Coniston Water, Ulverston, Windermere, Derwent Water, and at the Windermere Steamboat Museum, where two boats used in the film are still kept.

Whatever Happened to Harold Smith? (2000)

Peter Hewitt's delightful comedy is very much a North of England film, shot in Sheffield with a location trip to Blackpool, and offering a wonderful role for Tom Courtenay, little seen on the big screen in recent years. He plays Harold Smith, an ordinary northern man with special 'magical' powers. At the heart of the story, though, is the relationship between his son Vince

(Michael Legge) – who is into Travolta-style disco – and Joanna (Laura Fraser) who, he finds out, is a punk. The film delightfully mixes music, dodgy 1970s clothing and furniture, and some humour, and also has roles for Lulu (as Vince's mother), Stephen Fry and David Thewlis. Shooting took place on location around Sheffield (where the film's writer, Ben Steiner, comes from). A former steel factory, Richardson's, was turned into a mini-studio where the production team built all the interior rooms of the Smith house and the TV studio for the Roland Thornton (played by Mark Williams) show. An older Vince travels to Blackpool to throw his father's ashes from the Big Dipper, ending up with them spraying into the faces of Japanese tourists.

When Saturday Comes (1996)

Sean Bean does his muscular best as a brewery worker in Sheffield whose dreams of becoming a professional footballer are finally fulfilled, but – of course – not without damage to his personal life. Very much *Roy of the Rovers* stuff, but local boy Bean does the best he can and has Emily Lloyd on hand as his girlfriend, with Pete Postlethwaite also among the cast. Directed by Maria Gieste, the film was shot in and around Sheffield: look out for the Balti King Indian Restaurant in Broomhill. The film had a pretty poor reception, with the critics particularly brutal. James Cameron-Wilson in *Film Review* wrote: 'You can't believe any of this tosh for an instant; it's like *Rocky* Blu-Tacked to Northern England and washed down with Tennent's Extra.'

Withnail and I (1987)

Withnail and I has developed into a cult movie, and rightly so. Wonderfully written and directed by Bruce Robinson, its mixture of hard drinking, acerbic humour and hysterical rantings hit just the right mark for a young audience who discovered it a few years after its release in 1987 and relished it on video and at its occasional television and cinema outings. Richard E. Grant (Withnail) and Paul McGann (Marwood, the 'I' of the title) made their film debuts as the two wannabe actors living in a dank, dreary and dismal London of the late 1960s. Suffering from extreme cold and lack of money, they head for the remote country cottage belonging to Withnail's Uncle Monty (a glorious performance from Richard Griffiths). But they are hardly suited to the great outdoors and have a hilariously awful time dealing with locals, hills, fields and all things rural. The wonderfully dark humour of the script comes to the fore as they experience the countryside as a battleground. These are city guys who cannot handle lighting a fire or even walking across a muddy field (they soon have plastic bags over their feet), let alone deal with seemingly terrifying locals. Things go from bad to

worse when the amorous Uncle Monty becomes keen to romance Marwood. The film's brilliantly grim humour proves the perfect antidote to the bland sweetness of so many

other comedies. The film was shot in The Crown public house in the Market Square of Stony Stratford, Milton Keynes and memorably in the Penrith area of Cumbria and at nearby Crow Crag, as well as in the Lake District National Park.

Wuthering Heights (1992)

While this impressive version of Emily Brontë's classic didn't quite make a star of Ralph Fiennes (it was one of his first films), it certainly set him on the way, though we tend not to see him with long hair as a muscular romantic lead nowadays. Brontë had set the story in the moors above her home village of Haworth in Yorkshire, but for this film version director Peter Kosminsky used Broughton Hall, near Skipton, as the home of the Linton family, Thrushcross Grange. Other locations used included the Yorkshire Moors, East Riddlesden Hall, and Aysgarth Falls, where Cathy and Heathcliff speak of love. Fiennes does a fine job as Heathcliff, while Juliette Binoche plays an elfin Cathy Earnshaw. Other films of the story include the much-loved 1939 Hollywood version with Laurence Olivier and Merle Oberon, which was filmed entirely in the California hills; a Mexican version of 1954; and one of 1970 starring Timothy Dalton and Anna Calder-Marshall.

Yanks (1979)

Richard Gere was just about breaking through as a major Hollywood star when he headed over to England to make *Yanks*, the story of the romantic adventures of GIs billeted in Lancashire during the Second World War. The film was directed by John Schlesinger with a script by Colin Welland and Walter Bernstein. It was shot in Stockport and at Keighley Station in West Yorkshire.

wales

THE LOCATIONS OF WALES ARE PERHAPS AMONG THE LEAST appreciated in terms of the profile they have with film-goers. With ten thousand square miles of possibilities, Wales offers long expanses of unspoiled beaches, wild mountains, lush green valleys and traditional villages, but the proportion of films shot in the country that are acknowledged as Welsh productions is relatively small.

The growth in location shooting and media development in the region has led to a parallel growth in technical-support companies offering a full range of production services, from studios to crewing agencies. The facts that Caernarfon has been dubbed the 'Hollywood of Wales' and Cardiff now has a strong reputation as the largest media centre in the UK apart from London are helping to raise the area's profile. Wales supports three regional television stations, more than 80 independent production companies and more than 150 facility and media-support houses.

The sheer variety of types of location in a relatively small area has been a key factor in the success of Wales. The mountains of Snowdonia National Park (which prompted the nineteenth-century writer and traveller George Burrow to write 'perhaps in all the world there is no region more picturesquely beautiful') and the Brecon Beacons stand in fine contrast to the spectacular coastline of Pembrokeshire or the beautiful Clwydian Hills, and film-makers have a rich choice of stately homes, power stations, railways, lighthouses and farmhouses.

A healthy number of movies over the years have either very clearly been Welsh or have trumpeted their Welsh locations. Examples include *The Life Story of David Lloyd George* (1918), *Moby Dick* (1956), which was filmed at Ceibwr Bay near Fishguard and off the Pembrokeshire coast, *Tiger Bay* (1959), *Only Two Can Play* (1962), which was filmed in Swansea, *Under Milk Wood* (1972), *On the Black Hill* (1988), the Oscar-nominated *Hedd Wyn* (1991), *Second Best* (1993), *The Englishman Who Went Up a Hill But Came Down a Mountain* (1995), *Twin Town* (1996), *The Theory of Flight* (1998), *Up and Under* (1998), *Hilary and Jackie* (1998) and the recent *Rancid Aluminium* (1999).

Epic medieval movies that have made great use of Wales's castles and scenery include *First Knight* (1995), with Sean Connery, Richard Gere and Julia Ormond; two versions of *Prince Valiant*; Ron Howard's fantasy adventure *Willow* (1988), with Val Kilmer and Joanna Whalley; *Dragonslayer* (1981), which stars a young Peter MacNicol with Ralph Richardson; and even *The Vikings* (1958), starring Kirk Douglas and Tony Curtis, which was filmed in Caernarfon and the Menai Strait.

The rugged hills and valleys of Wales have doubled many times for the mountain ranges of India, with films as varied as *Elephant Boy* (1937), *The Drum* (1938) and even *Carry On Up the Khyber* (1968) saving money by skipping a trip to India. Other countries doubled in Wales include China for the moving Ingrid Bergman film *The Inn of the Sixth Happiness* (1958); the Carpathian Alps for the little-seen Michael Mann horror-thriller *The Keep* (1983); the Spanish coast for the wonderfully surreal *Pandora and the Flying Dutchman* (1951), which was filmed at Pendine Sands; the sands of Arabia for a section of David Lean's epic *Lawrence of Arabia* (1962), which made use of the Merthyr Mawr sand-dunes; and the Sino-Soviet border for the 1969 spy film *The Most Dangerous Man in the World*, which stars Gregory Peck and was filmed at Cwmdilli.

Terry Gilliam has twice visited Wales, in 1977 to shoot sequences of *Jabberwocky* in Chepstow and again in 1982 to shoot at Raglan Castle, near Abergavenny, for *Time Bandits*. Roman Polanski filmed his bloody version of *Macbeth* (1971) in Talsarnau near Harlech (doubling as Scotland) and Morfa Bychan near Porthmadog as well as Ffestiniog and on the Black Rock Sands. *The Lion in Winter* (1968), which stars Katherine Hepburn, Peter O'Toole and Anthony Hopkins, made use of stunning Marloes Sands near Pembroke as well as Pembroke Castle; and the martial-arts-fantasy

Snowdonia

The beautiful National Park in north Wales offers a plethora of stunning vistas of castles, valleys, coastline, mountains and sweeping meadows. The 840 square miles of unspoiled terrain offer a great deal for film-makers and over the years the area has been much used, often to double as remote foreign spots such as India or China.

Films: *Carry On Up the Khyber, First Knight, The Inn of the Sixth Happiness, Macbeth, Willow*

follow-up *Mortal Kombat II: Annihilation* (1996), which features Talisa Soto and James Remar, re-created its imaginary world at Dinorwig Quarry near Caernarfon and at Parys Mountain on Anglesey.

Several low-budget British Film Institute films – including *Elenya* (1991), directed by Steve Gough; *Madagascar Skin* (1994), directed by Chris Newby; and Andrew Grieve's *On the Black Hill* – have been shot in Wales. The Welsh-language television station S4C is relatively prolific, too, its films again made on comparatively low budgets. Titles include the Welsh-language *Hedd Wyn* (aka *The Armageddon Poet*), nominated for the Oscar for best foreign-language film in 1993. About the life of a young Welsh poet killed during the First World War, it was filmed in the Trawsfynydd area of Gwynedd. Others include *The Proposition* (*Y Fargen*) (1995), starring Patrick Bergin and Theresa Russell and filmed in Conwy and Pembrokeshire; *Chameleon* (1996), directed by Ceri Sherlock; and *Cwm Hyfryd* (*Beautiful Valley*) made in 1992 by Paul Turner and appropriately shot in the Rhondda Valleys.

Maurice Elvey made two films in Wales in 1918. *The Life Story of David Lloyd George* – which was recently restored and successfully screened by the National Film and Television Archive – features Norman Page and Ernest Thesiger. It was filmed at Llanystumdwy and at Criccieth, while *Hindle Wakes*, featuring Colette O'Neil and Ada King, was shot at Llandudno.

Equally early films make good use of Welsh locations. *The Last King of Wales* (1922), directed by George Ridgwell and featuring Charles Ashton and Malvina Longfellow, was filmed in Snowdonia; and an early version of the H. Rider Haggard novel *She* was made by Leander de Cordova on the north Wales coast starring Betty Blythe and Carlyle Blackwell. The classic science-fiction tale, *Things to Come* (1936), directed by William Cameron Menzies and featuring Raymond Massey, was partly filmed at Blaina near Ebbw Vale.

More recently, *Twin Town* (1996) was filmed in and around Swansea; while *House of America* (1997) starring Matthew Rhys, Sian Phillips and Lisa Palfrey, was shot in Glyn-neath, and with its hot soundtrack of new Welsh bands attracted a cult following. Made for just £1.5 million, *House of America* is about an eccentric south Wales mother (Phillips) and two of

Portmeirion

This unique Italianate village near Porthmadog is where the cult television series *The Prisoner* was shot. Designed by eccentric architect Clough Williams-Ellis in the early twentieth century, it was not completed until 1974. It features 70 acres of subtropical gardens, sandy beaches and wonderfully surreal buildings. The village has also been used for pop-video shoots: Supergrass filmed the video for 'Alright' there, and Manic Street Preachers made the video for 'This is My Truth' on the beach.

Film: *Under Suspicion*

her three jobless children, who start living a dream of escaping to the US to visit their father.

The James Gang (1997), though filmed in Wales, is actually about a Scottish family plotting a heist as a means of keeping the family together. Directed by Mike Barker and starring John Hannah, Helen McCrory, Jason Flemyng and Toni Collette, the setting of Penrhys, in the Rhondda Valley, doubled as the Scottish town the family escapes from. Filming also took place in Swansea and at Cardiff Docks. *Darklands* (1997) was something of a hit at several of the European horror-SF festivals, with its mix of action and evil cults in industrial south Wales. Directed by Julian Richards, it stars Craig Fairbrass as a Swansea reporter who gets drawn into investigating a nasty Druid cult. The film, which also stars Jon Finch and Rowena King, was shot in Swansea and at Port Talbot Steelworks.

Writer-director Justin Kerrigan's *Human Traffic* (1999), shot in Cardiff, stars John Simm, Lorraine Pilkington and Danny Dyer as a band of Welsh clubbers who just want to get high and have good times with friends. The drug element worried some critics, but the film clicked at the box office with younger audiences. *Rancid Aluminium* (1999), based on James Hawes's second anarchic novel with a screenplay by Hawes himself, was shot in Cardiff and Penarth, and on Barry Island.

selected films

August (1994)
Directed by and starring Anthony Hopkins (one of the greatest actors Wales has produced), this is an elegant version of Chekhov's *Uncle Vanya*, relocated to Wales of the 1890s. A visit by the head of a family and his much younger wife to the estate looked after by his brother-in-law leads to an examination of the stifled family. The film, also featuring Leslie Philips, Kate Burton and Hugh Lloyd, was shot on the Lleyn Peninsula.

Carry On Up the Khyber (1968)
For the Khyber Pass, read the Pass of Llanberis, making what amounted to a major piece of location filming. Producer Peter Rogers and his team rarely strayed from Pinewood Studios to film the series of fruity British comedies, but for *Carry On Up the Khyber* they made the trip to the Pass of Llanberis, which runs beneath Snowdon. The film is generally hailed as one of the best of the *Carry On...* films, and in fact it was the only one to make the BFI list

△ Behind the scenes while filming *The Dam Busters*.

of the hundred top British movies. It features the honourable Third Foot and Mouth regiment defending the Empire against the evil Khazi of Kalabar (played by the wonderfully over-the-top Kenneth Williams). In *The Drum* (1938) and *Elephant Boy* (1937), both of which cast Indian boy Sabu, Wales had already been chosen to replicate Indian locations, using the Harlech area in both cases.

The Dam Busters (1955)

This classic Second World War film starring Richard Todd, Michael Redgrave and Ursula Johns, and directed by Michael Anderson, is about the development of the bouncing bombs that were used successfully on a raid to destroy the Ruhr dams. The film was shot on location at Thirlmere in the Elan Valley in the Cambrian Mountains, Powys, which can be viewed in all their glory as the bombers embark on their practice runs.

△ Hugh Grant reaching the top of that hill... or is it a mountain, from *The Englishman Who Went Up a Hill But Came Down a Mountain*.

The Englishman Who Went Up a Hill But Came Down a Mountain (1995)

This lovely piece of whimsy was based on local folklore. In 1917 two English map-makers (played by Hugh Grant and Ian McNeice) come to a small Welsh village and end up announcing that the villagers' beloved mountain is just less than 1,000 feet high and therefore statistically is merely

a hill, so will not feature on future maps. The issue galvanizes the villagers, who set about carrying mounds of earth and rocks to the top of the hill to make up the missing 16 feet. The village is Llanrhaeadr-ym-Mochnant in North Wales, while the mountain is played by the nearby Gyrn Moelfre. The film, hot on the heels of Hugh Grant's success in *Four Weddings and a Funeral*, is full of charm and enjoyment, especially in its depiction of shrewd rural characters outwitting the urban officials. Also in the cast are Tara Fitzgerald, Colm Meaney and Ian Hart. The film caused a real stir in the locality and locals were recruited to take on roles along with the professionals, or to fill in as extras.

First Knight (1995)

This big-budget Arthurian epic features Sean Connery as King Arthur, Richard Gere as Lancelot and Julia Ormond as Guinevere, the woman who comes between them. Directed by Jerry Zucker (who made the comedy *Airplane*), this is a very Americanized Arthurian adventure that cost $60 million to make but took just $37 million at the US box office. As Geoff Brown wrote in *The Times*, it 'may look impressive on the surface; inside it is a mediocrity de luxe'. That surface look, though, comes mainly from the impressive work of production designer John Box, who brilliantly re-created Camelot close to a nuclear power station at Trawsfynydd Lake, near Ffestiniog in north Wales. His set allowed the home of Arthur to be approached via a stunning lake, while the film-makers also shot in the hills close to the town of Blaenau Ffestiniog, just north of Trawsfynydd. Further filming took place at St Albans Cathedral (for Arthur's and Guinevere's wedding) and at the National Trust's Ashridge Estate in the Chilterns in Hertfordshire, where a thatched medieval village was built.

△ King Arthur (Sean Connery) leads the way from Camelot (a mixture of a film set and a matte painting), in *First Knight*.

Zucker saw *First Knight* not only as an adventure but as a romantic, inviting look at medieval life. 'I always wanted Camelot to be a place where everyone would want to live.' Box worked with the art departments for five months creating Camelot, in mythical Lyonnesse, a hill village and various other sites. 'It's critical for the audience to feel this sense of Camelot, the

tradition of Camelot,' he said. 'It stands for hope – hope for better things in life, and that's why the tradition lingers on.' The nuclear power station at Trawsfynydd, no longer in use, became the exterior of Camelot.

Cinematographer Adam Greenburg helped Zucker actualize what he wanted to see in the finished film, and their work helped shape what appeared on the screen. 'Adam and I would go to the location on weekends and look at the different sets through the viewfinder,' Zucker said. 'We'd look for different places and angles and new ideas.'

Also in north Wales, a slate mine was pressed into service as the fortress lair of Arthur's foe, Malagant. 'I said, "No more corny castles,"' Box explained. 'I knew that there were slate pits in Wales, so I said, "Let's take Malagant under ground into his own strange, cavernous world."'

Hedd Wyn (aka The Armageddon Poet) (1991)

Though made in 1991, this impressive film only had a limited US release a few years later. As a Welsh-language film it was a surprise nomination for the best foreign-language film Oscar in 1993. Directed by Paul Turner, it is the well-made life story of a Welsh poet killed during the First World War who wins a prize posthumously for his poetry. Made by S4C, it stars Huw Garmon and Sue Roderick. *Hedd Wyn* was filmed in Snowdonia National Park, particularly in and around Trawsfynydd.

The Inn of the Sixth Happiness (1958)

Taiwan and China itself were possible locations for the filming of this big-budget biographical epic until director Mark Robson fell out with the

Chinese authorities and it was decided to build a walled Chinese city on farmland at Nantmor, near Beddgelert in north Wales. In the film Ingrid Bergman plays British missionary Gladys Aylward, who during the Japanese war helped rescue a large group of Chinese children by leading them to safety across the Yellow River. Also cast was acclaimed British actor Robert Donat (who had starred in Hitchcock's *The 39 Steps*), who died shortly after making the film.

The Keep (1983)

Michael Mann, who has gone on to rightful acclaim with films such as *The Last of the Mohicans*, *Heat* and *The Insider*, came to Wales to make this rarely seen horror tale, which features Ian McKellen and then little-known actors such as Scott Glenn, Gabriel Byrne and Jurgen Prochnow. The film is about German troops in 1941 who arrive to occupy a castle in the Carpathian Alps, only to discover that it contains an evil force. Mann made imaginative use of locations in Llanberis to replicate the Carpathian Mountains.

On the Black Hill (1988)

Based on the novel by Bruce Chatwin, *On the Black Hill* – though little seen on TV or video nowadays – remains a

powerful and beautifully shot story of a pair of twins and their farm, spanning a period of many years. The Black Hill itself is on the edge of the Black Mountains, close to Hereford, and director Andrew Grieve shot on the actual hill, though the film's farm (called The Vision in the story) was at Llanfihangel Nant Bran in the Mynydd Eppynt area. Grieve and his crew also filmed on the Brecon Beacons, and the film's town is Hay-on-Wye.

Prince Valiant (1954 and 1997)

There have been two different versions of the comic-strip medieval hero Prince Valiant, who is perhaps most distinctive for his pageboy haircut. In 1954 a young Robert Wagner made the perfect Prince Valiant, in a film directed by Henry Hathaway, with Janet Leigh his love interest and James Mason his dastardly rival. The film was

△ Planes attack the Chinese walled-city built near Nantmor, close to Beddgelert in Wales, from *The Inn of the Sixth Happiness*.

shot at the Menai Strait. In 1997 the prince, this time played by Stephen Moyer, returned to Wales to battle again with evil knights and the Vikings. This version, directed by Anthony Hickox, features Edward Fox, Udo Kier and Joanna Lumley, and is a German-Irish-UK-US co-production. It was filmed in various Welsh locations, among them Caernarfon, Penrhyn, Trawsfynydd, Blaenau Ffestiniog and Beddgelert.

Rancid Aluminium (1999)

Rancid Aluminium, directed by Ed Thomas has *Notting Hill* star Rhys Ifans playing Pete, a man whose business is going bust, whose sperm count is dodgy and whose relationship with Sarah (played by Sadie Frost) is on the rocks. He's having an affair with his secretary, Charlie (Dani Behr), and he spends far too much time in Harry's (Nick Moran, star of *Lock, Stock and Two Smoking Barrels*) coke den. Things don't look good! Then his Irish accountant and boyhood pal, Deeny (Joseph Fiennes), sets him up with a meeting with a mysterious Russian and his problems look as if they may be solved. Wrong! Cue more plot twists, a trip to Russia and Pete having to try to sort out the many complications in his life. Also in the cast are Tara Fitzgerald, Steven Berkoff and Keith Allen. Filming took place in Cardiff, on Barry Island and in Penarth (the bowling alley scene), as well as London, Gloucestershire and Poland.

Restoration (1995)

Michael Hoffman's opulent seventeenth-century costume drama *Restoration*, which stars Robert Downey Jr, Meg Ryan and Sam Neill, made use of a number of sites in Wales to replicate both London and some impressive mansions. Downey plays a well-bred young doctor and favourite of King Charles II who is ordered by the king to marry one of his mistresses – mainly so that the king can carry on seeing her. The film crew made good use of Caerphilly Castle to represent the Cheapside area of London and the waterfront for an impressive sequence of the Great Fire of London. Downey's character, Robert Merivel, visits a Quaker asylum, where he comes across the madwoman played by Meg Ryan. The asylum is actually medieval Tretower Court, near Crickhowell in Powys. The film also made use of Forde Abbey and its fine gardens, near Chard, Somerset; the Tudor manor house of Mapperton House in Dorset; and seventeenth-century Brympton d'Evercy in Somerset.

Solomon and Gaenor (1998)

Written and directed by Paul Morrison, *Solomon and Gaenor* is set in the Welsh valleys in 1911 at a time of racial unrest and tension. Gaenor (played

△ Robert Downey Jr, in a scene from *Restoration*, shot at Forde Abbey, near Chard in Somerset.

by Nia Roberts) who is from a family of strict chapel-goers, falls in love with a door-to-door salesman, Solomon (played by Ioan Gruffudd, star of the *Hornblower* television series). Initially he keeps his Jewishness from her, but as they gradually fall in love the truth comes out. The outraged community conspires to destroy the couple's happiness. The film was shot – in English- and Welsh-language versions, with the Welsh version receiving a best foreign language Oscar nomination – for six weeks in and around Cardiff, at Nant-y-Moel and at Clydach in the Rhondda. Two weeks were also spent shooting in Inverness, Scotland, for the concluding snow sequences.

Locations manager Bryan Moses said: 'My brief was to find locations with a 1910 look. That meant plenty of stone walls, old school buildings and council offices. We looked for stuff that had been built at the turn of the

△ Rhys Ifans (left) and his brother Llyr Evans take a drink in the hills overlooking Swansea, in *Twin Town*.

century and still looked relatively newish for 1910. For Gaenor's house we used a house that director Paul Morrison had bought in Wales a couple of years ago, specifically believing that the film would happen. It's a terraced house with a mountain on one side of it, which fitted in exactly with the script. And we used an old farmhouse in Caerphilly for six or seven locations, including a pub, a ruined church and a hayloft. For Solomon's parents' shop we converted the front of a house in the small village of Nant-y-Moel.'

Tiger Bay (1959)

Hayley Mills has her first role as a child actress alongside her father John in this sensitive melodrama. A lonely Cardiff child (young Mills) witnesses a Polish seaman killing his girlfriend, and she is then kidnapped by the killer.

Directed by J. Lee Thompson and filmed at Cardiff Docks, Newport and Talybont-on-Usk, this is an unusual police thriller that was a considerable box-office success on its release.

Twin Town (1996)

A down-and-dirty look at life in Wales, this was partly inspired by the success of the gritty Scottish film *Trainspotting*. No cosy Welsh culture here, and certainly no welcome in the valleys. Instead we get the antics of two delinquent brothers (one played by *Notting Hill* star Rhys Ifans in an early role, the other by his brother Llyr Evans), who are set on taking revenge on a local businessman and a crooked cop responsible for the deaths of their sister and parents. Before being cast in the film, brothers Rhys and Llyr went out and bought identical shirts from a charity shop in Notting Hill, had the same haircut and did a reading for the director; the next day they were told they had the parts. The film has plenty of black humour and some powerful scenes. Shooting took place in and around Swansea.

Under Milk Wood (1972)

Dylan Thomas wrote *Under Milk Wood* for the radio, and this impressive film version was steered to the big screen via the passion of Welsh actor Richard Burton, who also recruited Elizabeth Taylor, his wife at the time, to one of the key roles.

Thomas wrote a funny, though plotless, poem featuring a wealth of outlandish Welsh characters in the fishing village of Llareggub (read it backwards to get the proper gist of what it is about). Though it is commonly believed that Thomas's inspiration for the village came from Laugharne, where he lived and is now buried, the film-makers shot in Lower Town, Fishguard, on the north coast of Pembrokeshire. Burton plays one of the narrators, who spends a lot of time wandering the village and making observations about the local characters. Also in the cast are Sian Phillips and Peter O'Toole.

Up and Under (1998)

Writer-director John Godber, who made his name with TV dramas such as *Brookside* and *Grange Hill*, made his big-screen debut with the rugby film *Up and Under*. It's a rough-and-tumble comedy about an amateur rugby team in Humberside, in North-East England, and stars principally well-known television actors including Neil Morrisey, Samantha Janus, Tony Slattery, Griff Rhys Jones and Gary Olsen. It was shot on location at Llanharan Rugby Club, near Cardiff, which doubled for Humberside.

scotland

COMPRISING THE STARK BEAUTY OF THE HIGHLANDS, THE ROLLING greenery of the Lowlands and the windswept beauty of the magnificent islands, along with the urban landscapes of Glasgow and the Clyde and the elegant history of Edinburgh, it should come as no surprise that Scotland remains one of the most favoured regions for film-makers. Recent rousing successes – notably *Braveheart*, *Rob Roy* and even *Loch Ness* – pointed to a celebration of the history of Scotland, while contemporary tales such as *Trainspotting* (1996) and *The Debt Collector* (1999) displayed an awareness of modern issues. Scotland has the ability to be all things to all film-makers, but the country still contains an innate sense of its own very distinct character.

Despite a notoriously unreliable climate – which clearly remains one of the key things any producer will take into account when making a decision about where to mount a location shoot – Scotland quite simply offers the most breathtaking and diverse of locations. Perhaps more than any other area of the British Isles and Ireland, it has benefited from having the beauty of its countryside magnified across the silver screen.

In an official Edinburgh survey it was found that from an average film budget of $10 million, at least $3 million stays in the region, either directly through payments to local councils or police for their assistance, or indirectly via payments to crews and cast (especially extras), hotels, restaurants, shops, bars and local production facilities. At the time, one film official commented: 'It takes a lot of visitors to spend that much, even in tourist centres like Edinburgh. So naturally we want film-makers to come here. If they include a shot of the beauty of Edinburgh that sweeps across the world's cinema screens and gets people interested in spending their holidays here, then so much the better.'

Films like *Trainspotting*, *Shallow Grave* and *My Name Is Joe* offer a very different vision of Scotland from movies like *Local Hero*, *Mrs Brown* and *Braveheart*, but they still give the country a high profile. It is the latter films, though, that remain much more in the consciousness of audiences. The village and beach featured in *Local Hero* still draw visitors, the castles shown in *Mrs Brown* are constant tourist attractions, and the site of the medieval village built in the shadow of Ben Nevis and the Fort William locations for *Braveheart* are still popular spots.

The main industrial centres of Glasgow and Edinburgh have their own very active domestic production and ancillary-support operations (the long-running Edinburgh Film Festival has been a focus for film-makers for many years), and film-makers such as Bill Forsyth and Gillies MacKinnon have remained loyal to shooting in the region. The Scottish Film Commissions are extremely efficient and also well aware that the country's unique locations will always attract film-makers. Scottish film icon Sean Connery has been involved – sometimes overtly and sometimes just by his presence – in attracting interest in Scotland, and he is also active in plans to build a studio operation near Edinburgh.

In southern Scotland, consisting of the Borders region of Dumfries and Galloway, and Ayrshire and Arran, the misty lochs and gently undulating hillsides offer much for film-makers and have played host to films such as *Mrs Brown* (1997), *Mission: Impossible* (1996) and *Rob Roy* (1995). In fact, it is the very frontier nature of the Borders, acting as an often bloody boundary between England and Scotland, that shapes its character. The warm waters of the Gulf Stream lap the sandy beaches of Ayrshire, to create unique locations and a mild climate where palm trees and subtropical plants flourish along the coastline.

Directed by Robin Hardy, *The Wicker Man* (1974), stars Edward Woodward, Christopher Lee and Britt Ekland, and was shot at Dumfries, Plockton, Galloway, and on the Isle of Whithorn. More recently *My Life So Far* (1999), directed by Hugh Hudson and starring Colin Firth, Irene Jacob, Mary Elizabeth Mastrantonio and Malcolm McDowell, was filmed at West Loch Tarbet, midway down the Mull of Kintyre. The film is about a young

The Ellen Gowan Hotel, Creetown

In this classic cult horror film Edward Woodward plays a policeman who stays and drinks at the fictional Green Man Inn (where in the film Britt Ekland performs a sultry dance) on the supposed island of Summerisle, though in reality it is the Ellen Gowan Hotel at Creetown on the west coast of Scotland. A local story has it that Britt Ekland asked to buy one of the hotel's lavatory seats as a memento.
Film: *The Wicker Man*

boy growing up in a household populated by eccentrics and inventors.

The border region south of Edinburgh has played host to a variety of films. For instance, *Greystoke – The Legend of Tarzan, Lord of the Apes* (1984), was shot at Floors Castle; Scandinavian director Lasse Aberg filmed *The Accidental Golfer* (1991) in Manor Valley and the countryside around Peebles; and the BFI film *Speak Like a Child* (1997) was shot at Cove Harbour and St Abb's. Among its many settings, much of *Mrs Brown* was shot in the region, making special use of Duns Castle and estate, Manderston and Cove Harbour.

The centre of Scotland, which takes in the southern Highlands as well as the inland waters of Loch Katrine and Loch Lomond, offers rich variety to film-makers. Projects as varied as Alfred Hitchcock's *The 39 Steps* (1935), *Rob Roy* (1995), *Chariots of Fire* (1981) and even *Monty Python and the Holy Grail* (1975) have been shot in the area, making use of the ancient castles of Doune and Megginch, and St Andrews in Fife.

The Highlands and Islands, with their breath-taking beauty, have long been popular with makers of films and television programmes, as they offer long summer daylight hours, a cinematographer's light and a wealth of magnificent buildings, lochs, mountains, valleys and islands. Such films as *Braveheart*, *Local Hero*, *Hamlet* and *Mrs Brown* have been shot here. The region is often rugged and austere, and is sparsely populated, while on the coast there are unspoiled beaches in sheltered locations.

The beauty of the Scottish islands was highlighted in Jack Coufter's *Ring of Bright Water* (1969), starring Bill Travers and Virginia McKenna, about a man who buys an otter named Mij in London but decides to take it to Scotland to let it live in the wild. The film was shot in London and in and around Sandaig, Glenelg and Loch Hourn, close to the Isle of Skye.

Frank Launder filmed *The Bridal Path* (1959), starring Bill Travers and Bernadette O'Farrell, in the Western Isles and the Highlands. Disney, too, went there for its film *Greyfriar's Bobby* (1961), the true story, set in 1865, of a shepherd who travels to Edinburgh with his unswervingly loyal terrier; it was directed by Don Chaffey and stars Donald Crisp and Gordon Jackson. The monument to the real Greyfriars Bobby can still be found near the National Museum off Edinburgh's Royal Mile.

Michael Powell made the drama-documentary *The Edge of the World* (1937), starring John Laurie, Belle Chrystall and Eric Berry, on the island of Foula and the Shetland Islands. The film is about the 1930 evacuation of the island of St Kilda, though Powell could not film on St Kilda because it had been turned into a nature reserve. In 1939 he shot *The Spy in Black* (aka *U-Boat 29*), starring Conrad Veidt, Sebastian Shaw and Valerie Hobson, in the

Orkney Islands; and he later shot the much-loved *I Know Where I'm Going* (1945), starring Wendy Hiller and Roger Livesey, in Scotland, using locations on the Island of Mull as well as doing a lot of work back at the studio. In 1978 Powell made *Return to the Edge of the World*, essentially a re-release of the 1937 film that was book-ended with colour scenes of the director and cast revisiting Foula 40 years after they made *The Edge of the World*.

Stanley Kubrick made unusual use of Scottish locations for his science-fiction masterpiece *2001: A Space Odyssey* (1968). Though the film was mainly shot in London studios, Kubrick also used the landscape of the Hebrides. He shot aerial footage of the stark landscape to use in the scene when David Bowman (played by Keir Dullea) is transported to Jupiter against a backdrop of psychedelic-tinged landscapes. In contrast, Ben Nevis and the Cairngorms were called upon to represent the land populated by prehistoric man in Jean-Jacques Annaud's *Quest for Fire* (1981), in which the script consists totally of a series of grunts. It stars Everett McGill, Ron Perlman and Rae Dawn-Chong.

The action-adventure *When Eight Bells Tolls* (1971) was filmed at Duart Castle and at Tobermory on the Island of Mull, and, for a scene where a flare is fired into a cave from a helicopter, Fingal's Cave, Staffa. Directed by Etienne Perier and scripted by Alistair MacLean from his own novel, the film stars Anthony Hopkins and also features Jack Hawkins, Robert Morley and Nathalie Delon.

The much-loved *Whisky Galore!* (1949) (released in the US with the title of *Tight Little Island*) was directed by Alexander Mackendrick and shot on the lovely Island of Barra. Mackendrick filmed his ever-popular *The Maggie* (1953), the Ealing-style comedy about the savvy crew of a Glasgow 'puffer' (a coal-fired coaster boat) who try to convince a wealthy American to part with his cargo, around Bowmore and Port Askaig on the Isle of Islay, and also on the Crinan Canal near Lochgilphead in Argyll. In striking contrast, the critically acclaimed *Breaking the Waves* (1996), directed by Lars von Trier and starring Emily Watson, Stellan Skarsgard and Katrin Cartlidge, was a gritty, powerful drama shot in Glendale, Isle of Skye and Mallaig, as well as in the director's home country, Denmark.

The formation in the early 1990s of the Figment Films team of producer Andrew Macdonald, director Danny Boyle and writer John Hodge radically changed film-making in Scotland. *Shallow Grave* (1994), shot partly on location in Edinburgh using Scotland Street, Princes Street and Bridges Street, and on a set built in Glasgow, was a dark and clever comedy that indicated great things to come. *Trainspotting* (1996) proved just what a talented team they were. Adapted from Irvine Welsh's novel, it portrayed drug-taking youth with a verve and style that transported audiences. Its opening scene was filmed in Edinburgh from Menzies (now a Next shop) along Princes Street to Leith Street and Calton Road.

The thriving city of Glasgow has been the location for several recent films, including *Shallow Grave* (1994), *The Debt Collector*, *My Name Is Joe* (1998), *Trainspotting* (1996), *Gregory's Two Girls* (1999) and *Je M'Appelle Crawford* (1999). The city lays claim to being the gateway to Scotland and is well served in terms of communications, culture and a thriving media industry.

The comedy *Heavenly Pursuits* (1986) was filmed in and around Glasgow, starring Tom Conti as a remedial teacher called Vic who seems to have been achieving 'miracles' with his pupils but who is then rushed to hospital and told he has incurable brain cancer. Meanwhile Father Cobb is sent by the Vatican to canonize Edith Semple, founder of Vic's school, who has an authenticated miracle to her name. Vic continues to help his pupils and actually saves one from injury, ending up back in hospital – where miraculously his cancer is found to have been cured. The film (titled *The Gospel According to Vic* in the US), which also stars Helen Mirren, was shot at Queen's Park Secondary School and Notre Dame Primary School (to represent the school) and at Glasgow's Western Infirmary. Glasgow's city chambers were used for the Vatican scenes, while the Clydesdale Bank head office became the Vatican Bank.

Lynne Ramsey shot her powerful feature debut *Ratcatcher* (1999) on location in Glasgow, using a remarkable cast of inexperienced actors and receiving considerable critical acclaim. Set in 1970s Glasgow against the backdrop of a strike by rubbish collectors, the film is about the relationship between two dysfunctional youngsters, each trying to adjust to the problems in their lives.

Setting itself apart from Glasgow, Edinburgh presents itself much more as the artistic and cultural heart of Scotland (as well as being home to the Scottish Parliament), and has been dubbed the Athens of the North. The centre is divided into the Old Town (which dates from about the twelfth century) and the New Town, and it is this mixture of locales that has attracted film-makers. The traditional cobbled streets were seen in films such as *Jude* (1996), *Mary Reilly* (1995) and *The Prime of Miss Jean Brodie* (1969).

The revered British director Alfred Hitchcock went to Edinburgh to make typically hair-raising use of the Forth Bridge for the dramatic chase scene on the train in *The 39 Steps*, and the bridge was revisited for exactly the same scene in the 1960 remake, which had the infinitesimally different title of *The Thirty-Nine Steps*. Also in the city Peter Sellers and Robert Morley star in *The Battle of the Sexes* (1959), directed by Charles Crichton, about commercial war in the tweed business, which was shot in George Street and at various locations, including the Royal Scottish Academy.

Brigitte Bardot and James Robertson Justice star in *Two Weeks in September* (1967), which was filmed at Gullane Beach near Edinburgh, as well as in London; while the comedy *Restless Natives* (1985) was filmed at Edinburgh Bus Station, Victoria Street, Westerhailes, with its chase scene staged down the Mount, Princes Street and Hanover Street, from the top of the Scott Monument. Julia Roberts and John Malkovich were in town to shoot scenes for *Mary Reilly* (1994); among the Edinburgh locations used were Lower Carlton, St Stephen's Church, Greyfriars Churchyard and St Bernard's Crescent. Helena Bonham Carter stars in *Margaret's Museum* (1994), which was shot partly in Canada and partly in Edinburgh, using locations that included Craighouse and Lady Victoria Colliery Mining Museum at Newtongrange.

Scottish director Bill Forsyth filmed his early, distinctive – and exceptionally well-received – comedies in Scotland, and after a break making films in the US returned in 1999 to make the follow-up to an early hit. In 1979 he wrote and directed *That Sinking Feeling*, which signposted a talent to watch, but it was the charming comedy *Gregory's Girl* (1981) that really gripped critics and audiences alike; they loved the story of a gangling teenager (a young John Gordon Sinclair) and his attempts to deal with life and love. The film, which also stars Dee Hepburn and Clare Grogan, was shot at Cumbernauld.

'It takes a lot of visitors to spend that much, even in tourist centres like Edinburgh. So naturally we want film-makers to come here. If they include a shot of the beauty of Edinburgh that sweeps across the world's cinema screens and gets people interested in spending their holidays here, then so much the better.'

Next from Forsyth was *Local Hero* (1983), an uplifting mixture of whimsy and insightful humour that features a splendid cast (including one major US star, the veteran Burt Lancaster) and also captivates audiences with its beautiful coastal settings. The film was shot at Pennan in Aberdeenshire and at Camusdarrach in Morar. In marked contrast to the coastal beauty of *Local Hero*, next up was *Comfort and Joy* (1984), a dramatic yet funny story of ice-cream wars in Glasgow, filmed on location in the city.

After making the well-received films *Housekeeping* and *Breaking In* in the US Forsyth returned to Scotland to shoot sequences for his ambitious film *Being Human* (1993), about a man learning the meaning of courage

across four lifetimes, centuries apart. The film, which stars Robin Williams in the main role of Hector, also features Robert Carlyle, Hector Elizondo, and – in a very early acting role – a fresh-faced Ewan McGregor. Forsyth wanted a remote, prehistoric setting for the first segment of the film and chose Scourie in Sutherland (also shooting in New York, London, Morocco and California). The film, though, barely had a release, and received a very poor critical response. He wasn't to make another film until six years later when he returned to Scotland to make *Gregory's Two Girls*, again starring John Gordon Sinclair as the grown-up Gregory. The film also features Dougray Scott, Maria Doyle Kennedy and Fiona Bell.

There is a Western theme to several films that have been shot in Scotland. According to records, even two cowboy movies have been made in the country, both using locations in Stirlingshire. In 1926 the silent black-and-white film *The Last Frontier*, directed by George B. Seitz, was shot in Campsie Fells, Stirlingshire, with a cast including William Boyd and Jack Hoxie. It tells the tale of Wild Bill Hickok and his gun-blazing pals. In 1965 the Spanish film *El Hijo de Jesse James*, directed by Antonio del Amo, was filmed in Fintry in Stirlingshire with a cast including Mercedes Alonso and Raf Baldassarre.

In 1960 the classic Robert Louis Stevenson story *Kidnapped* was made into a rousing film, starring Peter Finch, James MacArthur, Bernard Lee and even a young Peter O'Toole. Directed (aptly) by Robert Stevenson, the film was filmed at Ardgour, Ballachulish and Glen Nevis. Writer-director Peter Watkins shot *Culloden* (1964), his highly innovative reconstruction of the 1745 Battle of Culloden Moor, on the actual moor, seven miles east of Inverness, adopting a documentary-style approach and recruiting local people to play the soldiers.

The eighteenth-century Scottish hero Rob Roy was the subject of a 1953 film, *Rob Roy, the Highland Rogue* (aka *Rob Roy*), directed by Alex Bryce and Harold French and starring Richard Todd, Glynis Johns and James Robertson Justice. The stirring tale was told again in the big-budget *Rob Roy* (1995), which stars Liam Neeson in the title role, along with Jessica Lange, John Hurt and Tim Roth. Directed by Michael Caton-Jones, the film

The Pennan Inn, Pennan

The success of Bill Forsyth's *Local Hero* attracted tourists from all over the world to the Aberdeenshire village of Pennan, the setting of the film's fictional Ferness Bay. Some came looking for a pint in the same bar that Peter Reigert hung out at with solicitor/hotel owner/barman Dennis Lawson. Several of the actors stayed at the inn, though for film purposes the exterior was a couple of houses with a pub sign on their side. The bar interiors were shot at Lochailort Inn, near Morar.
Film: *Local Hero*

was shot at Glen Coe, Glen Nevis, Loch Arkaig, Loch Earn and Loch Morar.

The Monty Python team have spent much time filming in Scotland under various guises. In 1975 Terry Gilliam and Terry Jones shared the directing duties for their first 'drama' feature film, *Monty Python and the Holy Grail*. Starring the usual gang, it was filmed at sites as varied as Doune Castle, Stirling, Glen Coe, Bracklin Falls and the Isle of Skye. The team returned for some scenes for *Monty Python's The Meaning of Life* (1983); and Michael Palin was back in 1982 for scenes for *The Missionary*, scripted by Palin and directed by Richard Loncraine. The film was shot at Ardverikie House, Loch Logan.

Ronald Neame used one of Scotland's most famous castles, Stirling Castle, as the backdrop for *Tunes of Glory* (1960), which stars Alec Guinness and John Mills as two army officers who clash because of their very different backgrounds. Filming also took place in and around Windsor. Another castle stars with Minnie Driver in *The Governess* (1998), a beautifully staged period romance directed by Sandra Goldbacher, about a Jewish governess who takes a job at a remote Scottish estate. Shot on location at Brodick Castle on the Island of Arran, the film also stars Tom Wilkinson and a youthful-looking Jonathan Rhys Meyers.

The big-budget action-adventure film *Mission: Impossible* (1996), directed by Brian De Palma and starring Tom Cruise, was shot in many locations in London, Prague and the US, but was initially stumped when it came for a spot to shoot the final action sequence of a fight on top of the Eurostar train as it rushes towards a tunnel. In the end the sequence was filmed on the Glasgow– Dumfries–Carlisle train line.

Above all, though, it was Mel Gibson's *Braveheart* (1995) that really focused international attention on the story of Scotland and the beauty of its landscape. Although many scenes were shot in Ireland, it was Scotland that benefited, to the extent that images from the film have become almost iconic.

selected films

The 39 Steps (1935)

One of the greatest films from Alfred Hitchcock, this is certainly far and away the best of the three movie versions of John Buchan's romping adventure novel, published in 1915. The wonderful Robert Donat is the innocent engineer caught in a heady web of intrigue after a mystery woman is murdered in his London flat. A wanted man, he escapes by train and subsequently on foot into the Scottish Highlands, before eventually returning to London to solve the mystery of the 39 steps. Most of the film was shot by Hitch in London's Lime Grove Studios – even the misty shots of the Scottish Highlands, complete with burbling brooks and woolly sheep. But even he couldn't duplicate in the studio the exteriors for the exciting chase on board the Flying Scotsman train. Trapped by the police on board the train, Donat pulls the communication cord and the train comes to a halt on the Forth Bridge. The police climb  out to hunt for him, but he hides behind the metal supports, then quickly manages to escape (time to suspend geographical belief here) straight into the Highlands. The magic of the film was heightened by the sexual chemistry between Donat and co-star Madeleine Carroll (who has the icy, blonde charm of the perfect Hitchcock leading lady), especially in the scene when, handcuffed together, they have to spend the night in a Scottish inn. Hitch pulls the surprises out of thin air as usual, and at the time of release he said: 'I am out to give the public good, healthy, mental shake-ups.' The Forth Bridge featured in the second version of the film in 1959, with Kenneth More this time playing Hannay, though when it was Robert Powell's turn to play the hero in the 1978 version the bridge was the Victoria Bridge over the Severn Valley near Bristol. This version, directed by Don Sharp, also shot at Castlemilk House near Lockerbie, Drumlanrig Castle, the Forest of Ae and Morton Castle, all in Dumfries and Galloway.

The Big Man (1990)

△ Mel Gibson issues instructions to his warrior cast on location in *Braveheart*.

This brutal Glasgow-set drama gave Liam Neeson a chance to practise his Scottish accent before playing the lead in *Rob Roy* in 1995.

Neeson plays an unemployed miner who finds the only way he can make money is to take part in illegal bare-knuckle fighting – something, of course, he is pretty good at. There is sometimes an uncomfortable mix of melodrama and social realism, but it remains a powerfully made film that rarely – pardon the pun – pulls its punches. Starring alongside Neeson are Joanne Whalley-Kilmer, Billy Connolly, Ian Bannen and Maurice Roeves. Directed by David Leland and based on William McIlvanney's novel, the film was shot in Glasgow and at Coaltown, Strathclyde. The opening scenes of Neeson and Whalley-Kilmer running through a park before police on horseback arrive was filmed at Glasgow's Tollcross Park.

Braveheart (1995)

Passionate and stirring, this nationalistic epic stars – of all people – an Australian as William Wallace, the Scot who leads a rebellion against the English king, Edward I. Images from the film have become strongly linked with the recent devolution of Scotland, and certainly Wallace's fiery speeches (some seemingly adapted from Shakespeare's *Henry V*) set the pulse racing. You can't help but dislike the nasty and arrogant Brits. There is a sense that history takes second place to dramatic structure, but there is no denying that this was Gibson's finest hour. Not only was his performance remarkable, he also directed the film, winning an Oscar for best director. But while the story is totally Scottish, at the time of shooting there was much controversy because the film-makers decided to do the bulk of the filming in Ireland, mainly because they could be supplied with hundreds of real soldiers for the massively staged battle sequences. Yet, though Gibson and his team used Dunsoghly Castle near Dublin to double as Edinburgh and Trim Castle to act as London and York, Scotland wasn't entirely ignored. A medieval village was built in the shadow of Ben Nevis, and some filming also took place at Fort William, Glen Coe.

▷ The *Chariots of Fire* runners take time-out to try on their Olympic uniforms.

Chariots of Fire (1981)

Oscar-winning *Chariots of Fire* is one of those British films that were shot all over the country, so it is hard to decide where best to slot it in terms of locations. But while filming took place in Liverpool, Berkshire and Buckinghamshire, it is perhaps the Scottish locations that are the most distinctive. Produced by David Puttnam, scripted by Colin Welland (who made the unfortunate 'The British are coming...' speech when he picked up his Academy Award) and directed by Hugh Hudson, the film is the patriotic and stirring story of Olympic runners Harold Abrahams (Ben Cross) and Eric Liddell (Ian Charleson) as they prepare for and take part in the 1924 Paris Olympic Games. Both are driven by religion (Liddell is a strict Scottish Christian and Abrahams the son of a Lithuanian Jew) and passion for their sport, and both have to make hard decisions to succeed. The famous sequence of the barefoot runners splashing across the sand and waves to the rousing music of Vangelis was supposedly in Broadstairs, Kent. In fact they were pounding along West Sands beach at St Andrews, Fife, and past the famous St Andrews golf-course clubhouse. Sma' Glen, just north of Crieff in Perthshire, is where Liddell takes part in Highland Games, and the Inverleith rugby club Stewarts-Melville provided the location for the memorable scene where Liddell preaches after taking part in a rugby match. He also discusses his faith with

his sister (Cheryl Campbell) during a walk in Holyrood Park in Edinburgh. Hudson shot the athletes' port departure for the games at Birkenhead in Liverpool, while the Bebington Oval athletics ground in the city was the spot for the restaging of the Paris games. Since Cambridge University would not allow any filming to take place there, Hudson shot the famous race around the courtyard at Eton College in Berkshire; while the scene where Nigel Havers' aristocratic Lord Lindsay is seen hurdling over fences on which are balanced glasses of champagne was filmed at Hall Barn, in Buckinghamshire.

Entrapment (1999)

Sean Connery obviously had a good time at Blenheim Palace while working on *The Avengers* because he returned to it for this enjoyable heist thriller (which he also produced), co-starring alongside Catherine Zeta-Jones. She is the insurance investigator trying to track down a wily old jewel thief (guess who?). The first part of the film covers their training and then a break-in at a well-guarded stately home (Blenheim), while the second half sees them trying to steal millions in Kuala Lumpur, Malaysia. Connery's Scottish castle/training centre is actually Duart Castle on the Island of Mull.

Duart Castle, the ancestral home of the Clan MacLean, was once one of a string of seven castles built by the clan chiefs as custodians of the west coast of Scotland, each able to communicate news of impending Viking or English invasions by way of a series of beacons lit to pass on the warning of danger. The present lord of the castle, Sir Lachlan MacLean, twenty-eighth chief of the clan, welcomed the cast and crew, especially Sean Connery, whose mother was born a MacLean.

Locals living near the castle were hoping that the film's success would help boost tourism. Hotelier Janice McGregor commented at the time of shooting: 'For all the time they have been filming we will probably get about five minutes of footage – but we're hoping when the movie comes out people will be curious and want to come to Mull.'

Gregory's Girl/Gregory's Two Girls (1981 and 1999)

The release of *Gregory's Girl* heralded a new comedy talent in the form of Scottish director Bill Forsyth. There is an honest and often joyful charm to *Gregory's Girl*, especially in the priceless performance of the young John Gordon Sinclair, who played the Gregory of the title. He is the inept goalkeeper in the school team who falls for the obvious charms of Dorothy (Dee Hepburn), the team's top scorer. He and his pals are in that awkward adolescent stage at which boys get tongue-tied and bumbling and girls get sophisticated. What he doesn't realize is that while he is chasing Dorothy,

she is setting him up with her best friend, played by Claire Grogan. Forsyth – who also scripted the film – shot *Gregory's Girl* in Cumbernauld, 14 miles from Glasgow, a new

△ A brooding Mel Gibson as *Hamlet*, with Dunnottar Castle in the background.

town designed to blend housing with fields and to separate main roads from housing. He used Cumbernauld's Abronhill High School as the teenagers' school, and shot in the area near by. Forsyth returned to Scotland to shoot *Gregory's Two Girls* (1999), which has Gregory (still played by John Gordon Sinclair), now a teacher, still typically troubled in his relationships with women, let alone the girls in his class.

Hamlet (1990)

Italian director Franco Zeffirelli made what was perceived as being the bold decision of casting Mel Gibson – then best known as an action hero –

as the brooding Prince of Denmark when he made *Hamlet*. But his decision paid off, and Gibson (as well as the splendid supporting cast that includes Glenn Close, Alan Bates, Paul Scofield and Helena Bonham Carter) received excellent notices and changed the opinion of many that he had a limited range. Richard Corliss in *Time* wrote: 'Funny thing is, *Hamlet* almost is perfect for Gibson, with his neurotic physicality and urgent baritone.' He went on to add that Zeffirelli's film was '...nicely realized in a sumptuous production'. Certainly, those stylish production values were much helped by the stunning Scottish locations, with Shakespeare's Elsinore being represented by Dunnottar and Blackness Castles (with some close-ups shot at Dover Castle in Kent). Dunnottar stands on cliffs overlooking the North Sea some 15 miles from Aberdeen, making for a highly photogenic location. Zeffirelli used Dunnottar for many of the exterior shots, while courtyard scenes were filmed at Blackness Castle, in West Lothian.

Highlander (1986)

Highlander may be fantasy nonsense, but it is extremely well-made nonsense that managed to strike a chord with audiences (and was especially popular with the video market), spawning several sequels and a long-running television series. Pop-video director Russell Mulcahy made the transition to the big screen by directing this swirling, complex and often exciting film, and he clearly had an eye for locations and shot structure. The film veers from fourteenth-century Scotland, via war-torn France of the Second World War, to modern New York, allowing itself the indulgence of set piece after set piece along the way. French actor Christopher Lambert plays Connor MacLeod, the Highland warrior who suffers an apparently mortal wound during a clan battle. When he recovers he is banished from his clan and only discovers his true nature when the dashing Ramirez (played by Sean Connery) reveals that they are both immortal and can only die if their heads are chopped off. The opening Scottish scenes of the clan castle were shot at the castle of Eilean Donan, located on an island in Loch Duich. It is a stunning spot and understandably much filmed. Filming also took place at Glen Coe (the clash of the clans), while the memorable scene of MacLeod and Ramirez practising their swordplay atop a mountain was shot by helicopter on Cioch on the Isle of Skye. When the duo take a run along a beach, it is at Refuge Bay at Cuartaig, Morar. Filming also took place at Loch Shiel at Glenfinnan and at Glen Nevis. *Highlander II: The Quickening* (1990) was shot totally in an Argentinian studio. Some scenes in *Highlander III: The Sorcerer* (1994) were shot in Scotland (at

Ardnamurchan, Glen Coe and Glen Nevis), as were some in *Highlander IV: World Without End* (2000).

I Know Where I'm Going (1945)

A Matter of Life and Death and *Black Narcissus* usually feature high on the list of people's favourite Powell and Pressburger films, but *I Know Where I'm Going* remains one of the most magical and romantic of any of their films. Perhaps because it was filmed in black and white, it retains an often unworldly, ethereal quality that lingers long after any viewing. It is a wonderfully simple story. A strong-minded young woman (played with zeal by Wendy Hiller) is heading to a Scottish island named Kiloran to marry her industrialist fiancé but is halted within sight of the island because of bad weather. She gets to know the locals of the harbour village and grows gradually closer to the laird of the island, Torquil MacNeil (played by Roger Livesey). For Kiloran, Powell used the island of Colonsay, south of Mull, and found other locations on Colonsay and the Island of Mull. The quay scenes were shot at Carsaig pier on Mull; the bar scenes at the Western Isles Hotel, Tobermory, Mull; and Erraig, the house where Hiller is initially taken in, is the House of Carsaig. Also featuring heavily are Moy Castle and Duart Castle. Though Hiller and the crew spent several weeks on location, Roger Livesey was busy on stage in London and did his work in a studio, a stand-in playing him for the long shots filmed in Scotland. Luckily, fog is a key character in the film and could hide a multitude of sins.

Hiller had mixed memories of her time making the film, saying: 'The location work on Mull was heaven – well, no, it wasn't really, because the war was still on and it was pretty hard going. Also, Roger wasn't there; he was in a play in London. There were his stand-in and me on Mull, mucking about in boats doing the water scenes for about a month or six weeks, though a lot of the storm scenes were actually shot in a studio tank.'

Local Hero (1983)

Such was the success of Bill Forsyth's *Local Hero* that the village setting became a tourist mecca for film fans. With its happy combination of easy charm, gentle whimsy and glorious locations it is easy to see why. The red telephone box on the Ferness harbourside became an almost iconic image for local cinema for a while, and given that the nub of the story is about tough city folk being drawn to the beauty of nature it is understandable that the tourism business was pleased with the results. A Detroit-based oil executive named MacIntyre (Peter Reigert) is sent off to Scotland to negotiate with the villagers of Ferness to buy their bay to be used as a refinery. As these were the days before mobile phones, the oil company boss Happer (Burt Lancaster) has to keep in touch with MacIntyre through the only public telephone in the village. What MacIntyre only gradually finds out is that the villagers are much savvier than he thinks and are keen to take the money and move out. The only stumbling block, though, is the old beachcomber named Ben (Fulton Mackay), who, it turns out, owns the beach. In the end the execs are won over by the beauty of their surroundings, and Happer decides to stay on while MacIntyre sadly returns to his barren Detroit apartment, plaintively emptying shells out of his coat pockets when he gets back. The final and moving shot is of the telephone in the box ringing as MacIntyre tries to call back his bit of Scottish happiness. For the village of Ferness, Forsyth used the village of Pennan in Aberdeenshire, while the supposed nearby beach is actually the Silver Sands of Morar at Camusdarrach in Morar, 200 miles away on the other side of Scotland. A Centenary Plaque now marks the famous red telephone box on the harbour wall. The village shop was actually at The Pole of Itlaw, Aberdeenshire. The scene in which MacIntyre and Danny (Peter Capaldi), his local contact, have to stop their car for the night because of dense fog was shot on the B862 on the south side of Loch Ness.

Loch Ness (1995)

While Loch Ness (and of course its monster) is the title of this amusing family comedy, in the name of art even this venerable loch had to be played by several other idyllic Scottish locations. In the film Ted Danson plays an American scientist on the hunt for Nessie who falls for the owner of a local hotel (played by Joely Richardson) and her youngster. The film features plenty of stunning shots of Loch Ness, but the fictional locale was made all the more interesting by director John Henderson, who added shots of Eilean Donan castle, on its island in Loch Duich, as well as factoring in a pier (at Lower Diabaig, at Loch Torridon, some 50 miles away from Loch Ness). Richardson's hotel can be found at Lower Diabaig, too, while the crew also filmed the villages of Fort Augustus, Foyers and Dores, all on Loch Ness. The

film-makers made a special trip to the Natural History Museum in London for one key scene.

Screenwriter John Fusco spend two months in 1985 living near the loch at Foyers gathering material for the script. 'When I first went to Loch Ness, I had a very romantic notion of what it was all about. When I was sitting near Urquhart Castle one day I saw the classic three hump phenomenon in the water and I seriously thought I'd seen this unique animal.'

When shooting started in September 1994, the crew were well used to the 'typical' British weather, but Loch Ness itself has its own weather system, with strong undercurrents, and can be calm at one end yet have breakers battering at the other. While filming at Fort Augustus, where the loch is reputedly at its most turbulent, a small boat carrying lights, a generator and two of the crew was suddenly capsized by a freak wave.

△ Actors Peter Riegert and Christopher Rozycki sit on the harbourside close to that famous telephone box, in *Local Hero*.

After filming at Loch Ness and in Inverness, the unit moved further north along the west coast to Lower Diabaig in Wester Ross. Location manager Mark Mostyn had hunted for three weeks to find the right spot. 'We visited every town and village on the map that touched on water, and found Diabaig at 8 a.m. on a Sunday morning,' he said. 'It took our breath away and was just what we'd been looking for.'

Prior to filming at Diabaig the production team arrived armed with alcohol and arranged a drink with the 50-strong population. 'At first a quiet get-together, the evening soon turned into a riotous knees-up, and the absence of a pub in Diabaig could explain why the beer barrels were drunk dry.'

Mission: Impossible (1996)

Like *Chariots of Fire*, the big-budget action-adventure *Mission: Impossible* is one of those films that were shot all over the country (in fact, further afield too, with filming taking place in the Czech Republic and the US). But while the London scenes are quite distinctive (part of the film is set in Liverpool Street Station), the climax of the film was actually shot in Scotland. Not that Scotland gets any mention in the storyline – the final scene is set on the Eurostar train as it heads towards the Channel Tunnel. But since filming the complex chase-fight sequence could not take place on the actual line, the film-makers had to find another location. They came up with the line from Kilmarnock to Dumfries as it snakes through the beautiful Upper Nithdale Valley, and with a few special effects it certainly makes an impact. Background footage was of the land between New Cumnock, Sanquhar and Thornhill near Dumfries. In the film top agent Ethan Hunt (Tom Cruise) finds himself framed when the rest of his Mission: Impossible team are killed in Prague. He sets about solving the mystery, and via a break-in at the CIA headquarters in the US, and a seedy London apartment, the climax is set for a final showdown on board the Eurostar. The closing sequences called for a fight to take place on top of the train as it heads towards the tunnel while being chased by a helicopter. Cruise slugs it out with the bad guy right until the end, with even the helicopter following into the tunnel. There are lots of special effects, and the action works well.

Mrs Brown (1997)

This acclaimed story about the true relationship between Queen Victoria (Judi Dench) and her loyal servant John Brown (Billy Connolly) is sensitively told, only hinting at the depths behind their friendship but playing out the story against a backdrop of awesome locations. It is the late nineteenth century, and the Queen is in mourning after the death of her beloved husband, Prince Albert, remaining in seclusion in Scotland. With public opinion turning against her,

John Brown, a former servant of the Prince, tries to help her, going against protocol and behaving in a totally unorthodox manner. It is in the beautiful Scottish countryside that the two ride and talk until the Queen begins to trust Brown. The relationship leads to scandal, with politicians of the day, including Disraeli (played by Antony Sher), asking questions. The initial scenes are set in Duns Castle and estate in the Borders, while filming also took place at nearby Manderston and Cove Harbour. Other scenes were shot at Lincoln's Inn Fields in London, at Wilton House near Salisbury (doubling as Windsor Castle), and at Victoria's own holiday home, Osborne House on the Isle of Wight.

My Name Is Joe (1998)

My Name Is Joe is very much a story of Glasgow and of those suffering in the underbelly of a tough city. Joe (played by Peter Mullan) is a recovering alcoholic who keeps sane by managing the worst football team in Glasgow and trying to find a little work on the side. When one of his players gets involved with local gangsters, Joe's actions threaten the lives of all concerned, as well as his budding love affair with social worker Sarah (Louise Goodall). The film was shot around Glasgow, and also at Inverary (in the scenes when Joe has to pick up a car for a band of gangsters).

Director Ken Loach said: 'The film came about because after *Carla's Song* we talked about doing a film that was rooted in this city and this landscape. And so it was to find a set of relationships that would reveal what is happening to people here. Because although there is great spirit, we are tearing ourselves apart in cities and certain areas like Glasgow.'

The Prime of Miss Jean Brodie (1969)

Edinburgh of the 1930s is very much a key character in this excellent adaptation of Muriel Spark's short story directed by Ronald Neame. Maggie Smith won an Oscar for her performance as the passionate but misguided schoolmistress Miss Jean Brodie, who, though well intentioned, proves to be but a poor influence on her favoured girls, her 'crème de la crème'. The fictional Marcia Blaine School for Girls was actually Donaldson's School for the Deaf, a building in Henderson Row, Edinburgh. Other locations used included Greyfriars Churchyard, close to Edinburgh Castle, while the 'home' of fellow teacher Mr Lowther (Gordon Jackson), which turns out to be a castle, is on the Delaney estate, along the coast from Cramond.

The Private Life of Sherlock Holmes (1970)

When Billy Wilder set about making *The Private Life of Sherlock Holmes* it was on the understanding that it would be released as a 'roadshow' movie, a film style popular in the 1960s that involved epic film-making, movies that ran for around three hours and screenings in cinemas on a reserved-seat basis. Other 'roadshow' movies included *It's a Mad, Mad, Mad, Mad World* and *Those Magnificent Men in Their Flying Machines*. But when Wilder finished his film – set to run for 'two hours and three quarters... with an intermission to give your kidneys a break' – the mood at the studios had changed, and he was ordered to cut the film to two hours. He eventually complied, and *The Private Life of Sherlock Holmes* was released at a running time of two hours and five minutes. It met with a poor response from critics and public alike. Since then, though, it has been re-evaluated and much made of the missing four major sequences, which can only be glimpsed on the subsequent laser-disc editions. For Wilder his Sherlock Holmes film was a labour of love. He had planned the project for years, and his first choices for the roles (Peter O'Toole as Holmes and Peter

Sellers as Watson) would have made fascinating viewing. The finished film, with Robert Stephens excellent as Holmes and Colin Blakely exuberant as Watson, is still a mesmerizing experience. In it the duo try to help a mysterious woman (Genevieve Page) search for her missing husband. Cue appearances by Queen Victoria and the Loch Ness monster (in reality, a submarine), and Holmes unravels a truly strange case. Wilder filmed at Loch Ness, in the ruins of sixteenth-century Urquhart Castle, which supplied the base for the secret plottings of the British Secret Service, run by Holmes's smarter older brother, Mycroft (played by Christopher Lee). During filming Wilder had to face the problem that a fake monster sank in the loch, never to be found again.

Regeneration (1997)

This moving adaptation of the First World War novel by Pat Barker was filmed largely at and around Overtoun House near Dumbarton. It doubled for the real-life Craiglockart Mental Hospital in Edinburgh, which has been so developed that it could not pass for a 1917 institution. Glasgow-based production

designer Andy Harris and his team handled the job of re-creating Craiglockart at Overtoun. Inherited by and now owned by the people of

△ Liam Neeson gets wet as the crew look on, in *Rob Roy*.

Dumbarton, the building had fallen into disrepair due to lack of funds, and the team basically had a shell to work with. It was at Craiglockart, used between 1916 and 1919 as a military hospital for shell-shocked soldiers, that the poets Siegfried Sassoon and Wilfred Owen met and became friends, with Owen writing twenty poems during his time there. For trench-warfare footage director Gillies MacKinnon filmed at Airdrie in Lanarkshire.

Rob Roy (1995)

Having brushed up his Scottish accent in *The Big Man*, Irish actor Liam Neeson was well equipped for the lead role in this ambitious film, directed with real verve by Scot Michael Caton-Jones. In the late seventeenth and early eighteenth centuries Rob Roy MacGregor turns outlaw rather than give in to the demands of the English. The international cast features Jessica

Lange as his wife and Eric Stoltz as his friend, while the English baddies are played with gusto by John Hurt and Tim Roth. The film-makers constructed an impressive Highland village near Ben Nevis but had to relocate to Perth after heavy rain ruined filming. Meanwhile a house for Rob Roy was built at Loch Morar, while the home of Hurt's evil character, the Marquis of Montrose, is actually Drummond Castle in Perth. Filming also took place in Glen Coe and at Crichton Castle, south of Edinburgh.

Trainspotting (1996)

With its extensive promotional campaign, pulsating soundtrack, exceptional performances and stylish filming, *Trainspotting* arrived on the film scene like an explosion. It is the dark, funny, sad and often sick tale of four young Scottish friends who share in drinking, drugs, theft and violence, against a backdrop of how truly awful drug addiction can be. Ewan McGregor gives a stunning performance as Renton, especially in the sequences when he finally tries to give up heroin, seeing hallucinations of a baby crawling across the ceiling and an imaginary game show in which Dale Winton asks AIDs-related questions of Renton's parents. Despite the darkness of the subject, the film-making team of director Danny Boyle, producer Andrew Macdonald and screenwriter John Hodge pack in lots of humour (Jonny Lee Miller's Sean Connery impersonation, for example) and some memorably stylized scenes. Though set in Edinburgh, most of the interiors and even exteriors were shot in Glasgow. An exception was the opening chase scene as Renton and Spud (Ewan Bremner) are chased from the shop Menzies (now a Next shop) along Princes Street to Leith Street and Calton Road. When the lads decide to do a little hill walking, they take the West Highland railway line to Bridge of Orchy under the shadow of Beinn Dorain, at Crianlarich (close to Loch Tay). The final scenes, when the boys take a trip south, were shot in London.

Whisky Galore! (1949)

Adapted from the novel by Compton Mackenzie, *Whisky Galore!* is based on the true story of the ship the SS *Politician*, which

struck rocks off the Hebridean island of Eriskay in 1941 carrying a cargo of whisky. The locals helped themselves to the cargo, and the incident inspired Mackenzie to write a wonderful story. When it came to filming, debut director Sandy Mackendrick shot totally on location (the first Ealing comedy to do so), and for the fictional island of Todday he used the island of Barra. The film sees the islanders desperate for whisky, with post-war rationing still in place, checking every new ship for the possibility of a new delivery. When a ship runs aground carrying 50,000 bottles, the islanders salvage and stash the valuable cargo. They manage easily to outwit the Customs and Excise officials and the local English Home Guard commander,

MOVIE LOCATIONS *scotland*

who look to recover the whisky. The main street scenes of the film were shot at the village of Castlebay, and Mackendrick also shot all around the island. Cast in the film were Gordon Jackson, Jean Cadell, James Robertson Justice and Basil Radford. The story was, of course, made somewhat lighter than the real-life incident, which saw several men jailed for stealing from the SS *Politician*. In 1993, though, 14 bottles from that original wreck were sold at auction in Glasgow for £12,012, so they were worth hanging on to. Mackenzie's follow-up book, *Rockets Galore!*, about a rocket-base coming to Todday, was made into a film in 1958. Directed by Michael Relph, it was also shot on Barra.

Because the island and village were so small, accommodation for cast and crew was limited during filming *Whisky Galore!*. Mackendrick recalled: 'Danischewsky [producer Monja Danischewsky] couldn't find a big enough house for us all. So he farmed out the experienced London actors into rooms and lodging houses with the islanders. This taught me something that I've used ever since, which is how to take professional actors, trained actors, and put them up against the amateur. The result is that they feed off each other. The professional actor give the scene pace, and the amateur keeps the professional actor honest.'

In the end the locals who acted in the film began to feel supremely comfortable in front of the camera. Actor Gordon Jackson recalled: 'We corrupted them all – they were high-powered actors and actresses by the time we left.'

The Wicker Man (1974)

The haunting British horror/thriller film *The Wicker Man* has gained cult status in the US, partly because it is an extremely well-made and often chilling film but also because of the supposed lost scenes that buffs clamour to see. The film opens in breath-taking style, with the dour policeman Sergeant Neil Howie (Edward Woodward) flying his seaplane over Skye and landing at the fictional island of Summerisle. He actually steps off his plane at Plockton, in Wester Ross on the mainland, a spot that later starred in the popular TV series *Hamish MacBeth*. Howie is there to investigate anonymous reports about a child who has vanished at Summerisle, but finds himself drawn into the strange community and the pagan ritual that forms the climax of the film. Laird of the island is Lord Summerisle, excellently played by Christopher Lee, whose fictional castle is actually Culzean Castle in Ayrshire. The final scene, where the surprise 'virgin' is offered for human sacrifice in the massive Wicker Man of the title, was shot at Burrow Head, a promontory on the south of Wigtownshire.

The Winter Guest (1997)

The directorial debut of actor Alan Rickman, *The Winter Guest* is a moving story of the relationship between two women, mother and daughter, played by real-life mother and daughter Phyllida Law and Emma Thompson. Law is trying to establish a relationship with her recently widowed, grieving daughter, but Thompson is as cold and unrelenting as the weather that grips their small Scottish village. The film (stunningly shot by cinematographer Seamus McGarvey) was made on location at Pittenweem and Crail, two beautiful, unspoiled fishing villages south of St Andrews. Rickman asked writer Sharman MacDonald to write the piece – which was first a play – after conversations he had had with actress Lindsay Duncan when they were on stage together in *Les Liaisons Dangereuses*, and she talked about her relationship with her mother.

scottish castles

Blackness Castle

On a rocky promontory a few miles east of Bo'ness on the Forth, this imposing castle once guarded the village of the same name, though in the seventeenth century it was used as a prison for distinguished prisoners. Released from military use after the First World War, it came into state care and was restored to its former glory.

Address: Blackness village, near Linlithgow, west of Edinburgh
Tel: 01506 834807
Film: *Hamlet* (courtyard scenes)

Brodick Castle

Some of the stones of Brodick are thought to date from Robert the Bruce's time, and it certainly dates back to the fourteenth century. It is thought, though, to have been attacked and levelled twice, and subsequently built into an impressive modern-looking castle incorporating an ancient tower house.

Address: near Brodick, Isle of Arran
Tel: 01770 302203
Film: *The Governess*

Culzean Castle

An outstanding castle and Ayrshire's premier tourist attraction, this outstanding castle is set in a fine country park, its towers rising elegantly above the sea cliffs. Nothing remains of the original fifteenth-century structure; in 1777 Robert Adam was commissioned to remodel it into a family home for the Earl of Cassillis. The top floor now accommodates bedrooms open to the public.

Address: near Turnberry, south Ayrshire coast
Tel: 01655 760274
Film: *The Wicker Man*

Drummond Castle

Standing on a rocky height three miles south of Crieff, overlooking Strathearn, Drummond Castle has at its heart a fifteenth-century keep. The tower has a seventeenth-century extension and was remodelled again in Victorian times. The main hall was badly damaged by Cromwell.

Address: near Crieff, valley of the River Earn, Perthshire
Tel: 01764 681257
Film: *Rob Roy*

Duart Castle

Standing on a peninsula jutting into the Sound of Mull, Duart Castle, dating from the thirteenth century, was built by Lachlan Lubanach MacLean. It was rebuilt and added to several times, but eventually fell into ruin. It was then reacquired by Sir Fitzroy MacLean in 1911 and lovingly restored.

Address: Isle of Mull, Argyll
Tel: 01680 812309
Films: *Entrapment, I Know Where I'm Going, When Eight Bells Toll*

Dunnottar Castle

Set on a promontory jutting into the North Sea, a mile from Stonehaven, Dunnottar Castle was built by Sir William Keith, Great Marischal of Scotland, who demolished a church in the process and found himself excommunicated for his efforts. An impressive defensive venue dating back to the fifteenth century, it was captured and recaptured several times but is now a privately managed ancient monument.

Address: Stonehaven, south of Aberdeen
Tel: 01569 762173
Film: *Hamlet*

Eilean Donan Castle

A stunning castle on a small island at the mouth of Loch Duich, opposite
Skye; this was the chief stronghold of the MacKenzies of Kintail, and is

thought to have been built in the thirteenth century. It was garrisoned by Spanish troops during an abortive Jacobite uprising in 1719 and battered to a ruin by three English warships. It remained ruined until early in the twentieth century, when reconstruction started.

Address: Dornie, Kyle, Wester
Tel: 01599 555202
Films: *Highlander, Loch Ness*

Floors Castle

This vast mansion overlooking the Tweed was largely designed by William Adam in the 1720s but had many Victorian modifications. Only some of the rooms are open to the public as it is still owned by the Duke of Roxburghe.

Address: Kelso, Roxburghshire
Tel: 01573 223333
Film: *Greystoke – The Legend of Tarzan, Lord of the Apes*

Stirling Castle

The poet Alexander Smith wrote of the castle that "Stirling, like a huge brooch, clasps Highlands and Lowlands together", and it is true that before unity between Highlander and Lowlander the castle played a vital defensive role. It was taken from Robert the Bruce by the English, and not until 1347 was it handed back to the Scots. After much rebuilding it fell into disrepair and declined in importance. In recent years it has been successfully restored and is once again an impressive sight.

Address: Castle Wynd, Stirling
Tel: 01786 450000
Film: *Tunes of Glory*

Urquhart Castle

This fourteenth-century ruined castle – a popular spot for Nessie-spotting – is atop a rock on the loch-side close to Drumnadrochit. It offers excellent views over the loch, though is rather bombarded by tourists in the height of the season (it is estimated it has more visitors than any other historic Highland site). It was built to guard the Great Glen and played an important role in the Wars of Independence.

Address: Drumnadrochit, Loch Ness
Tel: 01456 450551
Film: *The Private Life of Sherlock Holmes*

northern ireland

THE GRADUAL MOVE TOWARDS PEACE IN NORTHERN IRELAND HAS LED to an increase in the number of films being shot in the region, allowing the province's undoubted talent – both technical and creative – greater opportunity to shine through. Some five feature films were shot in Northern Ireland during 1997, and at the Cannes Film Festival of 1998 it was an uplifting sight to see so many films that originated there.

In previous years Northern Irish locations were largely underused by film-makers because of the Troubles. But the more films that have been produced in the region, the more film-makers have been made aware of the possibilities Northern Ireland has to offer. The more stability that the peace process offers, the more likely it is that the proximity to Ireland will open up possibilities of co-productions with the strong film industry there, and therefore access to the tax incentives and solid technical infrastructure that exist in the south. And while the ceasefire has led to a climate of change in terms of film production, the industry has also been aided by increased funding. The Northern Ireland Film Commission offers development loans to producers, with the key proviso that the project makes use of locations in the region. Producers also have access to National Lottery funding.

The countryside within easy access of both Belfast and Londonderry, never fully developed for tourism, has a wealth of options for film-makers seeking locations. The lakeland of Fermanagh is striking, as are the large inland Lough Neagh and Strangford Lough. Lovely seaside towns are scattered along the coast, while in the north are the hexagonal blocks of the Giant's Causeway. Inland, the Mourne Mountains run from the sea to the south-east, while the glens of Antrim are lush green valleys full of streams and trees.

In the past, even films and television programmes about the Troubles were almost invariably shot outside Northern Ireland, where there was an obvious reluctance to allow soldiers and masked men with guns to be filmed in the real city streets. (A rare exception was Carol Reed's *Odd Man Out* (1947), starring James Mason as a wounded IRA gunman on the run in Belfast.) The Canadian film *Born for Hell* (1976) (aka *Né pour l'enfer*), directed by Denis Heroux and starring Debby Berger and Christine Boisson, was filmed in Belfast and Hamburg.

Yet times change, and in 1990 Thaddeus O'Sullivan shot the moving *December Bride*, starring Saskia Reeves, Donal McCann and Ciaran Hinds, at Strangford Lough near Belfast. O'Sullivan went on to make the Belfast-set drama *Nothing Personal* (1995), set after the 1975 ceasefire and starring James Frain as a Protestant leader trying to deal with his one-time Catholic friend Liam (John Lynch).

Journalist turned novelist and now screenwriter Colin Bateman is linked with many of the new films coming out of Northern Ireland. He scripted *Jumpers* (1997), directed by Konrad Jay and starring James Nesbitt and Steven Brown, about unhappy people in a Belfast toyshop at Christmas; and in 1998 adapted his novel *Divorcing Jack* for the screen, attracting a heady cast that includes David Thewlis, Robert Lindsay and Rachel Griffiths. Bateman has also written the script for *Thanks For the Memories* (2000), a comedy starring the fine Brendan Gleeson and Amanda Donohoe.

> '*The reality of the present situation in Northern Ireland kept intruding into the fiction of the film during its production. We shot the funeral sequence in a very stylized way, and to do that on the first anniversary of the ceasefire in Belfast was very moving.*'
> Mary McGuckian, director,
> *This Is the Sea*

Belfast and Julie Walters have lead roles in the BBC film *Titanic Town* (1998), about a Belfast housewife who leads a struggle for peace after a neighbour is shot; and top British director Michael Winterbottom made the drama *With or Without You* (1999), starring Dervla Kirwan and Christopher Eccleston, at various Belfast locations, as well as at Magilligan Strand at Limavady. The countryside of Ulster is also on show to good effect in Mary McGuckian's powerful drama *This Is the Sea* (1998), starring Samantha Morton, Richard Harris and Gabriel Byrne.

If peace in Northern Ireland becomes more solid, it seems clear that film-makers from all over the world will want to take advantage of the province's locations. These are resources yet to be fully tapped, but if there is one thing that film-makers are good at, it is spotting an opportunity and going for it.

selected films

December Bride (1990)

December Bride marked the directorial debut of acclaimed cinematographer Thaddeus O'Sullivan, and this turn-of-the-century story of forbidden love and suppressed passion in a tiny Northern Ireland community is a powerful and enjoyable film. Saskia Reeves stars as a servant girl with an illegitimate daughter who flies in the face of her community by living in the same house as two brothers – played by Donal McCann and Ciaran Hinds – either of whom may be the father but neither of whom will she marry. *December Bride* was filmed on a small island in 20-mile-long Strangford Lough, close to Belfast. The film, based on the book by Sam Hanna Bell, also offered early roles for Dervla Kirwan (later to star in television's Irish-set *Ballykissangel*) and Peter Capaldi, and beautifully re-creates a cloistered community set against a stunning backdrop. The film was also shot in Dublin, which, ironically, doubled for Belfast.

O'Sullivan commented: 'I suppose the locals were bemused that there was a southern Catholic making a film of this book that they love and know as a study of the Presbyterian community in the north. But they were very helpful. They would say – usually over a pint – "Here's what I have to offer about this. I lived there, that's my farm," and that was their way of telling me that I didn't really know.'

Divorcing Jack (1998)

Set in a Northern Ireland of 1999 that is an independent state and whose people are united, *Divorcing Jack* makes no obvious reference to the Troubles but is instead a romp of a film, scripted by Colin Bateman and based on his bestselling novel of the same name. David Thewlis plays Dan

THE FUTURE'S BRIN

Starkey, a hard-drinking journalist whose antics find him embroiled in the machinations of a Tony Blair-like politician named Brinn (Robert Lindsay) who is heading for a landslide victory but whose past is rather murky.

△ David Thewlis in *Divorcing Jack*, with a picture of Robert Lindsay (as politician Brin) on the bus behind him.

There is much to enjoy (particularly Rachel Griffiths as a gun-toting nun). Directed by newcomer David Caffrey, the film was shot in Bangor, Belfast and Co. Down.

Brinn was created by Bateman when the Labour leader was still a humble backbencher, but during shooting the crew had reason to wonder if the Prime Minister had been upset by any comparison. When they were filming the scene where Starkey meets the girl in Belfast's Botanic Park

△ James Mason on the run in Belfast, in *Odd Man Out*.

shooting was constantly interrupted. It happened to be the same day that Blair and Gerry Adams did their historic handshake, and a fleet of military helicopters happened to spend much of the day hovering over the set.

Odd Man Out (1947)

Directed by Carol Reed, *Odd Man Out* (released in the US as *Gang War*) is an extremely well-made drama about an IRA gunman (played with dark passion by James Mason) who is wounded and on the run in Belfast. As he struggles through the city he is helped and hindered by various people. The impressive cast also includes Robert Newton, Cyril Cusack, Kathleen Ryan and F.J. McCormick. The film was partly shot in Belfast (the Crown Bar scenes were shot there).

Sunset Heights (1998)

Though shot in Northern Ireland, low-budget *Sunset Heights* is set in a nameless city in Ireland in the near future, a city in which there is an uneasy peace and where law and order are maintained by two rival gangs, the Boilermen and the Westies. Luke Bradley is an ordinary Joe with links to neither gang, but when his child is killed he joins forces with both gangs to try to find the killer. Suspicion leads to murder and on to further suspicion as Bradley, caught in the middle, strives to find the killer before everyone is destroyed. Written and directed by Colm Vila, the film features Toby Stephens, Jim Norton and Patrick O'Kane. Shot in Derry and Donegal, it is partly a gun-toting futuristic adventure and partly a comment on contemporary Northern Ireland.

St Ives (1998)

Shot under the working title of *All For Love*, this period drama, directed by Harry Hook, stars Jean-Marc Barr as Captain Jacques St Ives, a French hussar who is captured in the Napoleonic campaigns. He is sent to a prisoner-of-war camp in the Scottish Highlands, run by Richard E. Grant. While there, he falls for the charms of Anna Friel. Based on *St Ives* by Robert Louis Stevenson, the film also features Miranda Richardson and Tim Dutton. It was filmed partly on location at Castle Ward and Murlough National Nature Reserve, both in Co. Down.

Thanks For the Memories (2000)

Set in Ireland, this romantic comedy (also listed under the title of *Wild About Harry*) stars Brendan Gleeson as Harry McKee, a sleazy local TV chat-show host who has slipped from being an upright and loyal husband to Ruth (Amanda Donohoe) to a drunken, unfaithful slob. After a fight in a pub he attends his divorce proceedings, but promptly collapses. When he awakes from a coma a week later, he finds he has lost 25 years of memory, and despite

△ Julie Walters as the housewife
determined to make a difference,
in *Titanic Town*.

his middle-aged body he feels like an eighteen-year-old. As he starts to recover and have fun, his wife rediscovers the reasons why she married him. The film was directed by Declan Lowney, making his directorial debut, and scripted by Colin Bateman. Shooting took place partly in Co. Down.

This Is the Sea (1998)

Set in 1995, this is the story of Hazel Stokes (Samantha Morton), who lives in a rural community but is gradually allowed the freedom to visit Belfast. There she falls for a young west Belfast Catholic named Malachy McAliskey (played by Ross McDade), setting on course a chain of events that ends in disaster for both families and changes their lives for ever. Many scenes were filmed in rural Ulster, with shots of the Giant's Causeway and the glens of

Antrim, while filming also took place in Belfast. Directed by Mary McGuckian, the film depicts the prejudices of the religious divide.

McGuckian said at the time: 'The reality of the present situation in Northern Ireland kept intruding into the fiction of the film during its production. We shot the funeral sequence in a very stylized way, and to do that on the first anniversary of the ceasefire in Belfast was very moving. It become very personal then, for someone like Ian McElhinney [portraying the father of Hazel Stokes], who found that the events we were describing paralleled some of the experiences of his own community.'

Titanic Town (1998)

Titanic Town is loosely based on Mary Costello's autobiographical novel. The fictional character Bernie McPhelimy (played in the film by Julie Walters) moves into the Catholic Belfast housing estate of Andersontown, but she and her family are forced to move on because of Bernie's attempts to gather signatures for peace. When a neighbour is shot in IRA crossfire she and a number of women become involved in the peace campaign, with Bernie gradually taking a leading role. Bernie is based on a real woman who continued to live in west Belfast and who campaigned for peace. Shot partly in Belfast, *Titanic Town* was directed by Roger Michell. The film also stars Ciaran Hinds, Nuala O'Neill and Ciaran McMenamin.

With or Without You (1999)

Rosie and Vincent (played by Dervla Kirwan and Christopher Eccleston) are a contemporary Belfast couple desperately trying for a baby, but when all attempts repeatedly fail, their relationship becomes strained. Enter on to the scene French postal worker Benoît (Yvan Attal), who was Rosie's pen pal when she was a teenager. As the two begin to draw closer, Vincent feels increasingly upset and is in turn tempted by an old flame (Julie Graham). As Rosie and Vincent find themselves faced with hard decisions, their relationship heads towards breaking point. The film was shot at various Belfast locations, including Northern Ireland's new arts centre, the Belfast Waterfront Hall, where Rosie works on the information desk. The film-makers also shot on the stretch of beach at Magilligan Strand, Limavady, where the couple have an emotional showdown.

ireland

IRELAND HAS LONG BEEN A PRIME LOCATION FOR FILM-MAKERS, AS well as sustaining very active domestic film and television industries. The country is blessed with a variety of accessible locations, and as the desire to film there has increased so, too, has the infrastructure to support film-makers – so much so that backup can be provided for productions of all sizes, from the massive, such as Steven Spielberg's *Saving Private Ryan* and Mel Gibson's *Braveheart*, to modest and art-house films. Dublin has won renown as a centre for film-makers, and for many years was used as a double for Belfast for those wishing to make film or television dramas about the Troubles. Beyond the city, the landscape offers a multitude of options for creativity, from dramatic coastlines and secluded lakes to lush valleys and thick forests.

The Republic also offers a range of tax incentives to help cover every aspect of the film process, from the development of ideas and screenwriting through to actual production. Ironically, the recent successes of the Isle of Man – where *Waking Ned* was filmed, despite its Irish setting – has led to Ireland looking more closely at its own incentive schemes and at further development of studio facilities.

'For locations, I looked all around France, Ireland and England. Ireland had an area that looked exactly like Normandy. The landscape and the beaches were so similar it was uncanny.'
Tom Sanders, production designer, *Saving Private Ryan*

Like *Saving Private Ryan*, many films have used Ireland to represent other countries. Sam Fuller's Second World War drama *The Big Red One* (1980) used Irish beaches and countryside to represent northern France and the D-Day landing beaches, while Rob Reiner shot the fantasy film *The Princess Bride* (1987) in the

Republic as well as in the UK, as did Ireland-based John Boorman when shooting his fantasy films *Excalibur* (1981) and *Zardoz* (1974).

dublin

Ireland's capital is a delight for film-makers – great locations, historical buildings, excellent communications and plenty of Guinness – and has been used extensively. Sometimes it has been asked to represent other cities – it doubled for Berlin in the Richard Burton film *The Spy Who Came in From the Cold* (1965), for which Checkpoint Charlie was built at Smithfield Market – and has often stood in for Belfast, but more often it is simply that the story is set in Dublin.

Jack Clayton's *The Lonely Passion of Judith Hearne* (1987), which had memorable performances by Maggie Smith and Bob Hoskins, was shot in Dublin, as was John Huston's wonderful and moving *The Dead* in the same year. One year later Frank Deasy and Joe Lee filmed their low-budget thriller *The Courier*, starring Padraig Casey, Ian Bannen, Patrick Bergin and Gabriel Byrne, there.

Peter Chelsom filmed most of the sequences in his thoroughly enjoyable *Hear My Song* (1991) in Dublin (as well as London). The film, starring Adrian Dunbar (who co-scripted with Chelsom), Tara Fitzgerald and Ned Beatty, is about an impoverished Liverpool club owner who tries to convince tenor Josef Locke to visit England to sing. The trouble is, if he does

> **The Stag's Head, Dame Court, Dublin**
>
> Though the film is set in Liverpool, director Lewis Gilbert shot the Oscar-winning *Educating Rita* on location in Dublin. The memorable scene where Rita joins her mother and friends for a sing along in a local bar was shot in one of Dublin's oldest pubs, The Stag's Head. The exteriors, though, were of a rival establishment opposite, the Dame Tavern.
> **Film:** *Educating Rita*

visit England he will be arrested. The club is Merrion Hall, in Dublin's Merrion Square, while Locke is tracked down in western Ireland, the film-makers shooting the Cliffs of Moher in Co. Clare. The real Josef Locke attended the London premiere, at which he gave the audience a memorable rendition of 'Hear My Song'. Also on a musical note, Alan Parker shot his hit soul drama *The Commitments* (1991) in Dublin, with a cast of largely unknowns.

Stephen Frears filmed his highly enjoyable low-budget movie *The Snapper* (1993), starring Tina Kellegher, Colm Meany and Ruth McCabe, in Dublin, returning three years later to make *The Van* (1996), featuring Meany again along with Donal O'Kelly and Ger Ryan. Both films are adaptations of Roddy Doyle books, as was *The Commitments*, which – funnily enough – also featured Colm Meany.

Mike Newell, for his follow-up to *Four Weddings and a Funeral*, made the period drama *An Awfully Big Adventure* (1995) in Dublin, though its story was actually set in Liverpool (where some establishing shots were filmed). He brought Hugh Grant with him from *Four Weddings...*, casting him alongside Georgina Cates and Alan Rickman in this story of a theatrical troupe putting on a series of plays in 1947. Also in 1995 Michael Lindsay-Hogg filmed *Frankie Starlight*, his adaptation of Chet Raymo's novel *The Dork of Cork*, in Dublin (with a couple of trips to London and Texas thrown in for good measure). Corban Walker stars as a man suffering from dwarfism who is nicknamed Frankie Starlight by Matt Dillon's character.

David Keating's *The Last of the High Kings* (1996), starring Jared Leto, Christina Ricci, Gabriel Byrne and Stephen Rea, was shot in Dublin, Canada and the US, and concerns Dublin-based youngsters in the 1970s. Neil Jordan visited Dublin to film his big-budget *Michael Collins* (1996), and also shot his powerful drama *The Butcher Boy* there a year later (as well as shooting at Clones, Co. Monaghan). The film (based on the novel by Patrick McCabe) stars Eamonn Owens, Fiona Shaw and Stephen Rea. Sue Clayton dealt with two youngsters struggling to escape from their dismal estate when she made *The Disappearance of Finbar* (1997), filming at Tallaght in Dublin, as well as in Sweden and Lapland. Finbar finally succeeds by seemingly jumping off a bridge and vanishing, and is eventually tracked by his best friend to the arctic wilds of Lapland.

Though the story is very much Belfast-based, Jim Sheridan made his thoughtful and impressive film *The Boxer* (1997) in Dublin. It stars Daniel Day-Lewis as a former IRA man released from prison who takes up his old profession as a boxer and seeks to keep out of trouble. Trouble, of course, comes to him – in the form of his old love (played by Emily Watson) and the IRA men he has forsaken.

Paul Auster shot a scene from his directorial debut *Lulu on the Bridge* (1998) at the Ha'penny Bridge, with the rest of the filming taking place in New York. The film stars Harvey Keitel as a jazz musician whose life changes when he is shot. In the same year US director Jim McBride filmed *The Informant* in Dublin. Timothy Dalton stars as the eponymous IRA informant, with Cary Elwes the army officer who tries to protect him. More recently, Ewan McGregor has been playing the Irish writer James Joyce in *Nora* (1999), directed by Pat Murphy and filming in Dublin. The film explores Joyce's relationship with Nora Barnacle, played by Susan Lynch.

selected films

The Blue Max (1966)

Nowadays *The Blue Max* is one of those films that turns up reassuringly on a wet Sunday afternoon, allowing a flight of escapism as First World War air aces blast away in the skies over Europe before popping home for champagne and bit of love-making with the local lovelies. When it came out George Peppard was at the height of his popularity, and the film was quite a hit – the aerial dogfight sequences are certainly impressive. It is set in Germany in 1918, and Peppard is the low-born, lone-wolf air ace whose only ambition is to win the Blue Max, the highest medal of honour a fighter pilot can receive. He puts his desire above everything, even the safety of his colleagues. Ursula Andress plays his mistress, who, in one memorable sequence, manages to cover her breasts with a well-positioned towel as the two frolic in a bedroom.

The steamy sequences were shot at Dublin Castle, which was also used for the formal dinner-party scenes. The aerial fights were staged over Leixlip in Co. Kildare and Kilpedder in Co. Wicklow, with the aeroplanes taking off from Casement Aerodrome at Baldonnel and Weston Airfield, Leixlip. A few years later, Leixlip was the location for another First World War dogfight film, *The Red Baron* (1971), which was directed by Roger Corman and stars John Philip Law and Don Stroud. The ever-resourceful Corman even reused the vintage aircraft from *The Blue Max*.

The Commitments (1991)

When Alan Parker arrived in Ireland to make his adaptation of Roddy Doyle's book, he was embarking on a distinct change of pace from his previous US-based films. He was making a (for him) 'small' film featuring a cast largely made up of unknowns. He recruited the cast of The Commitments band from the local area, after deciding they should be musicians who wanted to act rather than actors who wanted to play a band member. The band is the brainchild of Jimmy Rabbitte (played superbly by Robert Arkins), who wants to create a band to play soul. The band, essentially a bunch of mismatches, gradually come together and end up playing beautiful music, but not without a lot of humour and incident along the way. *The Commitments* was a massive success internationally, with the soundtrack album equally as popular. The hall where The Commitments did their rehearsing was above a snooker hall in Lower Camden Street in Dublin, while the garden and interiors for Joey the Lips's mother's house is in Gardiner Street. Parker also shot in Sheriff Street, close to the docks, and at the Bray Head Hotel in the coastal resort of

MOVIE LOCATIONS ireland

Bray, just outside Dublin. The estate where Rabbitte lives was filmed at the rough Darndale estate in Dublin.

Alan Parker commented: 'There's this romanticized version of how Ireland's normally portrayed that I've steered well clear of. In actual fact, Dublin has one of the youngest populations in Europe, a huge working class who live in these places where the book is set. I didn't make anything up. I filmed the film in the place Roddy has written about. That is the Dublin I found.'

The Dead (1987)

John Huston's last film was his elegant version of James Joyce's short story *The Dubliners*, and it is rightly acclaimed as a refined and rich piece of work. Ironically, Huston was too ill to travel, so the Irish filming was directed by Seamus Byrne while the great director remained in Los Angeles to film the actors, who did all their work in a studio. The house that Joyce refers to in the story at 15 Usher's Island, Dublin, was the one actually used in the exterior filming, and Byrne also filmed (using artificial snow) in Henrietta Street, Temple Bar and Anglesea Street. He shot in Curragh, east of Kildare (for the graveyard scene) and Glendalough in Wicklow as well. The film is about two Irish spinsters who hold an annual winter dance for friends; at one such dance Gretta Conroy (a perfect performance by Anjelica Huston) recalls her love for a young man who died through his love for her.

Educating Rita (1987)

Though Willy Russell's tale is a Liverpool story, director Lewis Gilbert shot his film in and around Dublin. It doesn't matter too much: Julie Walters plays the ambitious hairdresser Rita with a Liverpudlian accent, and Michael Caine (as Frank, her tutor) plays a very good drunken Michael Caine. Rita is an Open University student reading English who has to attend private tutorials with the usually sozzled Caine. The college they are at is Trinity

△ The Commitments pose in their best gear in the rubble of a Dublin building site.

College, which offered lovely lawns and imposing buildings. Gilbert also shot in Burlington Road, Crosthwaite Park, and Stephen's Lane (where there is the little café that Rita goes to work in as a waitress). Russell adapted his two-person stage play into the film, and some critics felt that opening up the play didn't work. Audiences didn't agree, and the film was a box-office success.

The General (1998)

John Boorman re-created Dublin of 1984 for *The General*, the story of real-life Dublin folk hero Martin Cahill, a sort of Robin Hood figure who robbed from everyone in the city and eventually attracted the unwanted attentions of all sides, including both the police and the IRA. Brendan Gleeson gives a stunning performance as the poorly-educated but charismatic Cahill, gleefully robbing everyone and anyone, while playing a cat-and-mouse game with the police, who are led by Jon Voight (with a remarkably good Irish accent). Boorman – who shot in black and white on location in and around the city – had actually been robbed by Cahill years earlier, and among the things stolen was a gold record hung on his wall. Which is why that particular theft is re-enacted in the film. Kevin Spacey stars in a fictionalised version of the same story in *Ordinary Decent Criminal* (2000), directed by Thaddeus O'Sullivan.

In the Name of the Father (1993)

This controversial film is based on the story of the Guildford Four, convicted for the 1974 Guildford pub bombing but released fifteen years later when their convictions were overturned. Daniel Day-Lewis (who worked with writer-director Jim Sheridan on *My Left Foot*) stars as Gerry Conlon, one of the Four, and his story is the core of the film. Key characters are his father Guiseppe (played by Pete Postlethwaite), who is also later jailed, and his solicitor, played by Emma Thompson. Sheridan shot in Dublin and Liverpool (rather than Belfast and London, the real locations). He used Kilmainham Gaol in Dublin as the prison (though Mountjoy Prison and St. Patrick's Institution were also used for some exterior shots). The dramatic opening shot of a pub blowing up was filmed at Brunswick Vaults in Liverpool, while the scene where Conlon and Paul Hill are interrogated by police was shot at Sir Patrick Dun's Hospital in Merrion Square. The Old Bailey court in London was represented by St George's Hall in Liverpool, though the front exterior was Liverpool Museum.

Michael Collins (1996)

Neil Jordan wrote and directed this ambitious story about the Republican leader Michael Collins, with Liam Neeson giving a fine performance in the lead. After the failure of the 1916 rising against the British, Collins becomes a major figure in the Irish Republican Army and sets about negotiating an Anglo-Irish treaty. But he is repudiated by his former IRA colleagues and later assassinated. This is a big-budget production, extremely well staged by the talented Jordan and featuring an impressive cast that includes Julia Roberts, Aidan Quinn, Stephen Rea, Alan Rickman and Ian Hart. Jordan filmed in Four Courts, Dame Street, Grafton Street, City Hall, Dublin Castle and Trinity College in Dublin. He also shot at Hollywood, Co. Wicklow (for the interiors and exteriors of the Tuttys pub); South Pier, Dun Laoghaire (the scene where Neeson, Roberts and Quinn stroll along the pier); the Carlisle Grounds, Bray (the Croke Park set); and the Ha'penny Bridge in Dublin (the shot of the barge travelling down the river).

the rest of ireland

The Irish countryside has been used regularly by film-makers over the years, some, such as John Ford with his idyllic *The Quiet Man* (1952), relishing the lush greenery, others, such as Steven Spielberg, adapting the empty expanses (beaches in the case of *Saving Private Ryan*) to suit their own purposes. More recently Alan Parker shot his powerful version of Frank McCourt's book *Angela's Ashes* (1999) on location in Limerick and Cork.

In 1947 Michael Powell shot scenes for *Black Narcissus* in Galway, as well as in Horsham in Sussex. John Huston also made for Galway to film Paul Newman in *The Mackintosh Man* (1973). Much earlier he had shot scenes for *Moby Dick* (1956) at the fishing port of Youghal in Co. Cork. He used the port to represent New Bedford in Massachusetts, where Ishmael first signs up with Ahab. The film, which stars Gregory Peck (as Captain Ahab) and Richard Basehart, was also filmed at London studios and in the sea off Fishguard in Wales. One year before, Douglas Sirk, best known for his US melodramas, shot *Captain Lightfoot* (1955), a swashbuckling tale of Irish rebels in 1815, starring Rock Hudson, Barbara Rush and Jeff Morrow in Clogherhead, Co. Louth. The early scenes from Alan J. Pakula's *The Devil's Own* (1997) were also shot at Clogherhead. The film stars Brad Pitt as Frankie McGuire, an IRA man who has to escape from Ireland and heads to New York, where he ends up staying with a New York cop, played by Harrison Ford.

Michael Anderson filmed *Shake Hands With the Devil* (1959) in Dublin and Bray, Co. Wicklow, with a heady cast that includes James Cagney, Don Murray, Dana Wynter, Michael Redgrave and Glynis Johns. The film is set in 1921, when a surgeon (Cagney) is the secret leader of the IRA. Co. Wicklow and Newbridge, Co. Kildare provided locations for Pat O'Connor's acclaimed low-budget film *Cal* (1984). Set during the Troubles, it stars Helen Mirren, with John Lynch as the young Cal who acts as a driver for the IRA when they kill her policeman husband.

Bray in Co. Wicklow drew Neil Jordan when he was filming *The Miracle* (1991), starring Beverly D'Angelo and Donal McCann; and in 1992 he also shot key scenes for the successful *The Crying Game* in Ireland. He filmed the carnival scene at Bettystown, while other scenes were filmed in London (Dil's flat is in Hoxton Square, and the bar where Fergus and Jude plan the assassination is actually the Lowndes Bar, Chesham Street, Belgravia). The acclaimed film stars Stephen Rea, Forest Whitaker, Adrian Dunbar and Jaye Davidson as Dil. A few years previously he had shot his ghostly comedy *High Spirits* (1988) partly on location in Ireland, using exteriors of Dromore Castle in Co. Limerick for his fictional Castle Plunkett, though most of the filming was studio-based. Peter O'Toole stars as the owner of Castle Plunkett who tries to pitch it to tourists as a haunted castle. Unfortunately, his plans are hampered when real ghosts start arriving. Also in the cast are Daryl Hannah, Steve Guttenberg, Connie Booth and Liam Neeson.

John Boorman, who has lived in Ireland for many years, has shot several films in the country, including the strange and fascinating fantasy epic *Zardoz* (1974), which stars Sean Connery, and his tale of Arthurian legend, *Excalibur* (1981).

Directed by Ron Howard and starring Tom Cruise and Nicole Kidman, *Far and Away* (1992) is about impoverished Irish leaving their home country and heading to the open landscape of America. A rural village was built near Dunquin, against the backdrop of the Dingle peninsula, while Howard also shot at the stately home of Kilruddery, near Bray, and used Dublin to portray nineteenth-century Boston.

Gillies MacKinnon directed his lovingly shot story of thwarted love, *The Playboys* (1992), in the village of Redhills, in Co. Cavan (the village where the film's co-writer, Shane Connaughton, was brought up), with a cast including Aidan Quinn, Robin Wright and Albert Finney. In a small Irish village in the 1950s a travelling player (Quinn) and an alcoholic policeman (Finney) both fall in love with an unmarried mother (Wright). John Roberts preferred Co. Cork when he directed *War of the Buttons* (1994), filming on the coast at the fishing villages of Castletownshend and Unionhall. The story – based on the French novel by Louis Pergaud, and originally made as *La Guerre des Boutons* (1962) by Yves Robert – is about the rivalry between children's gangs. The youngsters' final battle takes place in the nearby ruins of Castle Freke.

Pat O'Connor made the impressive *Circle of Friends* (1995), based on Maeve Binchy's bestseller, on location at Inishoge and Thomastown, Co. Kilkenny, in Dublin, as well as at Burnham Beeches in Buckinghamshire, England. The film, about the lives and loves of three young Irish girls, stars Chris O'Connell, Minnie Driver, Saffron Burrows and Alan Cumming. In 1997 Mark Joffe shot another romantic drama *The Matchmaker*, starring Janeane Garofalo and Denis Leary, in Roundstone, Galway, as well as in the US.

The big-budget *Braveheart* (1995), directed by and starring Mel Gibson, was shot in Ireland after the production was offered access to real soldiers for the phenomenal battle sequences. Gibson shot the Irish parts of the film at Sally's Gap, Co. Wicklow; Trim, Co. Meath; and Ballymore Eustace, Co. Kildare. Steven Spielberg used Irish beaches in *Saving Private Ryan* (1998) for similar reasons, picking Curracloe beach, Ballinesker, Co. Wexford, to double as Omaha Beach for those powerful opening scenes of the Normandy landings.

selected films

Angela's Ashes (1999)

Alan Parker's bold and moving film adaptation of Frank McCourt's best-selling book is a remarkable achievement. Parker has brilliantly re-created the Limerick of McCourt's childhood and – as he often manages to do – drawn exceptional performances out of the children in his cast. The younger Frank is played by two actors – Joe Breen as Young Frank and Ciaran Owens as Middle Frank – while Emily Watson is the mother Angela and Robert Carlyle the father Malachy. The film is about the McCourt family, who leave their New York tenement to return to Ireland, in particular the poverty-ridden streets of Limerick. Told from Frank's viewpoint, it is a moving, harrowing, funny and uplifting narrative as the family struggle to survive.

△ Stanley Kubrick surveys his troops, for a scene in *Barry Lyndon*.

Alan Parker wrote about the film: 'The production designer, Geoffrey Kirkland, and I travelled all over Ireland to seek out our locations. One of the negative aspects of the thriving economy in Ireland (the so-called "Celtic Tiger") is that it has become more and more difficult to make a period film there. What little period architecture the country once had has either been torn down or rebuilt in a modern manner, and only the most obvious Georgian architecture survives...

'In short, a nightmare for a design department set the task of creating a world of 60 years ago. Limerick, the real centre of our story, offered us the beautiful Georgian crescent, with O'Connell's statue, adjacent to South's pub and the River Shannon... the damp heart, and, in many ways, the silent villain of our story. Even the Shannon itself offers fewer and fewer riverbank views as the city hurtles into modernity, changing the historic riverscape... I had

some experience working in Ireland on *The Commitments* and, as with that film, it was obvious that a patchwork quilt, a mosaic of different places, would have to be put together to replicate the Limerick of 60-odd years ago accurately.

'For these reasons we decided also to film in Cork, a city that has retained its narrow, cobbled streets and is also, handily, close to Cobh Harbour, which for a century and a half had seen 100,000 Irish families emigrate to the US, and to where Angela, Malachy, Frank, Malachy Jr and Eugene McCourt conversely return. It is also close to Ardmore, the main Irish studios, where we were to build many of our interiors.'

Parker and his team built the cobbled Roden Lane exterior set, with its 30 dilapidated cottages, on an empty Dublin building site, just 100 yards from the River Liffey, next to the Collins Barracks Museum. As Parker commented: 'I can only think that the future bands of "McCourties", their "movie version" website maps in hand, are going to be disappointed visiting the film's Roden Lane on Benburb Street, because, alas, it took just two days to demolish it and return it to a building site.'

Barry Lyndon (1975)

Though much of Stanley Kubrick's glorious version of William Thackeray's novel was shot in Ireland, the director decided to move shooting to the UK after much of the work had been done, owing to terrorist threats. The film, though, retains many of those Irish scenes and is therefore imbued with a sense of Irishness despite the fact that many scenes depicting stately homes were filmed in England. It stars Ryan O'Neal as the rakish eighteenth-century gentleman of fortune, Barry Lyndon. The impressive cast also includes Marisa Berenson, Patrick Magee, Hardy Kruger and a young Steven Berkoff. The Irish locations include Cahir Castle in Co. Tipperary, while in England Kubrick filmed at Wilton House, near Salisbury, at Longleat House in Wiltshire and at Petworth House in Sussex.

△ Richard Harris oversees his land, in the powerful drama *The Field*.

Excalibur (1981)

Arthurian legend has long been something of an obsession for John Boorman, and you can often detect references to it in his films. With *Excalibur* he seized the chance to tell the full story in his own style, and he revelled in creating a fantastic sense of atmosphere for Arthur and his Knights of the Round Table. Though Camelot was built at Ardmore Studios in Bray, numerous other Irish locations feature in the film. The opening scene of Uther Pendragon (a young Gabriel Byrne) entering the castle of his rival during a siege thanks to the magic of Merlin (Nicol Williamson) was shot at Cahir Castle, on a promontory in the River Suir in Tipperary. Some filming was done around Co. Wicklow; the battle between Arthur (Nigel Terry) and Lancelot (Nicholas Clay) was filmed at Powerscourt Waterfall; the wedding of Arthur and Guinevere (Cherie Lunghi) was staged at

Childers Wood, Roundwood. Boorman also filmed at the Rock of Cashel in Co. Tipperary, Derrynane in Co. Kerry and at the Sally Gap area of the Wicklow Mountains.

The Field (1991)

Jim Sheridan's *The Field* is no piece of Irish blarney. Instead it tells the harsh and brutal story of men who live with and by the land, and shows how powerful the link with the land can be. Set in the 1930s and based on John B. Keating's play, the film stars Richard Harris (in his first major role for some ten years) as tough farmer Bull McCabe, who is prepared to kill in order to retain a rented field that his family has farmed for generations, and which an American (played by Tom Berenger) wants to buy. The strong cast also includes John Hurt, Sean Bean, Frances Tomelty and Brenda Fricker, though it was the heart stoppingly powerful performance by Harris that attracted attention. For the suitably isolated location Sheridan filmed in and around Leenane, a small village on Killary Harbour Lough that had the rough and spartan quality he wanted.

The film-makers were able to transform Leenane into the fictional Carraigthomond of 50 years ago in the matter of a few short hours because the village had changed so little. Sheridan chose it precisely because it was so untouched, and when comparisons with *The Quiet Man* were made, he said: 'This is even more remote. More rural. More savage.'

Henry V (1944)

Laurence Olivier's glorious colour film of Shakespeare's *Henry V* was planned as a stirring and patriotic tribute to those fighting in the Second World War. And patriotic it certainly is, with Olivier rarely as physically powerful and handsome, and the battle scenes magnificently staged. The structure is bold and experimental, and the adaptation by Olivier and Alan Dent brings out

△ The muddier side of film-making. On location filming *Henry V*.

the best of the play. The hard-to-please American critic Pauline Kael wrote: 'His production – it was his first time out as a director – is a triumph of colour, music, spectacle and soaring heroic poetry, and, as an actor, he brings lungs, exultation, and a bashful wit to the role.' The opening scenes are of the play being performed on stage at the Globe Theatre in 1603, but gradually the camera pulls back and the whole production opens out thrillingly to tell the story of Henry leading his men to a final battle at Agincourt in 1415. Wartime England ruled out access to a suitable English location, and there certainly wouldn't have been enough men for his ambitious battle scenes. So Olivier shot in neutral Ireland, hiring enough extras to complete his roster of more than 700 soldiers for the fighting. The Battle of Agincourt itself was staged at Powerscourt estate at Enniskerry, south of Dublin.

Into the West (1992)

Into the West is a touching and extremely well-made story of two young boys named Ossie and Tito who are led on a mystical journey away from their Dublin home by a magical white horse, Tir na n'Og, which seems to represent the spirit of their dead mother. Their alcoholic father (memorably played by Gabriel Byrne) has to hunt for his children and as a result eventually comes to some sort of redemption. The boys' journey takes them from Dublin's Ballymum estate through Co. Wicklow and finally on to Turlough Hill in the Wicklow Mountains and their mother's grave. Along the way they take in landmarks such as Powerscourt Waterfall, Lea Castle and Portarlington.

The Mackintosh Man (1973)

John Huston went to Ireland to film his spy thriller *The Mackintosh Man*, starring Paul Newman, Dominique Sanda, James Mason and Harry Andrews. The film, based on Desmond Bagley's novel *The Freedom Trap*, was scripted by Walter Hill and is about a government spy (Newman) sent to prison to establish links with a criminal gang, and who then escapes. Huston filmed scenes in Galway (the sequences in the safe house, the bar and the car chase) as well as in London and Malta.

My Left Foot (1989)

Sublime performances abound in Jim Sheridan's powerful and often poignant story of the life of Irish painter and writer Christy Brown, crippled from birth by cerebral palsy. Daniel Day-Lewis won an Oscar for his performance as the older Christy, while the rest of the cast are all excellent. The film is told in flashbacks, so right at the start we see the grown-up Christy, grumpy but with a twinkle in his eye, at a reading from his autobiography (filmed at Kilruddery House, near Bray). The story moves back to his early years in the packed Brown home (exteriors shot at St Kevin's Square, Bray), and how his talents first expressed themselves. With a pencil gripped between his toes, he manages to write a few words. The scenes of Christy taken to the pub by his father and of the boys playing football in the street (Christy as goalkeeper, stretched out in front of the goal) are all memorable. Equally good are the later sequences when Christy's art comes to the fore, but so, too, do his increased frustrations. The scene where he creates a rumpus at a restaurant when he finds that his doctor (Fiona Shaw) is to marry was shot at Locks Restaurant, in the Portobello area of Dublin.

The Quiet Man (1952)

John Ford's deeply personal and ultimately romantic *The Quiet Man* must go down as one of the loveliest presentations of rural Ireland. It may be a little rose-tinted at times, packed with blarney and four-leafed clover, but it remains a thoroughly enjoyable film experience, and is worth viewing just for the epic fist-fight that dominates the closing stages. When Ford got the go-ahead to make his long-planned film, he took with him to Ireland the starry cast of John Wayne, Maureen O'Hara and Victor McLaglen, and topped it up with the likes of Barry Fitzgerald, Ward Bond and Mildred Natwick.

▷ Daniel Day-Lewis gives a powerful performance as Christy Brown in *My Left Foot*.

Wayne plays Sean Thornton, the quiet man of the title who returns home from America to settle in rural Ireland close to the fictional village of Innisfree. But his buying back his family's former land infuriates fellow farmer Red Will (McLaglen), who wanted to buy the land himsef. Things get more complicated when Will's sister (O'Hara) and Thornton fall for each other. In the epic fight between Thornton and Will the pair fight their way across fields and along the village street (where they stop for a quick drink), gathering an audience as they go. For his Innisfree, Ford used the village of Cong, while he also used the nearby land around Ashford Castle, close to Lough Corrib in Co. Galway. He filmed the rousing horse race on the sands of Tully Strand in Connemara. In 1990 a Spanish documentary entitled *Innisfree* took a trip back to the Irish locations of *The Quiet Man*.

Ryan's Daughter (1970)

Director David Lean took a year to shoot *Ryan's Daughter*, an epic tale of romance set against the backdrop of the Irish Rebellion of 1916. The film took two Oscars – for Frederick A. Young's stunning cinematography and for John Mills' impressive performance as the village idiot Michael – and though critics didn't warm to it, the film was undoubtedly a potent advertisement for the beauty of Ireland. Lean, a past master of filming epics (*Lawrence of*

Arabia and *Doctor Zhivago*), shot almost entirely on location on the Dingle peninsula in Co. Kerry. His team built the fictional village of Kirrary on an exposed hill close to the village of Carhoo, while Lean made good use, too, of the beautiful stretches of sand at Inch Strand, close to Dingle, and at Coumeenoole Strand in the Dunquin area. He also filmed in Co. Clare and at Barrow Strand, north of Tralee. The film – which runs for a prodigious 206 minutes – is about a village schoolmaster Charles Shaughnessy (Robert Mitchum), whose wife Rosy Ryan (Sarah Miles) grows increasingly frustrated with their relationship and falls instead for Major Doryan (Christopher Jones), the commander of the local British garrison.

Sarah Miles recalled her time on location: 'To me, personally, it was a hard slog: up at five o'clock on that hill every single day, waiting for the rain to stop. I probably had the toughest time of all because I was always there – if not working, then doing weather cover of some sort for the second unit [working on secondary location shots], and it was enormously hard work. But there were some wonderful bonuses; there were some great characters in it, and having all of these extraordinary, egomaniacal people in the little town of Dingle, sitting there waiting for the rain to stop.'

▷ Tom Hanks and Steven Spielberg on the Irish beach used to represent Omaha Beach in *Saving Private Ryan*.

She remembered the reaction from locals when the producers asked if they wanted the constructed village to be left intact. 'They said, "Take the fookin' lot down. We're sick of the lot of ye!",' she said. 'We'd got most of it down when they came back to us. "We've had a little meeting and we've decided we want the village after all, so would ye kindly put it back up again. We realize now how valuable it'll be for the tourists." Sorry, old chap! We did manage to keep the schoolhouse intact, though, and thousands of people trail over it every year to see where *Ryan's Daughter* was made.'

Saving Private Ryan (1998)

Steven Spielberg's massively staged story of a band of GIs sent out on a mission to find one Private Ryan shortly after the Normandy landings was an epic and powerful achievement, and it rightly attracted acclaim, awards and attention when it was released. It is essentially a small story set against an enormous backdrop. A squad of men, led by Tom Hanks, is ordered to find Private Ryan (played by Matt Damon), who is fighting somewhere ahead of the main American advance line. It turns out that his brothers have all been killed elsewhere in the war, and the government doesn't want another Ryan son to die. The opening twenty minutes are purely harrowing and

breathtakingly filmed scenes of the Normandy landings, evoking the terror of jumping off a landing craft into a hail of bullets and explosions. Spielberg had assistance from the Irish government in the form of real soldiers to act in these scenes – which is why he used Curracloe Beach, Ballinesker, Co. Wexford to represent Omaha Beach. Spielberg created the devastated French town where the final fight is staged at a former British Aerospace aerodrome at Hatfield, Hertfordshire; and converted a farm building near Marlborough, in Kennet, Wiltshire, into an Iowa-style farmhouse for the scene of Mrs Ryan being told of the death of her sons. The storming of the machine-gun nest, the half-track ambush and the shots of the squad walking across a large field were filmed at Thame Park in Oxfordshire.

Afterwards Tom Sanders, the film's production designer, recalled: 'For locations, I looked all around France, Ireland and England. Ireland had an area that looked exactly like Normandy. The landscape and the beaches were so similar it was uncanny. We had to have beach access, so we were looking for a place with a harbour. We needed a particular kind of tide to have a certain amount of beach left when the tide was in, for the crew on the beach.

'Also, we needed a location where we could house a 1,000-man army and a 45-man crew. Having worked in Ireland before, we knew we could hire its army, which was a key element. Without a trained army to jump out of the boats and storm the beach, we'd have to train lots of extras.'

Recalling those stunning opening sequences of the landings, actor Barry Pepper remembered: 'One day we were out there on the boats and the Irish Sea was really rough. It was a cold, stormy day, and the Higgins boats were slamming pretty hard, bouncing and pounding through the surf; the chop was like four- to five-feet swells. We were getting really upset, in reality, not our characters. We were just very nervous about the water and being in the boats, and we got this incredible feeling of impending doom. It gave me this minute sensation of what it must've been like out there. It was really scary for me. My mind just started to wander and think about how afraid those young guys must have been.'

At Hatfield the crew had to build the ruined French village from scratch. Production designer Tom Sanders said: 'When we started there, this was a grass field. We decided that it would be better to build a river for environmental reasons and for control. We started from scratch, dug the river back here, and put in the bridge. We had to build these buildings because we couldn't find anything like this in Europe. It's all historically accurate.'

The Secret of Roan Inish (1994)

John Sayles filmed his magical *The Secret of Roan Inish* on location in Donegal. The tale, starring Jeni Courtney, Mick Lally, Eileen Colgan and John Lynch, is about a young girl who persuades her family to move to a seal-inhabited island off Donegal where their ancestors once lived. The film has a rare magic all of its own, and is shot in an unsentimental manner, with stunning cinematography by Haskell Wexler, who pulls together beautiful wildlife footage of the seals and gulls that populate the area.

Zardoz (1974)

John Boorman's science-fiction fantasy – which features Sean Connery spending his time wandering around wearing only a pair of leather underpants and some large boots – is set in a post-industrial future of 2293. The earth is just a harsh wasteland in which the Elite live in luxury and control the remaining Brutals by commanding the Exterminators, who retain both intelligence and memory. Connery plays an Exterminator who finds out the truth behind the Exterminator god Zardoz, a massive flying head that brings them weapons. Zardoz, it turns out, is a control device created by the Elites, with its name taken from *The Wizard of Oz*... Get it? The film was shot largely in the Sally Gap area of the Wicklow Mountains.

the bond films

JAMES BOND IS THE MOST BRITISH OF HEROES. FROM HIS STYLISH Aston Martin to his elegant Savile Row clothes, he is the perfect English gentleman – a gentleman, though, with a dark and deadly edge. All the James Bond movies except two (the laughable *Casino Royale*, which starred both David Niven and Woody Allen as Bond, and the *Thunderball* remake *Never Say Never Again*) have been made by Eon Productions, a decidedly English company with its head office in Piccadilly and production offices at Pinewood Studios.

Bond, of course, travels the world in his crusade against evil, happily dispatching bad guys in countries including Jamaica, the USA, Russia and Greece, and even taking the odd trip into space to rid the world of dastardly wrongdoers. In most of the nineteen Eon-produced Bond movies, though, he has usually found time to visit a few British locations – sometimes just for a game of golf or for yet another romantic assignation; at other times for a thrilling chase or to slug it out with a villain or two.

▷ Pierce Brosnan as Bond, with Denise Richards as Dr Christmas Jones, emerge typically unscathed from a pipeline explosion, in *The World Is Not Enough*.

As might be expected, the Bond film-makers have often utilized UK locations to represent some far-flung spot featured in the story (as varied as the South China Sea or a Russian railway line). However, the UK plays a much more important role in the most recent Bond movie, *The World Is Not Enough*, which features the Millennium Dome at Greenwich in London.

The first Bond film, *Dr. No* (1962), was a massive hit with audiences. It brought stardom to Sean Connery and proved wrong those critics who thought

that the pulp-fiction spy would not work on the big screen. It initiated a series of films that has outlasted the different actors chosen to play Bond (despite the fact that most polls still hail Connery as the ultimate Bond actor) and continues to appeal to all generations and nationalities. Interestingly, the first film did not use any British locations. The majority of the film is set in Jamaica, the country where Bond author Ian Fleming had a home, Goldeneye, in which he wrote the books. The remaining scenes were all studio-shot, with especially memorable the initial – and much-imitated – sequence where Bond first introduces himself. 'The name is Bond... James Bond.'

While certain films in the series did not use exterior UK locations extensively (such as *The Spy Who Loved Me*, *Moonraker* and *Licence To Kill*), other Bond films did make increasing use of local locations. They were:

From Russia With Love (1963, Sean Connery as Bond)

Though shot largely in Turkey, certain classic sequences were filmed in the UK.

- The opening scene where Bond is stalked by Robert Shaw's blond-haired killer was shot in the gardens behind Pinewood Studios' administration building.
- The sequence with Bond dallying with Sylvia Trench was shot at Hurley, in Berkshire, England.
- An exterior chase sequence late in the film was shot in Scotland.
- The SPECTRE mansion was in fact the Pinewood Studios' administration building.

Goldfinger (1964, Sean Connery as Bond)

Mainly set in mainland Europe and the US. Regarded as Bond at his best.

- The classic opening pre-credits sequence features Bond emerging from the water wearing a wetsuit with a fake duck on his head. He proceeds to blow up a storage tank complex, which is actually at Stanwell, outside London.
- When Bond plays his game of golf with Goldfinger (who has the

memorable Oddjob as his caddy), they are
playing at Stoke Poges golf
club in Buckinghamshire.

△ Sean Connery and Lois Maxwell
at the Dover ferry terminal, in
Diamonds Are Forever.

- The scene when Goldfinger's Rolls-Royce is
being shipped overseas was filmed at Southend Airport in Essex.

Thunderball (1965, Sean Connery as Bond)

Time for fun and games in the UK, before heading off to the sunnier climes
of the Caribbean.

- When Bond is sent to the fictional Shrublands health farm to get himself back
into condition, he is actually staying at Chalfont Park House, Chalfont Park,
Buckinghamshire.
- The scene In which bad guy Count Lippe is killed by a leather-clad woman who
uses a rocket-firing motorcycle to blast him as he pursues Bond's Aston Martin

DB5 was shot at Silverstone racetrack in Northamptonshire.

You Only Live Twice (1967, Sean Connery as Bond)

Mainly shot in Japan, with a wicked script by Roald Dahl.

- Bond's aeroplane-crash sequence was shot at Finmere Aerodrome in Buckinghamshire.

On Her Majesty's Secret Service (1969, George Lazenby as Bond)

Notorious – though fun – because of Lazenby's Bond, and also for being the film in which Bond ties the knot.

- The scene in which Bond visits M at his residence was shot at a Thames Lawn mansion, Marlow, Buckinghamshire.
- The sequence when Bond visits the College of Arms to learn more about heraldry was shot at the actual College of Arms in London.

Diamonds Are Forever (1971, Sean Connery as Bond)

The last of Connery playing Bond for Eon (though he returned in the so-so *Never Say Never Again*). Mostly set in the US by way of the Netherlands.

- The scene in which Bond assumes the identity of diamond smuggler Peter Franks was shot at the Customs section of Dover ferry terminal.

For Your Eyes Only (1981, Roger Moore as Bond)

Set mainly in Greece, with unforgettable underwater scenes.

- The scene in which Bond kills Blofeld by dropping his wheelchair-bound body into an industrial chimney was shot at Becton Gasworks, London.
- The scene in which Bond visits his wife Tracy's grave was filmed at Stoke Poges Church, Buckinghamshire.

Octopussy (1983, Roger Moore as Bond)

India and mainland Europe are the key venues for this gimmicky Bond adventure.

- The South American military base where Bond escapes in a miniature jet aircraft was represented by RAF Northolt just outside London.
- The sequences on board the escaping train when Bond has to fight various bad guys as he tries to reach a ticking nuclear bomb were shot at the Nene Valley Railway, near Peterborough.

A View To A Kill (1985, Roger Moore as Bond)

Bond fights atop the Eiffel Tower before heading to the US.

- The entrance to the mine run by bad guy Zorin, which is shown in a sequence with Grace Jones atop yet another ticking nuclear device, was filmed at the Amberley Chalkpits Museum in West Sussex.

The Living Daylights (1987, Timothy Dalton as Bond)
Eastern Europe and Afghanistan are the locations for the first Dalton Bond.
- The Secret Service estate where agents are guarding a top rival spymaster with secrets to spill, and which is infiltrated by one of the killers, was shot at Stonor House, Stonor.

GoldenEye (1995, Pierce Brosnan as Bond)
Set mainly in Russia before a trip to the sunshine and Cuba for the final showdown. The first of the Brosnan Bonds.
- The glimpsed exterior of M's offices is the actual MI6 headquarters situated on the banks of the River Thames near Vauxhall in London.
- St Petersburg Airport is actually the Royal Enclosure at Epsom Racecourse, Epsom, Surrey.
- The train depot from which 006's armoured train departs is a sugar factory in Peterborough; while the sequence in which Bond manages to stop that same train was shot along part of the Nene Valley Railway line.
- When Bond visits rival Russian spy Zukovsky (played by Robbie Coltrane) at his nightclub (and, yes, that is Minnie Driver in the background murdering a country-and-western tune), they are actually inside The Snake Ranch in Chelsea, London.

Tomorrow Never Dies (1997, Pierce Brosnan as Bond)
Mainland Europe and South-East Asia are the locations as Bond teams up with the Chinese to defeat the media-mogul bad guy.
- Bond at Oxford was filmed at New College and Brasenose College, Oxford.
- The exterior of baddie Carver's media headquarters is actually the IBM head office near Heathrow Airport in London.
- Carver's print complex, from which Bond has to fight to escape, is an amalgam of Harmondsworth Quays Printers, Westferry Printers and the *Financial Times* Building, all in London.
- The interior shots for the sequence in which Bond drives his BMW by remote control around a multi-storey car park was filmed at Brent Cross Shopping Centre in London.
- Certain sequences in the South China Sea were represented by the English Channel just off the coast of Portsmouth Naval Base.

The World Is Not Enough (1999, Pierce Brosnan as Bond)

Many spots in the UK were used for the nineteenth Bond film, though the crew also shot in France, Spain, Turkey and Azerbaijan.

- The actual MI6 building by the Thames again plays the exterior of the Secret Service building.
- A motor-boat chase along the Thames was shot at the actual locations and features many recognizable London landmarks, including the Houses of Parliament and Docklands. The Millennium Dome is seen in the climax of the pre-credits fight sequence.

● The hi-tech Scottish castle that acts as the
temporary MI6 headquarters is actually Eilean
Donan Castle, Dorrie, Scotland.

△ Filming the thrilling boat chase
along the Thames for *The World Is
Not Enough.*

● The pipeline explosion scene was filmed at
Hankley Common, Thursley, near Guildford, and at Black Park, Iver,
Buckinghamshire.

the
carry on...
films

THE INNOCENTLY BAWDY *CARRY ON...* FILMS ARE CLASSICS OF BRITISH comedy. From *Carry On, Sergeant* in 1958 through to *Carry On, Columbus* in 1993, the comedies were the longest-running and most successful series of comedy films in the history of British cinema. Granted, the final two (*Carry On, Emmanuelle* and *Carry On, Columbus*) were probably misguided attempts to recapture past glories, but at their peak in the 1960s and 1970s the *Carry On...* films kept the country laughing.

They are distinguished by several key characteristics. They had a team of superlative comedy actors, including Sid James, Barbara Windsor, Kenneth Williams, Joan Sims, Kenneth Connor and Charles Hawtrey, who appeared regularly. The scripts are based on sexual innuendo and broad comedy, and the films were made on very low budgets and rarely strayed to exotic locations – preferring to stay studio-bound, or at a push to film in woods or fields near the studio.

In all, 31 *Carry On...* films were made and released, including a compilation film entitled *That's Carry On* (a very obvious tribute to the popular *That's Entertainment* films) fronted by Kenneth Williams and Barbara Windsor. And despite the fact that their heyday was some years ago, constant exposure on television – either as full-length films or in the popular *What A Carry On!* compilation series – and accessibility on video has kept the films popular with new generations.

Though the *Carry On...* creators, Gerald Thomas and Peter Rogers, tended to favour shooting at Pinewood Studios (where the films were viewed initially as the poor neighbour to other productions), at times the *Carry On...* team used special locations. The following list highlights a few of those films:

Carry On... Don't Lose Your Head (1966)

The *Carry On...* team left Pinewood to film sequences at Waddesdon Manor, six miles from Aylesbury, Buckinghamshire (so they didn't travel too far really). It is one of the few country houses in the UK with the look of a French château. The film is a play on the Scarlet Pimpernel story of dashing aristocrats saving victims from French revolutionaries, with Sid James as the gruesomely named Black Fingernail.

Carry On... Follow that Camel (1967)

A *Carry On...* version of P.C. Wren's famous *Beau Geste* story, has the team – this time bolstered by a US star in the form of Phil Silvers – supposedly off to the Sahara Desert. The team spent three weeks filming at Camber Sands and Rye in Sussex (the longest location shoot in the series' history); to help the re-creation of the desert producer Peter Rogers brought in a few fake palm trees and borrowed a camel named Sheena from Chessington Zoo. Phil Silvers was gradually losing his sight, so as well as his trademark glasses he also wore contact lenses. At times Silvers and co-stars Jim Dale and Peter Butterworth could be seen searching for lost lenses on the beach at Camber Sands.

Carry On Up the Khyber (1968)

One of the best loved – and most praised – of the *Carry On...* films, it pokes fun delightfully at the notion of Englishmen in India during the Raj. Shooting called for the team's furthest trip from Pinewood – to a spot in Snowdonia that could double as the Khyber Pass. The same spot doubled for China in the Gregory Peck film *The Most Important Man in the World*, which was shot shortly after the *Carry On...* team left.

Carry On Camping (1968)

Shot straight after *Carry On Up the Khyber*, this film was back to Pinewood, moving out only as far as nearby fields for the classic campsite scenes. This supposedly summer movie was in fact shot in October and November, and the mud in the fields was sprayed green to try to make it look more like grass.

Carry On Loving (1970)

Sid James and Hattie Jacques run the Wedded Bliss agency, providing an excuse for lots of sexual innuendo as various couples try to get together. The film is essentially a reworking of *Carry On Regardless*, and in fact the exterior location in Park Street, Ealing, was used for both Sid's Helping Hands agency in *Carry On Regardless* and the Wedded Bliss agency in *Carry On Loving*.

MOVIE LOCATIONS *the carry on... films*

Carry On at Your Convenience (1971)

Actresses Joan Sims and Dora Bryan would often be mistaken for each other, but they were happy to play up to this misconception. When the team were filming in Brighton they stopped at Dora Bryan's hotel, Claridges, and Bryan ran to Sims shouting, 'Oh, Dora!' and Sims to Bryan shouting, 'Oh, Joanie!' Actor Richard O'Callaghan, who stars in the film, recalled: 'For *Carry On At Your Convenience* we were in Brighton for three or four days, and as far as I could tell all these films were made on a terrible shoestring. Most of the location work was done on the Pinewood lot. So when we actually got a trip to Brighton, most of the regulars were saying: "Oh? Are we actually going somewhere away from Pinewood?" They were quite amazed that they had decided to spend money and go off down to Brighton, where they had to put us up in hotels.'

◁ Peter Butterworth, Kenneth Williams and Phil Silvers (left to right) enjoy the Sahara Desert (aka Camber Sands, Sussex), in *Carry On... Follow That Camel.*

Carry On Abroad (1972)

The team heads off to a holiday hotel in Spain – or perhaps not! As actress June Whitfield recalled: 'I was delighted when offered a part in *Carry On Abroad* and wondered where in sunny Europe we would be filming. Alas, the location turned out to be a car park at Pinewood.'

Carry On, Girls (1973)

The twenty-fifth film in the series and a trip back to Brighton for the gang. A beauty contest is organized in the fictional seaside town of Furcombe (Brighton), leading to lots of the expected innuendo as the sexes battle it out. The scene with the young Robin Askwith, a sexily dressed Margaret Nolan and a keen Peter Butterworth was shot on Brighton beach, with the Palace Pier visible in the background.

the hammer films

THE NAME HAMMER WILL BE LINKED WITH BRITISH HORROR FILMS for ever. From the 1930s through to the late 1950s the company made a whole variety of productions, but it was a move to Bray Studios and the making of a science-fiction film based on a BBC series that changed its course. The success of *The Quatermass Experiment* (1955) signalled a move towards a new form of British horror, and, in a way, Hammer was reborn.

In 1957 *The Curse of Frankenstein* was made, and a year later *Dracula* arrived – Hammer was making its mark on British cinema with its mixture of horror, blood, suspense and (especially in later years) sex. Through the 1960s until the mid-1970s Hammer established a strong reputation for a very distinctive style of horror, attracting audiences and substantial popularity along the away.

Like the *Carry On...* films, Hammer productions were distinguished by modest budgets, use of a regular group of actors (headed by Christopher Lee and Peter Cushing) and a marked reluctance to leave the safety of the studio sets and backlot. Also like the *Carry On...* team, the Hammer team did make occasional trips for location filming (though usually just a few miles away rather than hundreds) and demonstrated a remarkable ability to make the best of limited resources.

The Quatermass Experiment (1955)

Already a hit six-part BBC series, the story was adapted for the big screen and Brian Donlevy and Jack Warner recruited to give it larger appeal. Directed by Val Guest, it follows the frightening events when a lost rocket returns to earth with its sole survivor strangely changed. Much of the film was shot in and around Windsor, while Chessington Zoo doubled as London Zoo and Westminster Abbey was actually Bray Studios.

Quatermass 2 (1957)

A sequel to *The Quatermass Experiment*, with Professor Quatermass (again played by American Brian Donlevy) working on a new rocket launch but distracted by an evil infection caused by meteorites falling on the fictional town of Winnerden Flats (in fact the new town of Hemel Hempstead). The film was also shot at the Shell Haven oil refinery on the Essex coast.

The Curse of Frankenstein (1957)

First of the Gothic horrors with which Hammer will always be associated. Count Frankenstein is played by Peter Cushing, while Christopher Lee meets the Hammer requirement of a very tall man with 'some knowledge and experience of movement and mime' for the role of the monster. The film was shot at Bray Studios, with occasional trips to the nearby River Thames for exterior shots. The prison frontage was built on to the entrance of the main house at Bray.

Dracula (1958)

The release of *Dracula* (shot on the modest budget of £81,412) secured the Hammer horror reputation, with Christopher Lee perfect as the toothy Transylvanian. The film, directed by Terence Fisher, was shot at Bray in just 25 days, with trips to nearby country roads for the coach sequences. Visiting photographers were asked to photograph Lee only from behind when they visited the set for fear that a front view would spoil the surprise element when the film was released.

The Hound of the Baskervilles (1959)

Peter Cushing is Holmes and Christopher Lee takes out his fangs to play the goodie, young Henry Baskerville, this time. Surrey's Frensham Ponds were used as Dartmoor (though brief insert shots of Dartmoor and Holyport were also cut into the film), and Dartmoor and the Baskerville home were also built at Bray. The film had a so-so response, and no more Hammer Holmes films were made.

The Curse of the Werewolf (1961)

In a period setting Oliver Reed plays the hapless young man who turns into a werewolf in a Spanish village named Santa Vera (the crew made use of a Spanish set at Bray that was being built for a subsequently cancelled film

called *The Inquisitor*). The film was also shot on location at Black Park and Egham in Surrey.

Captain Clegg (1962)

Planned as an adaptation of Russell Thorndike's *Dr Syn* novel (ironically, Disney was shooting a version at the same time, and legal wranglings meant the character's name had to be changed to Dr Blyss), the story is about pirates and smugglers in England in 1776. Peter Cushing plays the evil Dr Blyss. As well as at Bray, the film was shot at Copstone Mill in Buckinghamshire and made inventive use of the deconsecrated Braywood Church near Bray.

The Phantom of the Opera (1962)

The ever-excellent Herbert Lom is the Phantom in this Hammer version. Initially the producers had grand ambitions of using Covent Garden Opera House as a location (after all, its budget was £180,000), but they had to settle finally for Wimbledon Theatre as well as sets at
Bray.

◁ Oliver Reed suffering from *The Curse of the Werewolf*.

The Damned (1963)

Acclaimed director Joseph Losey directed this chiller about an American (MacDonald Carey) who is attacked by a gang of motorcycle thugs (led by Oliver Reed) and when recovering meets a dastardly scientist who keeps radioactive children beneath his clifftop laboratory. The film was shot in Weymouth and Portland Bill in Dorset.

The Evil of Frankenstein (1964)

Peter Cushing returned to play the Count, but this time round it was New Zealand wrestler Kiwi Kingston who had the makeup applied to portray the monster. The film was shot largely at Bray, though locations were also used at nearby Oakley Court, Black Park and the wonderfully named Monkey Island Lane.

The Nanny (1965)

Hammer signed 57-year-old Bette Davis to play the evil nanny in this adaptation of Evelyn Piper's psychological thriller. The film was shot at Elstree Studios (the producers had to arrange for a local pub to open early in the morning for Bette to down a couple of large scotches before filming started) as well as location visits to Regent's Park and a school near Radlett.

△ Christopher Lee gets his teeth into another juicy Dracula role.

Rasputin the Mad Monk (1966)

Christopher Lee adopted long hair and a straggly beard to play an evil Rasputin, with *Dracula, Prince of Darkness* sets reused to double as Russia. Director Don Sharp also shot four days of exteriors at Black Park.

The Plague of Zombies (1966)

Hammer tackled one of the few remaining horror genres it hadn't previously covered with this tale of the walking dead, which stars André Morell. The film was shot at Bray, with four days' location work (in the sweltering heat,

which caused problems for the actors heavily made up as zombies) at nearby Oakley Court.

Dracula has Risen from the Grave (1968)

Christopher Lee returned as the Count, with direction provided by Freddie Francis. The film was shot at Pinewood Studios, with location work at Black Park and on the slopes of Box Hill, Surrey (acting as the hills running up to Dracula's castle, which was inserted later by artists).

The Vampire Lovers (1970)

While Peter Cushing was still on board, it was the arrival of scream queen Ingrid Pitt as the seductive vampire that heralded a change of direction for Hammer, as it headed for a more explicit and exploitative format. The film was shot at Elstree Studios as well as at the nearby clubhouse of Moor Park golf club (eagle-eyed viewers can glimpse tennis courts in one scene).

historic houses

national trust properties
Enquiries: 020 8315 1111
E-mail: enquiries@ntrust.org.uk
Website: www.nationaltrust.org.uk

Ashridge Estate
An estate that runs across the borders of Buckinghamshire and Hertfordshire along the ridge of the Chiltern Hills. The woodlands and downland offer a variety of flora and fauna.
Address: Ringshall, Berkhamsted, Hertfordshire
Tel: 01442 851227
Film: *First Knight* (medieval village built on the estate)

Castle Ward
An eighteenth-century mansion of a schizophrenic nature: the west front is classical and the east front Gothic, reflecting the different tastes of the first owner and his wife. A lovely walled, landscaped park runs down to the shores of Strangford Lough.
Address: Strangford, Downpatrick, Co. Down, Northern Ireland
Tel: 028 4488 1204
Film: *St Ives* (aka *All for Love*) (exterior scenes)

Chiddingstone Village

It is easy to understand why the National Trust decided to preserve

Chiddingstone, with its enchanting cobbled streets and the well-known Chidding Stone, from which it takes its name.
Address: Chiddingstone, Kent
Info: 01892 890651
Film: *A Room With a View* (the parish of Summer Street)

Claydon House

Claydon, originally Jacobean but remodelled in the 1750s, has been in continuous occupation by the Verney family for more than 350 years. It is an extraordinary building, with many lavish rooms beautifully decorated with motifs based on oriental birds, with summerhouses and pagodas in the park.
Address: Middle Claydon, near Buckingham, Buckinghamshire
Tel: 01296 730349
Info: 01494 755561
Film: *Emma* (ballroom scene)

Cliveden

A stunning house with an estate overlooking the River Thames, once the home of Nancy, Lady Astor, it is now let as an hotel. The current house, the third to be built on the site, was constructed by Charles Barry for the Duke of Sutherland in 1851. The grounds contain beautiful riverside and woodland walks, and a lovely series of gardens.
Address: Taplow, Maidenhead, Berkshire
Tel: 01628 605069
Info: 01494 755562
Film: *Carrington, Chaplin*

Compton Castle

A fortified manor house, home of the Gilberts for most of the past 600 years, it was built between the fourteenth and sixteenth centuries. One owner, Sir Humphrey Gilbert (1539–83), was half-brother to Sir Walter Raleigh. It boasts battlements, a medieval great hall and a sheltered stone courtyard.
Address: Marldon, Paignton, Devon
Tel: 01803 872112
Film: *Sense and Sensibility* (exterior of Mrs Willoughby's home)

Dyrham Park

Dyrham was constructed between 1691 and 1702 for William Blathwayt, William II's Secretary of War and Secretary of State, and the rooms have been little altered since Blathwayt furnished them. The domestic rooms have been

△ The Beaufort Hunt gather outside Dyrham Park in a scene from *The Remains of the Day*.

restored, allowing a fascinating glimpse behind the scenes of an impressive home.

Address: Near Chippenham, Wiltshire

Tel: 01179 372501

Film: *The Remains of the Day* (exterior of Darlington Hall in Beaufort Hunt scene)

East Riddlesden Hall

Set in the Aire Valley, this enchanting seventeenth-century West Riding manor house contains elegant furniture and furnishings and also has a lovely garden designed by Graham Stuart Thomas, as well as a picturesque duck pond.

Address: Bradford Road, Keighley, West Yorkshire

Tel: 01535 607075

Film: *Wuthering Heights* (Heathcliff's home, sheep-shearing and weaving scenes)

Formby beach

A glorious stretch of unspoiled coastline between the sea and Formby town, it combines rolling sand-dunes and pine woods and is home to many birds and plants. It is also one of the few places left in Britain where people may catch a glimpse of a rare red squirrel.

Address: Victoria Road, Freshfield, Formby, Merseyside
Tel: 01704 878591
Film: *Hilary and Jackie* (setting of the holiday scenes in the opening shots)

Fountains Abbey

This unique site comprises the ruins of a twelfth-century Cistercian abbey, an Elizabethan mansion and a fine Georgian water garden. The garden has temples, cascades and ornamental lakes, while nearby is a medieval deer park, home to some 500 deer.

Address: Fountains, Ripon, North Yorkshire
Tel: 01765 601005
Film: *The Secret Garden* (Fountains Hall was the exterior of Misselthwaite Manor)

Ham House

A 1610 house that has featured in court life over the years and is famous for its elegant interiors and collections of fine textiles, furniture and paintings. The seventeenth-century garden is being restored.

Address: Ham, Richmond, Surrey
Tel: 020 8940 1950
Film: *Spice World* (scene featuring Scary Spice in her silver suit)

Lanhydrock

This fascinating Victorian country house is full of atmosphere, partly created by a seventeenth-century gatehouse and north wing. The garden has a collection of camellias and rhododendrons.

Address: Bodmin, Cornwall
Tel: 01208 73320
Film: *The Three Musketeers*, *Twelfth Night* (Olivia's house and garden)

Little Moreton Hall

One of the country's most famous timber-framed moated manor houses, it opens into a cobbled courtyard. Of special interest are a knot garden, and wall paintings in the main hall. The property also features an open-air theatre and organizes ghost tours.

Address: Congleton, Cheshire
Tel: 01260 272018
Film: *Lady Jane* (banquet and brothel sequences)

Lower Brockhampton House

The house lies at the heart of the 1,700-acre Brockhampton Estate, where there are traditional farms and areas of woodland. The moated manor house itself was built in the late fourteenth century and has a timber-framed gatehouse and a ruined chapel.

Address: Bringsty, Herefordshire
Tel: 01885 482077
Film: *Shadowlands*

Mompesson House

This elegant eighteenth-century house has a notable oak staircase, impressive plasterwork and fine furniture. Outside the house is a walled garden with a pergola.

Address: The Close, Salisbury, Wiltshire
Tel: 01722 335659
Film: *Sense and Sensibility* (Mrs Jennings' London residence)

Montacute House

Magnificent state rooms are a main feature of this Elizabethan house. They include a long gallery (the largest of its type in England); the house also boasts distinctive carved parapets and elegant chimneys. Outside, the formal garden is surrounded by a landscaped park.

Address: Montacute, Somerset
Tel: 01935 823289
Film: *Sense and Sensibility* (the Palmers' home)

St Michael's Mount

This castle is set dramatically on a rocky island just off the coast, approached by a causeway at low tide, and was originally the site of a Benedictine priory. It was converted to a private house in the seventeenth century and offers impressive furnishings and features.

△ Saltram House in Devon

Address: Marazion, near Penzance, Cornwall
Tel: 01736 710507
Film: *Twelfth Night* (Orsino's castle)

Saltram House

This impressive George II mansion stands in a landscaped park. The remarkable state rooms retain many of the original contents, including fine plasterwork, furniture, china and paintings. The eighteenth-century gardens feature an orangery and several follies. After the release of *Sense and Sensibility* Saltram saw visitor numbers boosted by 39 per cent, an increase entirely due to the film, as the house had not been marketed in any other way.

Address: Plympton, Plymouth, Devon
Tel: 01752 336546
Film: *Sense and Sensibility* (Norland Park, the Dashwoods' estate)

Stowe Gardens

These landscaped gardens were established in the Georgian era, with temples, arches, monuments and a Palladian bridge. The main house is occupied by Stowe School.

Address: Buckingham, Buckinghamshire
Tel: 01280 822850
Film: *The World Is Not Enough* (cemetery scene)

Waddesdon Manor

A Renaissance-style château built by Baron Ferdinand de Rothschild in the 1870s, it is notable for fine collections of portraits and decorative art. Outside, the landscaped gardens are famous for their fine views. The wine cellars contain thousands of bottles of vintage Rothschild wine.

Address: Waddesdon, near Aylesbury, Buckinghamshire
Tel: 01296 653211
Film: *An Ideal Husband* (exterior scenes of carriages and horse riders on Rotten Row, Hyde Park, London)

english heritage properties

Enquiries: 01793 414910
E-mail: members@english-heritage.org.uk
Website: www.english-heritage.org.uk

Aydon Castle

One of the finest examples of a thirteenth-century manor house, Aydon Castle overlooks the steep valley of the Cor Burn. Built as an undefended house during a rare time of peace in the borders, it was later fortified.

Address: Corbridge, Northumberland
Tel: 01434 632450
Film: *Elizabeth*

Chiswick House

One of England's finest Palladian villas, Chiswick House is close to the centre of London, in beautiful gardens. The Palladian style was pioneered in England by Inigo Jones, and Chiswick House was designed by the third Earl of Burlington.

Address: Burlington Lane, Chiswick, London
Tel: 020 8995 0508

Film: *The Servant* (exterior shot)

Dover Castle

This fortress, originally an Anglo-Saxon defence, was strengthened in 1066 by William of Normandy. Under Henry II it was totally rebuilt into a fortress of commanding style overlooking the sea.

Address: Dover, Kent
Tel: 01304 201628
Film: *Hamlet*

Kenwood House

Set in Hampstead Heath, Kenwood is a lovely neoclassical house containing many impressive paintings and offering gorgeous views. The house was remodelled by Robert Adam between 1764 and 1773, when he changed the original brick house into a majestic villa.

Address: Hampstead Lane, North London
Tel: 020 8348 1286
Films: *101 Dalmatians*, *Mansfield Park*, *Notting Hill*

Kirby Hall

Built from local Weldon stone, Kirby Hall is an Elizabethan mansion with courtyards, galleries and a great hall, while the gardens are regarded as among the finest in England.

Address: Deene, near Corby, Northamptonshire
Tel: 01536 203230
Film: *Mansfield Park*

Northington Grange

Northington Grange was one of the earliest Greek Revival houses in Europe, though its structure has changed over the years. The core of the house was designed in 1809 by William Wilkins. The house is surrounded by a naturalistic landscaped park with a lake.

Address: Northington, near Winchester, Hampshire
Film: *Onegin*

Old Wardour Castle

A late-fourteenth-century six-sided castle designed in the French style, it was badly damaged during the Civil War. It is now one of the most attractive ruined castles in England.

Address: Near Tisbury, Wiltshire
Tel: 01747 870487
Film: *Robin Hood: Prince of Thieves* (Robin's father's castle)

Osborne House

The tranquillity of the Isle of Wight was perfect for Queen Victoria and Prince Albert, who termed Osborne House 'a place of one's own, quiet and refined'. Overlooking the Solent, the house is dominated by two Italian-style towers. The royal couple bought the land in 1845, employing Thomas Cubitt to design and build the house. After the release of *Mrs Brown* the property experienced an increase in visitors of 25 per cent. A video screening of the film is shown regularly.

Address: East Cowes, Isle of Wight
Tel: 01983 200022
Film: *Mrs Brown* (the second half of the film is set at Osborne)

Wingfield Manor

This large, ruined country mansion was built in the mid-fifteenth century. Mary Queen of Scots was imprisoned here in 1569, 1584 and 1585, but it has been unoccupied since the 1770s. It remains a memorable location.

Address: South Wingfield, near Alfreton, Derbyshire
Tel: 01773 832060
Film: *Jane Eyre*

other properties

Alnwick Castle

Northumberland's impressive Alnwick Castle is probably the finest example of a castle that has developed into a stately home, and in Victorian times it was described as 'the Windsor of the North'.

Address: Alnwick, Northumberland
Tel: 01665 510777
Film: *Becket, Elizabeth, King Arthur and the Spaceman, Mary Queen of Scots, Robin Hood: Prince of Thieves*

Hatfield House

The home of the Cecil family for some 400 years, Hatfield House was built on the site of a mansion where Elizabeth I spent much of her childhood.

Address: Hatfield, Hertfordshire
Tel: 01707 262823
Film: *Batman* (the interiors of Wayne Manor), *Greystoke: The Legend Of Tarzan, Lord of the Apes, Shakespeare in Love* (doubled as Greenwich Palace)

Knebworth House

Knebworth House was originally a modest brick Tudor manor but was transformed in the 1840s into a Gothic-style Victorian building.

Address: Knebworth, Hertfordshire

Tel: 01438 812661

Film: *Batman, Eyes Wide Shut, Haunted Honeymoon, Jane Eyre*

Wilton House

This beautiful country house is frequently used by film-makers, who are drawn by stunning interiors (the Double Cube Room and the Cloisters are often filmed) and its extensive grounds.

Address: Wilton, Salisbury

Tel: 01722 746720

Film: *Barry Lyndon, The Bounty, The End of the Affair, The Madness of King George, Mrs Brown, The Portrait of a Lady, Scandal, Sense and Sensibility*

useful addresses and movie tours

IF YOU ARE INTERESTED IN FURTHER INFORMATION REGARDING TOURS, opening times or about some of the specific locations, here follows a list of useful contact numbers and addresses that will be a good starting-off point.

selected contacts

British Film Commission
2nd floor, Queens Yard, 179a Tottenham Court Road, London W1P OBE
Tel: 020 7224 5000
Fax: 020 7224 1013
[also provides access to the UK's regional film commission network]

British Film Institute
21 Stephen Street, London, W1P 1PL
Tel: 020 7 255 1444
Fax: 020 7436 7950

British Tourist Authority
Thames Tower, Black's Road, London, W6 9EL
Tel: 020 8846 9000
Fax: 020 8563 0302

English Heritage
23 Savile Row, London, W1X 1AB
Tel: 020 7973 3000
Fax: 020 7973 3001

Historic Houses Association
2 Chester Street, London, SW1X 7BB
Tel: 020 7259 5688
Fax: 020 7259 5590

Historic Scotland
Longmore House, Salisbury Place, Edinburgh, EH9 1SII
Tel: 0131 668 8600
Fax: 0131 668 8888

Isle of Man Film Commission
Department of Trade & Industry, Illiam Dhone House,
Circular Road, Douglas, Isle of Man, IM1 1PJ
Tel: 01624 685 864
Tel: 01624 685 454

London Fim Commission
20 Euston Centre, Regent's Place, London, NW1 3JH
Tel: 020 7387 8787
Fax: 020 7387 0799

National Trust
36 Queen Anne's Gate, London, SW1H 9AS
Tel: 020 7222 9251
Fax: 020 7222 5097

National Trust – Wales
Trinity Square, Llandudno, Gwynedd, LL30 2DE
Tel: 01492 860 123
Tel: 01492 860 233

National Trust – Northern Ireland
Rowallane House, Saintfield, Ballynahinch, County Down, BT24 7LH
Tel: 028 9751 0721
Fax: 028 9751 1242

MOVIE LOCATIONS *useful addresses*

National Trust for Scotland

28 Charlotte Square, Edinburgh, EH2 4DU
Tel: 0131 243 9300
Fax: 0131 243 9501

Northern Ireland Film Council

21 Ormeau Avenue, Belfast, BT2 8HD
Tel: 028 9023 2444
Fax: 028 9023 9918

Northern Ireland Tourist Board

St Anne's Court, 59 North Street, Belfast, BT1 1NB
Tel: 028 9024 6609
Fax: 028 9031 2424

Scottish Screen

249 West George Street, Glasgow G2 4RB
Tel: 0141 302 1700
Fax: 0141 302 1711

Scottish Tourist Board

23 Ravelston Terrace, Edinburgh, EH4 3EU
Tel: 0131 332 2433
Fax: 0131 343 1513

Wales Tourist Board

12th Floor, Brunel House, 2 Fitzalan Road, Cardiff CF2 1UY
Tel: 029 2049 9909
Fax: 029 2048 5031

movie tours

Gentle Journeys

This company offers a varied programme of movie-themed tours both in London and outside the city, giving people the chance to visit the locations of films such as *Chariots of Fire, The End of the Affair, Four Weddings and a Funeral, The Madness of King George, Notting Hill, Shadowlands, Shakespeare in Love* and *The World Is Not Enough*.

Contact: Gentle Journeys, Park House, 140 Battersea Park Road, London SW11 4NB
Tel: 020 7720 4891
Fax: 020 7720 0250
E-mail: tours@gentlejourneys.co.uk
Website: www.gentlejourneys.co.uk

The Full Monty Tour

The *Full Monty* trail includes the working men's club where the final strip took place, the site of the famous canal scene, and the location where the steelworkers try to get fit and ready for the ordeal to come.

Itinerary available at the Tourist Information Centre in Sheffield.
Tel: 0114 273 4671

index

Page entries in *italics* refer to photographs.
Please note most locations are listed within their county, under 'locations'.